The names of the sicknesses/which may be healed by these bathes.

The casting of children out/ before the dewe tyme appoynted by nature.

The stoppinge of the longes and shortnes of breth when a man can not take breth/except he sit right vp.

The hardnes and binding of the bellye/ when as a man can not go to the stoole without Physick.

The palsey when as a man is quite num all the partes of his body/and hath nether mouing nor healing.

Impostemes and gatheringes of humors together with swellinge.

The running gout which runneth frō one ioynte to an other.

The defenes or dulnes of hearing.

The windines or singing or tinginge of the eares

The brusing that cummeth by falling or beating.

The stone in the kidnes.

The stone in the blader.

Hard lumpes and swellinges.

The Cancre.

The headache of a cold cause.

The head ache of an hote cause.

The Rewm or Pose or Catar.

The stopping of the brayne with euell humors.

Scarres and foule markes of sores or woundes.

The Colike.

The fallinge sicknes.

Crampes and drawinges together brawnes and synewes or streching furth to muche of the same.

The trimbling of the hart.

The foulnes of the skin and scuruines.

The puffinge vp of the legges with wind.

The hardnes of any place in the body.

The often and to much making of water called Diabetes.

The leannes of the hole bodye.

Agues after the mater is made rype and digested.

Tertian agues.   Quartane agues.

Fistules or hollow or false vnder creepinge sores.

Al kindes of isshues or flixes.

The stickinge of yron in a bone or in the fleshe.

Breaking or bursting of bones.

Membres that are made num with colde.

The knobbes and hard lūpes that are made by the french pockes.

The lousnes and watering of the gummes.

The emrodes and pyles.

The mygram or headache in the one halfe of the head.

The diseases of the liuer.

Bursting or breakinge.

The bottel dropsey in the stomach.

The general dropsey throw all the body/running betwene the fell and the fleshe.

The iaundes or guelsought.

The coldnes and stopping of the liuer.

The sciatica or hancheuel.

The lepre vpon the skin.

The hardnes of the milt / or the cake in the left syde.

Wormes in the bellye.

Membres that are num and fele not.

The madnes called melancholia.

The hurting of the memorye or forgetfulnes.

THE HOSPIT[A]
OF THE NAT[ION]

MB

THE HOSPITAL OF THE NATION

The Story of Spa Medicine and the
Mineral Water Hospital at Bath.

by
ROGER ROLLS
with photography by
CLIVE QUINNELL

BIRD PUBLICATIONS

Published by Bird Publications 1988
1, Trim Bridge, Bath, Avon, BA1 1HD

Designed and produced by LMA Southampton.
Tel. (0703) 37311

ISBN 0 9513219 00

CONTENTS

PREFACE AND ACKNOWLEDGEMENTS

Bath has become the great hospital of the nation, frequented by all the valetudinarians whose lives are of any consequence to the commonwealth.
Tobias Smollett. 1752.

As its title suggests, this book is about a hospital but in the sense that Tobias Smollett used the phrase, the hospital of the nation was Bath itself. The Royal National Hospital for Rheumatic Diseases was founded at Bath in 1738 and is one of the earliest hospitals in the world to specialise in the treatment of arthritis and rheumatism, two diseases traditionally improved by the hot waters of Bath. It is also the first truly national hospital to be founded in Great Britain, admitting patients from all over the country. At first called the Bath General Hospital, it later became known as the Royal Mineral Water Hospital until it adopted its present title in 1935. To avoid confusion, the author has used the title *Mineral Water Hospital* throughout the book, regardless of the chronological period under discussion.

The book not only deals with the early history of the hospital but looks at the way in which medicine developed in the most famous of all English spas. It also looks at patients and their diseases and the various treatments which were offered at Bath. The author has extensively researched the hospital archives which contain the complete series of minutes relating to the weekly meetings of the Committee of Governors which administered the institute's affairs until the inception of the National Health Service in 1948. A number of the illustrations have not appeared in print before and Clive Quinnell has spent many hours assembling his camera on top of rickety scaffolding or kneeling on uncomfortable floors in art galleries to obtain the illustrative material for this book. The author is equally grateful for his help in tracking down the various documents and records which the hospital possesses. He is also indebted to Mrs Jane Root of the Bath Archaeological Trust who not only helped catalogue the hospital archives but spent many hours in various county and city record departments in search of original material relating to the hospital's early years.

Much of the recent history of the hospital, particularly relating to its research and post-war resurrection, has been published by Dr George Kersley who was largely responsible for the hospital's survival in the early NHS years. The author is grateful to Dr Kersley for the help and encouragement he has given during the preparation of this book. The author also wishes to thank the many people who have helped, and in particular the following: Dr Alistair Robb-Smith, William Shupbach at the Wellcome Institute for the History of Medicine, Neill MacLaren, Dr John Guy, Kate Clarke, Mrs Joyce and the staff of the Bath Reference Library, Paul Cresswell, Dr Denis Gibbs, David Falconer, Charles Gordon, Gerald Chown, John Kirkup, Dr Audrey Heywood, Simon Hunt of the Bath Museums Service, Victoria Barwell and Barbara Milner at the Victoria Art Gallery, Bath, Mr Belsey at Gainsborough's House, Sudbury, staff at the British Library and National Portrait Gallery, London, Evelyn Newby of the Paul Mellon Foundation for British Art, Christopher Couchman, Anthony Trollope-Bellew, Rita Quinnell, B.R. Doshi of A.H. Hale Ltd., Richard Baggaley and Dr Myles McNulty. Laurence Bardy, Joy Book and Judith Elswood helped with some of the typing and Jock Grant gave assistance on word-processing. Lyndsey Denham and staff at LMA have been extremely patient in the course of the book's production. My final thanks must go to my wife for her support and literary comment during the course of the project.

BATH. 1988.

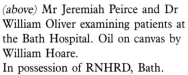

(above) Mr Jeremiah Peirce and Dr William Oliver examining patients at the Bath Hospital. Oil on canvas by William Hoare.
In possession of RNHRD, Bath.

(left) Working drawings of the Coat of Arms granted to the hospital by the Royal College of Arms in 1988.

CHAPTER ONE
Beggars and Bathers

There are many reasons why people still visit Bath. Some come to admire the elegance of the honey-coloured crescents and terraces which cascade down the hillside; others prefer to be tempted by the glittering window displays of Milsom Street or feast at one of over fifty dining establishments. In many respects the air of Georgian England still pervades the city, but the modern visitor, thirsting to re-live this bygone culture is unwittingly spared the seamier side of the Augustan era. No longer do beggars impede the flow of prosperous shoppers. The scars and scabs of disease-ridden children and maimed soldiers, limping their way to the hot springs, no longer prick the consciences of tourists and residents as they did two centuries ago. The scene was very different then: lame and crippled, from all walks of society and all parts of Britain, converged on Bath in such numbers that the pavements almost groaned in sympathy.

One hobbled, another hopped, a third dragged his legs behind him like a wounded snake, a fourth straddled betwixt a pair of long crutches like a mummy of a felon hanging in chains, a fifth was bent into a horizontal position like a mounted telescope, shoved in by a couple of chairmen, and a sixth was the bust of a man set upright in a wheel machine.[1]

By the time Tobias Smollett wrote these words in 1771, hundreds of ailing people were annually flocking to Bath to immerse themselves in the mineral water bubbling incessantly from the famous geothermal springs. They came to be douched, pumped and sprayed with it, to inhale its vapour or simply savour what Charles Dickens once called "the taste of warm flat irons." They expected to be relieved of their illnesses by absorbing an etherial quintessence which was released as the waters emerged from the mysterious subterranean world of brimstone fires. They were certainly relieved of their money by the bevy of medical gentlemen who followed in their wake, swooping like eagles on gullible and desperate invalids. A visitor in 1709 had remarked that the physicians were very numerous but good natured and that he was cured of more diseases in one week than he had suffered in the rest of his life.[2] But a lot of visitors arrived penniless and were so destitute that they could afford neither bed nor board in the city.

CHARITY BEGINS AT HOME

Not all had genuine illnesses: faked convulsions and exaggerated limps were common tricks used by beggars to elicit sympathy and prey on the charitable spirits of the rich who were coming to Bath in increasing numbers each year. There were probably far more who were genuine, for whom the expense of accommodation and medical fees were just too much for them to bear: charity was their only hope.

It was such hope that led a young woman from the Somerset village of Priddy, perched high on the Mendip hills, to come to Bath in the summer of 1694. As a result of a birth injury, she suffered from a condition called choreo-athetosis or, in the words of the contemporary physician who saw

(*opposite*) Travellers in front of the Royal Crescent. From an engraving by Watts. 1794.

1

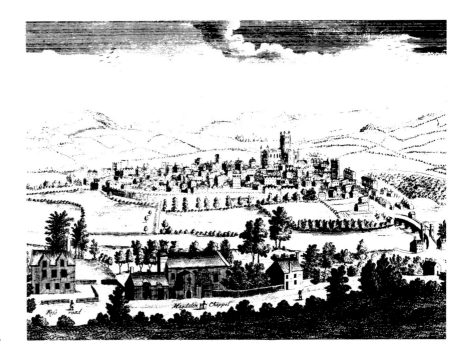

Bath in the early 18th century,
printed for Dr Richard Mead, a
Governor of the Mineral Water
Hospital.
Courtesy of Avon County Libraries.

her, "when she endeavoured to move her right arm in any direction
(especially upwards) or to lay hold of anything, such odd and antick motions
would be in that arm and hand as if she were about to act the
Changeling."[3] As a result of her handicap, she had had to give up her
work as a maid and eked out a miserable existence making stockings, a
skill she had learnt to do using only her left hand. She had struggled the
twenty miles to Bath, probably on foot, in the hope of finding a hospital
in which she could be admitted without charge. The poor woman could
not afford to stay in Bath without financial assistance but the only hospital
for such patients at this time was a tiny place which restricted admission
to men. With nowhere to stay, she had no choice but to return home
without so much as getting a finger immersed.

As early as the sixteenth century, the huge annual flux of poverty-stricken
invalids had become such a headache to the Corporation that the Mayor
petitioned Parliament to safeguard the interests of the city.

A great number of poor and diseased people do resort to the city of Bath... for some
ease and relief of their diseases at the baths there... The inhabitants are greatly overcharged
with the same poor people to their intolerable charge. Therefore no diseased or impotent
poor person living on alms... shall resort or repair from their dwelling place to the said
city of Bath and to the baths there for the ease of their grief unless such person be not
only licenced so to do by two Justices of the Peace in the county where such person doth
dwell but also provided for by the inhabitants (of their own parish). The inhabitants of
Bath shall not in any wise be charged by this Act with the finding or relief of any such
poor people.[4]

This Act effectively transferred the burden of supporting poor persons
seeking treatment from the citizens of Bath to the person's own parish.
It also helped to control the number of beggars entering the city as anyone
who arrived at the gates without a licence could be punished and treated
as a vagabond.[5] Removal of "malingerers" served to focus social
awareness on those genuinely in distress through illness and fostered greater
benevolence from charitably-minded individuals. Persons with chronic skin
disease were particularly unfortunate for they were still branded as "lepers"
and would have found great difficulty in getting accommodation. In 1576,
John de Feckenham who was the last Abbot of Westminster purchased
three tons of timber and four tons of lathes at his own expense "to build

a howse for the poor by the whote bathe," later to be known as the Leper Hospital.[6] Feckenham, ever mindfull that physicians' fees were beyond the means of less fortunate individuals even wrote a "booke of sovereign medicines... chiefly for the poor which hath not at all times the learned phisitions to hand." He had plenty of good advice for bathers:

Before you enter the Bathe, fyrst emptie your Bellie and make water, therefore Purge yorselfe with the Soluble broth made with ye Powdre which you have for the purpose.

See that altogether whyle you tarry in Ye Bathe and longer that you avoyde Copulation and Fornication, that is the use of Women.

Look on Ye Bathes as a verie admirable and Merciful work of Divine Providence, designed for ye benefit of People diseased with Lepre, Pokkes, Scabbes and Great Aches as well as yorselfe. Therefore worship God who made these fountains, for He alone can Bless it to your Health because He also is Ye Author of that very Distemper that bring Ye hither.[7]

A few years later, benevolence flowed in every direction from the hand of Thomas Bellott, secretary to Lord Burleigh. Bellott spent his entire fortune on charitable deeds in the city "and left his kinsman nothing."[8] He contributed generously to the restoration of the Abbey Church:

The Chapel ornaments, the Floor,
The benches, windows, seat and door
Call Bellott father; and the bell
Rings Bellott though it rings a knell.

He also founded and endowed the small hospital on which the poor girl from Priddy had pinned her hopes. Opening in 1609, it provided accommodation for twelve poor strangers who required treatment at the baths. Only men were admitted and each received a weekly allowance of 7 groats[9] during their stay which was limited to four weeks. A married couple acted as Master and Matron and were expected to "curteously welcome and intreate the said poor," keep the building sweet and clean,

(*above*) Front elevation of Bellott's Hospital, from Gilmore's map of the city. 1692-94.

(*below*) Interior of old Bellott's Hospital shortly before its demolition.
Watercolour by unknown artist.
Early 19th century.
Courtesy of Bath Municipal Charities.

make the beds and see to the furniture. [10] A medical practitioner was paid an annual salary of one pound to examine prospective residents and advise the mayor if they were not suitable for admission. In 1652 Dr Tobias Venner was appointed physician out of the proceeds of a bequest by Viscount Scudamore to give medical advice both to patients at Bellotts and to "such honest poore people as shall yerely resort unto the said city and take physic for cure and remedie of his and her diseases." Dr Venner(1577-1660) whose book, *Via Recta ad Vitam Longam* - The right way to a long life, ran to several editions may properly be considered as Bath's first hospital consultant.

Bellotts is in many respects the embryo of later hospitals in having attached medical staff and a limit on the length of stay, and in being an institution for the accommodation of persons undergoing treatment. This distinguishes it from the other so-called hospitals in the city at this time which were merely refuges for the poor and aged. Visitors who could afford to pay stayed at one of several lodging-houses in the city. Many of these were owned or rented by medical men who ran them like private nursing-homes. The finest of all the lodgings was the Abbey House which stood on the east side of the King's bath and was demolished in 1755 to reveal Roman baths under its foundations.

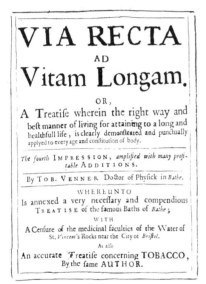

(*above*) Frontispiece to Venner's book.

(*above right*) The Abbey House, from Gilmore's map. 1692-94.

(*right*) Portrait of Dr Tobias Venner.

The names of the sicknesses/which may be healed by these bathes.

The casting of children out/ before the dewe tyme appoynted by nature.

The stoppinge of the longes and shortnes of breth when a man can not take breth/except he sit right vp.

The hardnes and binding of the bellye/ when as a man can not go to the stoole without Physick.

The palsey when as a man is quite num all the partes of his body/and hath nether mouing, nor healing.

Impostemes and gatheringes of humors together with swellinge.

The riming gout which rinneth fro one

Crampes and drawinges together brawnes and synewes or streching furth to muche of the same.

The trimbling of the hart.

The foulnes of the skin and scuruines.

The puffinge vp of the legges with wind.

The hardnes of any place in the body.

The often and to much making of water called Diabetes.

The leannes of the hole bodye.

Agues after the mater is made ripe and digested.

Tertian agues.   Quartane agues.

Fistules or hollow or false vnder creepinge sores.

Al kindes of isshues or flixes.

The stickinge of yron in a bone or in the flesshe.

Breaking or bursting of bones.

Members that are made num with colde.

The knobbes and hard lumpes that are made by the french pockes.

The lousnes and watering of the gummes.

The emrodes and pyles.

(left) List of diseases cured by the Bath waters. From William Turner's "The Book of the Natures and Properties of the Baths of England".

(below) Frontispiece to Turner's book.

BATHS OF BRIMSTONE

The revival of interest in Bath as a spa owed much to the writings of Dr William Turner whose publication *The Book of the Natures and Properties of the Baths of England* in 1562 is the first definitive treatise on the subject by an English author. Turner was a fairly exceptional man whose religious convictions made it necessary for him to take refuge abroad when the ecclesiastical climate became uncomfortable. As well as being a physician, he produced an outstanding herbal in three volumes, wrote a book about birds and was Dean of Wells Cathedral. His travels in Europe gave him the opportunity of visiting Continental spas which were flourishing on a far grander scale than those in England. Indeed, Turner was so disgusted by the sad state of affairs in his own country that he wrote that he "was ashamed for any stranger who has seen the foreign baths to look upon our baths." He doubted whether the "unnatural unkindness of the rich men of England is to be more displayed which, receiving such good turns from the Almighty God now, after they know that the baths are so profitable, will not bestow one halfpenny for God's sake on bettering and amending them that diseased people that resort thither might be better helped. There is enough money spent on cock-fightings, tennis playing, parties, banquettings, pageants and plays, serving only for a short time of pleasure... but I have not heard tell of any rich man hath spent upon these noble baths, being so profitable to the whole Commonwealth of England, one groat in twenty years."[11]

The virtues of the Bath waters lay, according to Turner, in the presence of sulphur, a misconception which was perpetuated by generations of physicians well into the eighteenth century. "Bathes of brimstone soften the sinews, suage the pain that a man hath in defying the going often unto the stool and when he cometh thither can do little or nothing. They scour and cleanse the skin wherefore they are good for the white and black

(*above*) The Cross Bath, c1738 by
John Fayram.
Courtesy of Avon County Libraries.

morphews (i.e. pimples), for leprosy and scabs, scurf, for old sores and blotches and for the falling of humours into joints.'' As if this was not impressive enough, he lists about sixty more diseases which include such diverse conditions as dropsy, windiness and tinging in the ears, the French pox, the palsy, trembling of the heart, wormes in the belly, forgetfulness and infertility. The reputation for curing the latter proved attractive to certain English monarchs and Royal visits helped to popularise the town as a resort. Queen Catherine, wife of Charles II, visited in 1663 but bathing was of no avail. Twentyfour years later, King James II dispatched his wife to the city to try the effect of the waters. Happily for the royal couple, Queen Mary gave birth to a son though whether this was due to the brimstone or the beaux in the bath, we cannot be sure. Certainly the Cross Bath at that time was an invigorating place for visitors:

Here is performed all the wanton dalliance imaginable; celebrated beauties, panting breasts and curious shapes, almost exposed to public view; languishing eyes, darting killing glances, tempting amorous postures, attended by soft music, enough to provoke a vestal to forbidden pleasure, captivate a saint and charm a Jove. The vigorous sparks present the ladies with several antick postures, as sailing on their backs, then embracing the elements, sink in rapture and by accidental design thrust an arm. . . but where the water concealed, so ought my pen. The spectators in the galleries please their roving fancies with this lady's face, another's eyes, a third's heavy breasts and profound air. In one corner stood an old letcher whose years bespoke him no less than three score and ten, making love to a young lady not exceeding fourteen. [12]

(*right*) Mary of Modena.
Courtesy of Earl Spencer.

The Cross Bath was one of several baths in the city. In William Turner's time there were at least five. The King's, Cross and Hot baths beyond the precincts of the old monastery and two others, the Abbot's and the Prior's baths, which have long since disappeared. Several new baths were constructed after the Dissolution. One was known as the Queen's bath and was built beside the King's bath. This bath was removed in the 1860's when the site was excavated to reveal the circular Roman plunge bath underneath. Another was annexed to the Hot Bath, so called because it was originally the smallest and hottest of the baths. This annexed bath was built for the exclusive use of residents at St John's hospital and appears to have been destroyed in 1597 when "certain leud and disordered persons of base sorte and condition did on Shrove Tuesday last in tumultuous sorte assemble themselves together and shutting the doors of the Hott Bathe unto them, did digg up the springhead of the said bathe and have either destroyed yt or at least drawn yt awaye as that yt may not serve soche good use as heretofore it hath done."[13]

The Leper's Bath lasted longer. It too was annexed to the Hot bath and was described by John Wood as a "place of resource for the most miserable objects that seek relief from the healing fountains, that cistern is proportionally mean, obscure and small."[14] Both the Hot and Leper's baths were demolished when John Wood's son replaced them in 1776 with the old Royal Baths, built slightly to the east of the original baths which were apt to subside into the spring-head.

The largest bath was the King's bath and remained the least altered until its floor was removed in 1979 to allow excavation of the underlying Roman reservoir. The floor has not been replaced and the present water level is much lower than before, leaving the sides of the King's bath exposed.

The King's and Queen's Baths, 1672, Thomas Johnson. From an original drawing in the British Museum.

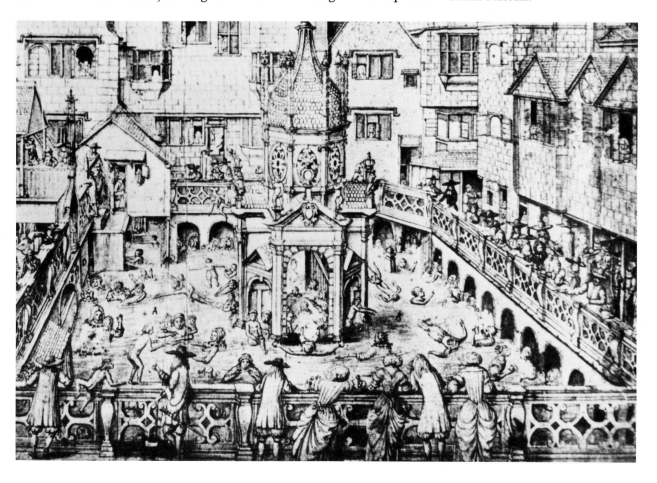

The view by Thomas Johnson shows the central arched structure known as the kitchen[15] and elegant and ornate buildings encroaching on all sides. A visitor at this time could see "young and old, rich and poor, blind and lame, diseased and sound, English and French, men and women, boyes and girles, one with another, peep up in their caps and appear so nakedly and fearfully in their uncouth postures as would a little astonish and put one in mind of the Resurrection."[16]

By the end of the seventeenth century bathers were developing a greater sense of decorum and ladies entered the baths in garments of yellow canvas which were "stiff and made large with great sleeves like a parson's gown; the water fills it up so that it is borne off that your shape is not seen. It does not cling close as other linning which looks sadly in the poorer sort that go in in their own linning. The gentlemen have drawers and waistcoats of the same sort of canvas."[17]

Whereas most visitors to Bath in the seventeenth century came to take the waters for reasons of health, the seasonal influx in Georgian times was motivated as much by a desire for pleasure as it was for the relief of illness, though some of the pleasures were themselves the cause of illness. Venereal disease was amongst that long list of illnesses which the city's liquid assets could cure. "If they can't be cured by drinking and bathing here," claimed Dr Oliver, "they will never be cured anywhere."[18] As an eighteenth century medical student from Philadelphia observed: "It was an almost endless task to ennumerate the various diseases and infirmities the advocates of these waters pretend they have removed; whatever may be their real virtues, two thirds of the company who visit them do it entirely from the influence of fashion and to alleviate an insurmountable itch for pleasure which they enjoy in the highest perfection."[19]

Visitors in the Pump Room. From a painting by Humphrey Repton in the Victoria Art Gallery, Bath. Courtesy of Bath Museums Service.

If the antics of high-spirited bathers were not sufficient entertainment, there were many more diversions to suit all tastes whether it be promenades or pornography, banquets or balls or simply spending all morning breakfasting and all afternoon buying items in shops.[20] Bath attracted a complete cross-section of eighteenth century society eager to spend what money it had.

Every upstart of fortune, harnessed in the trappings of the mode, presents himself at Bath. Clerks and factors from the East Indies, loaded with the spoil of plundered provinces; planters, negro-drivers, and hucksters, from our American plantations, enriched they know not how; agents, commissaries, and contractors who have fattened, in two successive wars, on the blood of the nation; usurers, brokers and jobbers of every kind; men of low birth and no breeding have suddenly found themselves translated into a state of affluence... all of them hurry to Bath because here without any further qualification they can mingle with the princes and nobles of the land.[21]

Neither was there any shortage of beggars. They began drifting back to Bath in ever growing numbers after 1714 when the old Elizabethan *Act* effectively regulating their presence in the city expired. Once again the more privileged citizens had to distinguish between paupers with genuine medical needs and malingerers, "to discriminate real objects of charity from vagrants and other imposters who crowd both the church and the town to the annoyance of the gentry residing here and who ought to be, by the care of the magistry, expelled and punished."[22]

What was needed was a hospital, where the admission procedure could be so tightly regulated that only those with illness deriving benefit from the Bath waters and who could be vouchsafed by a responsible person as being deserving of charity would be permitted entry. This would allow other idle folk who came to Bath to extort money from fashionable visitors to be effectively disposed of without troubling the consciences of the rich.

PHILANTHROPISTS AND GAMBLERS

The eighteenth century has the reputation for spawning philanthropists. Certainly the growth of organised voluntary effort and care of the sick must be one of the better characteristics of the period. But underneath the wave of philanthropy there lies an inevitable degree of self interest on the part of subscribers and donors. Self interest always plays some part in social awareness - there but for the grace of God go I – and rich men were neither exempt from ravages of disease nor from financial ruin, two facets of life which must have been all the more evident to visitors at Bath, flanked on the one side by invalids and on the other by gamblers. Gambling was such an important aspect of the city's life that in 1706, fifty known gamesters and sharpers were reported to have arrived in Bath from London.[23]

One of these gamblers was a man called Richard Nash who in time became one of Bath's best known characters. Beau Nash was born at Swansea in 1674. His father, hopeful of giving him a good education sent him to Oxford where, according to his biographer Oliver Goldsmith, "he soon showed that though much might be expected from his genius, nothing could be hoped from his industry" and he was sent down. After a rather unsuccessful try at being a soldier and a lawyer, he visited Bath in 1705. Not long after his arrival, the city's Master of Ceremonies was killed in a duel and the persuasive Nash was appointed in his place. Nash wielded tremendous influence on the social behaviour of the city's visitors and had a great propensity for extracting money from people, particularly ladies. Though he grew rich on the proceeds of gaming, not all the money he collected

Richard "Beau" Nash. Pastel portrait attributed to Benjamin Morris. RNHRD.

(above) Engraved portrait of
Ralph Allen. 1693-1764.
Courtesy of Bath Museums Services.

(below) Prior Park.

lined his own pockets and he was amongst the initiators of the scheme to found the Bath Mineral Water Hospital. One can argue that Nash, as the moulder of fashionable Bath, was keener than anyone to rid the city of the beggars who, to use Wood's expression, teased people of fashion, but one should remember that Nash's considerable efforts in fund-raising were primarily to benefit the sick poor; removal of malingering indigents could have just as easily been effected without the expense of a large hospital.

Restoring the health of working men and women did have economic implications in an age obsessed with material prosperity and commercial success. The early years of the eighteenth century mark the rise of the nouveau rich man whose social mobility over two or three generations could transport his family from humble origins to immense social and material elevation; men like Ralph Allen who originated from a quite humble Cornish family and by his own ingenuity and effort became wealthy enough to commission his country mansion at Prior Park, three miles from the centre of Bath. There were lots of self-made men emerging at this time, benefiting from the growth of manufacturing industries and world trade. They often employed a large workforce with many skilled and semi-skilled individuals amongst it. Businesses were dependant on these men and women to work effectively and economically so there was a constant worry that any decline in the health of the working population might create a

(left) Sir Joseph Jekyll (1663-1738). Courtesy of British Library.

(below) Portrait of Lady Elizabeth Hastings (1682-1731) by Kneller. Courtesy of Queen's College, Oxford.

(bottom) Henry Hoare (1677-1725). Courtesy of Courtauld Institute.

shortage of available labour and lead to disastrous wage increases. It is therefore not surprising to find the nouveaux richs well represented amongst the inaugurators of a proposed hospital where working men and women from all over Britain, precipitated into impecuniary circumstances by illness, could be rehabilitated from physical handicap and cured of their incapacities.

Beau Nash's London bankers, Henry and Benjamin Hoare and local banker, property developer and colonial trader Richard Marchant were both involved in the scheme at an early stage. Henry Hoare was also a founder of the Westminster Hospital (1715), the country's first voluntary hospital. His father Richard, who founded the banking firm was a frequent visitor to Bath for reasons of health and was in the habit of having several crates of bottled Bath Water delivered to his London house each year. Hoare's enthusiasm for the Waters might even have caused him to influence some of his customers to extend beneficience. Lady Elizabeth Hastings (1682-1731), renowned for her philanthropic deeds, and Sir Joseph Jekyll were two more wealthy people who became involved with the Hospital scheme at an early stage. Both were amongst the clientelle of Hoares' Bank.[24]

Sir Joseph Jekyll, Master of the Rolls, seems to have been equally possessed of philanthropic zeal but in a somewhat different manner for one feels he was motivated by knowing what was best for the poor. The poor begged to differ and Judge Jekyll, who was also Honorable Member for Reigate became one of the most unpopular politicians of his time. He was the champion of the Gin Act which imposed swingeing duty on the spirit in an attempt to stamp out drunkenness on the streets of London. The mob were so incensed by this piece of legislation that they threatened to burn down Jekyll's residence and the unfortunate man was obliged to enlist the help of sixty soldiers to protect his property.

INDIGENT SEEKERS OF THE CURE

His interest in founding hospitals led him to get involved with the inauguration of the General Infirmary at Northampton near his country seat. Jekyll was an enthusiastic do-gooder to the end. In his will, he bequeathed his entire fortune to relieve the National Debt. Unfortunately, the National Debt stood at £8 million while his fortune amounted to a mere £20,000. As one wit observed, Judge Jekyll might just as well have tried to stop the flow of water under Blackfriars Bridge with his wig.[25]

In the years between 1716 and 1723, Jekyll got together a number of interested persons to start raising money for a hospital in Bath. Unfortunately, their attempts to find a suitable plot on which to build proved fruitless and in 1723, with a fair number of subscriptions already collected, Jekyll and other eminent worthies including the Lord Presidents of England and Scotland called a meeting in Bath to announce that funds would be used to "provide for poor lepers, cripples and other indigent persons resorting to Bath for cure, well recommended and not otherwise provided for." The £270 so far collected was invested in South Sea Bonds and the income used for renting and fitting up apartments for invalids, and for other incidental expenses. A committee of thirteen was chosen to administer the charity and decide who should receive relief. Paupers who were turned down could expect a raw deal, for "the magistrates of Bath were in the strongest terms, called upon by the contributers (of the charity) to expel and punish vagrants and imposters."[26]

The committee of thirteen were supposed to meet each month to approve requests for relief. Six of the committee were medical practitioners. The eldest, a seventy-three year old Cornishman physician called Richard Bettenson (1651-1724) had made money from property development in the city. His beneficence had already extended to a substantial donation towards a marble case for a drinking fountain in the Pump Room.[27] He had scarcely been elected when he died and his place was taken by an apothecary, Francis Bave whose physician brother Charles was also one of the committee members. The Bave family were wealthy and influential in Bath and had strong medical connections.

LARGER THAN LIFE

The other medical members of the committee included Drs John Beeston (1674-1725) and John Quinton (d.1743), both rather shadowy figures, though Quinton published a two volume treatise extolling the virtues of the Bath Waters.[28] Another member, the larger-than-life Dr George Cheyne (1671-1743), was so large that he weighed over 32 stones on his arrival in Bath. This did not deter him from publishing "An Essay on Health and Long Life" warning against excesses of food and drink.

Cheyne was one of the most popular physicians of his time, not just in Bath but amongst a wide selection of personalities both in medicine and the arts. Samuel Johnson, John Wesley, Alexander Pope, David Hume and Samuel Richardson all consulted him at one time or another. He was also Ralph Allen's and Beau Nash's doctor though the latter seems to have held a cynical view of his treatment for when Cheyne asked Nash if he had followed his prescriptions, Nash replied ''If I had, sir, I should have surely broken my neck for I threw them out of an upstairs window.'' Cheyne could be equally disparaging about his patients – ''Folks use their physicians as they do their laundresses, send them their linen to be cleaned in order to be dirted again.''

George Cheyne and a surgeon called Jeremiah Peirce (1696-1765) were the only two medical men on the original committee who were still alive when the hospital opened. Peirce became a Governor and remained senior surgeon until 1761. Little is known of this man's background or how he came to be elected to the original committee at a relatively early age. By 1738, Peirce was well established as a surgeon in Bath. A year before he had reported the case of a patient with a tumour of the knee whose leg he had amputated. This was published by the Royal Society[29] of which Peirce was a fellow. He owned a tiny villa on the end of Lansdown, designed by John Wood and called Lilliput Castle. (It has since been extensively enlarged and renamed Battlefields).

(above) Jeremiah Peirce. Detail from a painting by William Hoare. RNHRD.

(left) Dr George Cheyne (1671-1743), after Van Diest. Courtesy of British Museum.

Surprisingly, only one clergyman seems to have been involved with the founding committee, the archdeacon of the city, Dr Hunt. This contrasts with other provincial voluntary hospitals of the period where clergy were often the prime movers of such charities. The foundation of the Bath Mineral Water Hospital owes more to the enthusiasm and generosity of businessmen like Ralph Allen and Richard Marchant, to property speculators like Humphrey Thayer, a London druggist who had bought undeveloped land in Bath during the early eighteenth century, and ultimately to local medical practitioners like William Oliver and Jerry Peirce who themselves were property speculators.[30] After all, the Bath medical fraternity was the corner stone of Bath's principle industry, the health trade, and its members were sufficiently influential in the affairs of the city and its rich visitors to insure the success of the proposed new hospital at Bath, the first truly national hospital in the country. There was only one problem: nobody on the Committee could agree on how or where to build it.

Detail from ''The Knights of Baythe or the One Headed Corporation'', a satirical view of Bath councillors published in 1763. The apothecaries amongst the council are depicted with drug jars in place of faces whilst the surgeons have skull heads and wield knives. Courtesy of Avon County Libraries.

(above) View of Bath. Detail from
an early 19th century engraving.

(left) Builders in 18th century Bath.
Detail from an engraving by Watts.

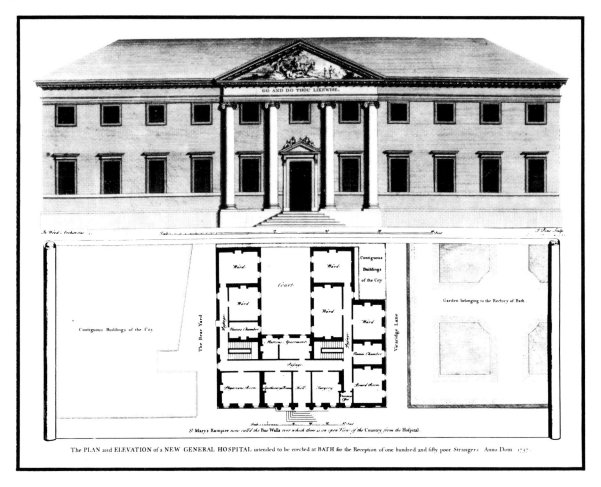

GO AND DO THOU LIKEWISE.

The PLAN and ELEVATION of a NEW GENERAL HOSPITAL intended to be erected at BATH for the Reception of one hundred and fifty poor Strangers Anno Dom 1737

THE Ufefulnefs of HOSPITALS for the Reception of *Sick People*, is fo well known, that it is needlefs to fay any Thing of it. The frequent and noble Benefactions to *St.* THOMAS's and *St.* BARTHOLOMEW's in *London, &c.* fhew the Conviction People have, after long Experience, that fuch Donations are *True Charity.* It is upon this general Principle of *Relieving the Poor and Diftreffed*, that many well-difpofed Perfons have fet on foot, and hope to eftablifh, an *Hofpital* at BATH : And what more particularly moved them to promote this Work, was the Confideration, that in many Cafes the *difeafed Poor* might there recover their Healths, which they could not do from any other Charity, or by any other Means whatfoever. The Care of the *Phyfician*, the Affiftance of the *Surgeon*, and the Medicines of the *Apothecary*, may be had in any other Part of the Kingdom ; but *the Benefit of the* BATH *Waters, in their full Virtue*, can only be enjoy'd at the *Fountain-head.* The Expence, indeed, of living at BATH long enough to receive a Cure, is greater than moft Parifhes are able or willing to defray ; and therefore they chufe rather to fupport their *poor Cripples*, by a fmall Allowance at Home, than be at the Charge of endeavouring their Relief by maintaining them at BATH. Few Parifhes are free from fuch Perfons, who, by the Lofs of their Limbs, are become a Burden to Themfelves and their Neighbours, and drag on an uneafy Life, which, by God's Bleffing on the *Charity* here propofed, might be render'd comfortable to themfelves, and profitable to the Publick. It would be endlefs to enumerate the many different Cafes in which the like good Effects of this *Charity* might reafonably be expected ; and furely, a Confcioufnefs of having been the Inftruments, under GOD, of the Reftoration of fuch Objects from Mifery to Eafe, from Impotence to Strength, and from Beggary and Want, to a Capacity of getting an honeft Livelihood, and comfortable Subfiftence, would be fo fincere a Pleafure to all good Minds, that they muft think it cheaply purchafed by a generous Contribution towards fo good a Work. But though the Relief of our miferable Fellow-Creatures might be fufficient to induce all good-natur'd Perfons to promote this *Charity*, efpecially thofe who have themfelves felt the Benefit of thefe *healing Waters* ; yet it may not be amifs to mention another very great Advantage that will accrue to the Publick from fuch an *Hofpital* being founded at BATH: All Phyficians allow, That the greateft Certainty that can be attain'd to in the Knowledge of the Nature and Virtues of any Medicine, arifes out of the Number of Obfervations of the Effect it has on *Human Bodies* in *different Circumftances.* The World is indeed greatly indebted already to many worthy and learned Gentlemen of the *Faculty*, who have publifh'd their Obfervations on the BATH *Waters*, and given the Hiftories of their *Patients* Cafes with great Exactnefs : Thefe Hiftories are very valuable, and greatly affift the prefent Practitioners in the Performance of the many Cures which numberlefs living Witneffes can now teftify that they have received upon

the Place : But furely, if the Knowledge of the Nature and Efficacy of thefe *Waters* could ftill be render'd more extenfive and certain, it would be doing great Service to every individual Perfon, who may hereafter, in any Country or Age, have Occafion for their Ufe. Nobody can doubt but that this *Hofpital* will greatly contribute towards this defirable End, who confiders, that Perfons of higher Rank are too often negligent of their own Health ; and, by no means, fo exact in taking their Medicines, abftaining from Things which hurt them, and ftaying a due Time, as could be wifh'd, and is indeed neceffary, in order to give the Phyfician a fufficient Opportunity either of doing them all the Service their Cafe would admit of, or of making Obfervations for the future Benefit of others. Whereas in this *Hofpital* every Perfon will be under his Government and Direction in all Circumftances regarding his Health ; fo that a few Years will furnifh more Hiftories of Cafes, which may be depended upon, (if the Phyficians keep due Regifters of the *Sick* under their Care) than any Man's private Practice could have done in an Age : And it is to be hoped, that the Succefs which may reafonably be expected from the Regularity of thefe *poor Creatures*, may induce others of better Condition voluntarily to imitate them in the Management of Themfelves, that they may receive the like Benefits. Every body may therefore fee how great an Advantage this *Hofpital* will be to the Publick : The *Sick* will be healed, many *Parifhes* eafed of the Burden of their ufelefs *poor Cripples*, and the Knowledge and Ufe of the BATH *Waters* will be greatly improv'd to the Benefit of all fucceeding Generations.

IT being neceffary, for the Promoting, Carrying on, and Supporting this *Charity*, that Perfons of Honour and Reputation fhould take it into their Protection and Guardianfhip, the Contributors prefent have **agreed**, That every Perfon contributing Twenty Pounds, or any Sum exceeding that, towards this *Charity*, fhall be admitted a Governor of this *Hofpital.*

IT is propofed by the Contributors prefent, to build an *Hofpital* capable of **Receiving** and commodioufly **Entertaining** One Hundred and Fifty *Poor Diftreffed Perfons.*

THE Expence of Building the faid *Hofpital*, according to the above **Draught**, and of Furnifhing the fame with Beds, and other Neceffaries, it is thought, upon the moft moderate Computation, will amount to the Sum of Six Thoufand Pounds.

ANY Perfons inclin'd to encourage this Undertaking, are defir'd to fend their Contributions to RICHARD NASH, Efq; FRANCIS FAUQUIER, Efq; and Dr. OLIVER, at *Bath* ; or Mr. BENJAMIN HOARE, Banker, at the *Golden Bottle* in *Fleet-ftreet, London* ; or leave their Subfcriptions with Them for the Ufe of this *Charity* : And they may be affur'd, that all fuch Donations fhall be faithfully applied to the Purpofes intended

by the Donors, and a Monthly Account publifh'd by Mr. HOARE of all fuch Donations.

EFFECTUALLY to prevent any poor Perfons coming to *Bath*, and being burdenfome to the Town, under a Pretence of defiring to be admitted into the faid *Hofpital*, the following Order for fuch Admiffion is agreed on, *viz.*

THE Perfon propofed fhall firft have his Cafe drawn up by fome Phyfician or fkilful Perfon in his Neighbourhood, which, being duly attefted by the Minifter and Church-Wardens of the Parifh he refided in, and tranfmitted to the Phyficians of the faid *Hofpital*, together with the Age of fuch Perfon, fhall by them be carefully confidered and examined ; and if they find that the Perfon is a proper Object of this *Charity*, they fhall fignify fuch their Judgment to the Minifter of the faid Parifh ; and fo foon as there is a Vacancy in the faid *Hofpital*, fhall notify it to him by Letter, for the Perfon to come within a limited Time, who is to bring back thefe Letters of the Phyficians to the Minifter; *by which* he or fhe is to be admitted into the faid *Hofpital* ; and if any Perfon fhall come to *Bath*, under Pretence of propofing himfelf to the *Hofpital*, contrary to this Order, he fhall not only be refufed Admittance, but be treated as a Vagrant, with the utmoft Severity of the Law.

EVERY Parifh fending a Perfon to the *Hofpital*, fhall fupply him with Thirty Shillings, which, upon his Admiffion, fhall be lodged in the Hands of the Treafurer of the *Hofpital*, to defray the Charge of his Funeral, in cafe he dies in the *Hofpital* ; or to be returned to him whenever he is difcharged from thence, to anfwer the Expence of his Journey to his own Abode.

WHENEVER any Perfon is propofed to the Phyficians of the *Hofpital*, and is adjudged by them to be a proper Object, he fhall be immediately minuted down to fucceed to the next Vacancy that fhall happen ; and every Perfon fo minuted, fhall abfolutely fucceed in his Turn, any Intereft or Application from any Perfon whatfoever notwithftanding.

THESE Articles are all that are now thought neceffary to be fettled by the Contributors prefent ; but as foon as the Foundation of the *Hofpital* is laid, (publick Notice whereof will be given in fome of the Papers) General Meetings of the Truftees and Contributors will be appointed, for them to confider and fettle fuch farther Regulations as they fhall then judge to be for the Good of this *Charity.*

THESE Articles are fubmitted to the Judgment of the Publick: And all Perfons are defired to give their Opinions as to any Alterations or Additions, to promote the Good which is intended by all the Contributors.

CHAPTER TWO
A Magnificent Pile

It is difficult to imagine how Bath appeared in the early eighteenth century. It certainly bore very little resemblance to the city as seen today. The mediaeval wall, though in a deplorable state, still bounded most of the city's perimeter. Within these confines lay a city "of no more than fifteen streets, four inferior courts, five open areas of a superior kind, four terrace walks, sixteen lanes, three alleys, four throngs, and two bridges." [1]

Almost all the houses standing in the city at that time have since been demolished, many during the eighteenth and early nineteenth centuries when there was a programme of intensive rebuilding. The old walled city has literally gone to ground, following the fate of its Roman predecessor. With the exception of a short length on the north side of the old town, and the east gate, the borough walls remain only as streets.

THE ARCHITECT ARRIVES

To this small confined town, its buildings crowded around narrow muddy streets and passageways, its resident population no more than three thousand inhabitants, there came a young architect who was to do more than anyone to transform the place into the elegant city which endears itself to the countless numbers of visitors who annually frequent the place today. It was in the spring of 1727 that John Wood, at the age of twenty-three, quit London to take up residence in Bath.

Curiously for a man who achieved so much distinction as an architect, little is known about Wood's early life. He was certainly working in London before his removal to Bath. He was employed there by Lord Bingley who engaged him to assist in the construction of a new town house in Cavendish Square. In 1725, Bingley asked Wood to design the gardens of his country seat, Bramham Park, in Yorkshire and this has given rise to a misconception that Wood himself was a Yorkshireman. There is no evidence to support this supposition, and current opinion suggests that his family were local and his father and brother worked as builders in Bath. [2]

Lord Bingley was not the only person with an interest in developing real estate in London. The Duke of Chandos, who lived in such great state that his ninety-strong household included a private orchestra of sixteen musicians, had also chosen Cavendish Square as a site for one of his town houses. One can imagine that Chandos, who later employed Wood at Bath, became acquainted with the promising young architect while he was enjoying the patronage of the Duke's neighbour. There were other London acquaintances who proved useful to Wood after he left the city: the rich druggist Humphrey Thayer, who later became a Commissioner of the Excise, and a wealthy surgeon, Robert Gay, both of whom owned considerable portions of land in Bath. Gay had actually represented the town in Parliament between 1719 and 1721.

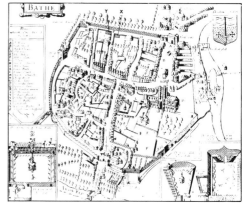

(*above*) Speed's map of 1610 showing the mediaeval layout of the city.

(*opposite*) Broadside advertising the proposed hospital at Bath, published in 1737. The ground plan depicted was not the one finally chosen by Wood. RNHRD.

The Circus, one of John Wood's masterpieces. From a painting by J.R. Cozens. 1773.
Courtesy of Avon County Libraries.

ROME REVISITED

It is not difficult to see how the enthusiasm for developing real estate spilled out amongst these gentlemen who owned undeveloped plots in the increasingly popular West Country spa town. In the company of the fancifully inventive Wood, always dreaming of rebuilding the place as a second Rome and talking of creating one of the "Wonders of the World amongst the Productions of Art,"[3] these gentlemen must have become all the more excited by the possibilities which development of their provincial plots might offer. In reality, when it came to the business of signing contracts, the landowners opted for more modest schemes. The wealthy Duke of Chandos engaged Wood to rebuild part of St John's Hospital and adjacent land and to make there the finest lodging house in town, while Gay requested him to build a street on his land to the north of the town. Meanwhile, Humphrey Thayer employed him to design the plans for streets on the sites of the Abbey Orchard and old Bowling Green.

IN CIRCLES AND SQUARES

Thayer's involvement as treasurer of the Appeal to fund the proposed Mineral Water Hospital provided Wood with another opportunity: he was chosen to design the hospital and look for suitable ground on which to erect it. Wood was attracted to an open piece of ground just south of the town near the river, called the Ambrey. This site is now occupied by the Technical College theatre but in those days it provided a vegetable garden for one Samuel Broad. The proposed building required an area of sixty-seven square feet and Wood offered the trustees two versions, one quadrangular and the other circular. Both versions incorporated a bath in their design which was to be supplied with thermal water flowing down a conduit from the Hot Bath. The buildings could accommodate a maximum of sixty patients.

It was suggested that three of the trustees, Mr Thayer, Mr Martin and Beau Nash, visit Robert Gay, who owned the land, and persuade him to bequeath it to the hospital after his death. Gay took a rather dim view of this proposal, not through any want of charitable benevolence but rather that a hospital would not be the sort of structure likely to "improve" the parts of his estate lying about the city. It was not until he had been convinced by Wood that the designs would not "hurt the intended works" that he finally agreed to offer the trustees his inheritance.

Meanwhile the trustees were still arguing over the designs. Sir Joseph Jekyll, who had been associated with the charity since its very early days, thought the building was much too small and proposed that they renegotiate with Gay for more land. Gay, who by now must have felt his patience stretched as much as his benevolence, did not even bother to reply to their letter. It was either to be a small circular hospital or no hospital at all. In the late spring of 1731, advertisements showing Wood's circular design were printed and distributed[4] in an effort to attract donations for the charity and a lawyer, Richard Collibee, was engaged to handle the conveyancing of the land. It looked as though the new Mineral Water Hospital was about to take off. Then came an unexpected snag. Collibee reported that the tenant, Samuel Broad, was subleasing the ground from a city councillor called Rosewell Gibbs who insisted that the charity buy out his term of the lease which had another eight years to run. There appears to have been some dispute over this, probably on account of the sum involved, and while this was dragging on, one of the trustees who opposed the hospital being built on this site bought the remainder of the lease himself and refused to vacate possession. This extraordinary piece of gazumping completely frustrated the trustees' plans so that they had no alternative but to look for a new site.

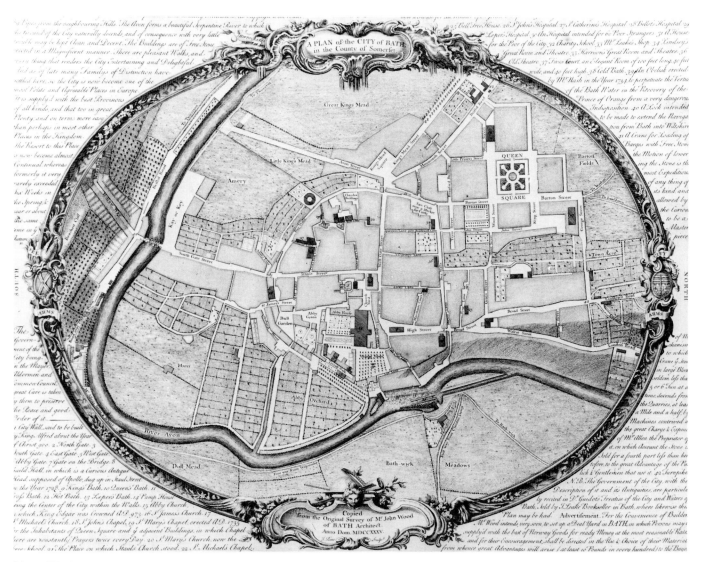

Plan of Bath, c1735, showing the
site of Wood's proposed circular
hospital near the river.

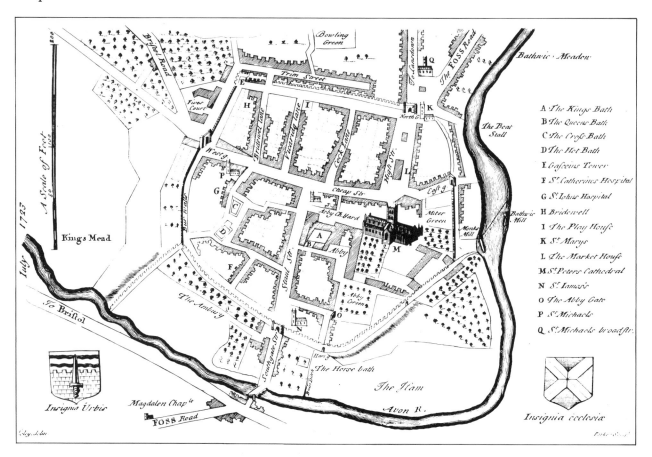

The following labels appear on the map:

A *The Kings Bath*
B *The Queens Bath*
C *The Cross Bath*
D *The Hot Bath*
E *Gascoins Tower*
F *St Catherines Hospital*
G *St Johns Hospital*
H *Bridewell*
I *The Play House*
K *St Marys*
L *The Market House*
M *St Peters Cathedral*
N *St Iames's*
O *The Abby Gate*
P *St Michaels*
Q *St Michaels broad Str.*

Plan of Bath 1723. The final site chosen for the hospital was on the site of the old playhouse. (I) Courtesy of Avon County Libraries.

THE PLAYHOUSE REPLACED

Seven years were to pass before the trustees could agree on a new site. Ironically, it was as a result of legislation introduced by Sir Joseph Jekyll, who was then MP for Reigate, that this particular site became available, though his Bill had nothing to do with hospitals. Politicians were the butt of satirical plays in the eighteenth century just as much as they are lampooned and ridiculed on television today. Both government and opposition were spared no mercy. By 1737 they had had enough and an Act was passed which required all playhouses to be licenced by the Lord Chamberlain. Many small provincial theatres failed to obtain a licence and were closed. This did nothing to stop the offending productions as they merely went underground and continued to flourish. Certainly this is what happened in Bath where the old Playhouse, built in 1705, was forced to close.[5] The building occupied a most desirable piece of land just inside the city's northern boundary and enjoyed open views across the fields which then sloped upwards towards Lansdown, as yet undeveloped and providing a panorama of open countryside: the ideal site for a hospital.

The trustees moved quickly and negotiated a purchase of the land from the owner, Mrs Cairne. The tenant of the theatre, Mr Dillon, was offered £21 to leave and financial inducements were also laid before the tenants of other buildings on the site. The proprietors of the White House in Vicarage Lane would not accept anything less than £100 and William Boyes who rented some stables next door appears to have held out for a similar amount and insisted that he be allowed to take away the rack, manger and the break-post standing in the building. This hardly worried the Trustees for as soon as the various buildings were vacated, they were promptly demolished and by June 1738, the site was ready for the foundations to be excavated.

FOR THE SAKE OF ORNAMENT

John Wood's designs for the new hospital had already been made public in February when a broadside appealing for donations was engraved. This showed the front elevation and ground floor plan of the proposed building. In fact, the final plan differed considerably from that which was published. Wood explained that the first plan was merely "for the sake of ornament and to gain a point in the purchase of the land"[6] though exactly what this point was remains a mystery.

The final design adopted had a ground plan in the shape of a trapezium, the east and west side being skewed at an angle of four degrees with the north front. To our neat and ordered twentieth-century minds, this may seem a rather curious plan but eighteenth century builders thought nothing of such angulations. Vicarage Lane meets Upper Borough Walls at an angle, so it was only right and proper that the hospital should follow the line of these two streets.

Wood's original hospital, "a magnificent pile of building in the Ionic order," had three storeys, the entrance on the north side being to the principal, or first, storey as is usual in Georgian architecture. The north front has a tetrastyle frontispiece in its central elevation which supports a pediment, the tympanum of which was to have been decorated with a bas relief of a scene depicting the parable of the Good Samaritan. The Trustees engaged a sculptor called Vincent Matthysens to execute the design and although he was paid thirty pounds for his services, the committee got no more than a model and some drawings. Perhaps his fee for the real thing exceeded the budget. Matthysens did manage to produce some finished products which were commissioned by Ralph Allen a few years later. These stone panels depict men blasting rock and other scenes of General Wade's road-building exploits in Scotland. They can still be seen at Prior Park College.

Expanded view of the hospital as it might have looked in 1742.

A. Queen's Ward
B. Apothecary's Bedroom
C. Apothecary's Shop
D. Matron's Bedroom
E. Matron's Parlour
F. Surgeon's Room
G. Committee Room
H. Register's Room
I. Steward's Room
J. Princesses' Ward
K. Porter's Lodge

(*above*) Model of the hospital facade as it would have appeared in 1742. Constructed by Alyson Carter.

The north side, at least below the level of the cornice, has changed the least since the hospital was first built though much of the original stonework has been replaced. The first cornice had largely crumbled away by 1850 and had to be restored. The original windows had sashes with thick Georgian glazing bars. Two of the original sashes survive on the west side but the rest have been replaced by plate glass. (The old sashes were sufficiently well-preserved to find use in the construction of the hospital's greenhouse during the nineteenth century).[7] At the same time the Committee wanted to enlarge the upper storey windows. They were fortunately advised by the hospital architect to refrain. Some of the side windows were heightened at this time and the reveals splayed to allow more light in. The west side was altered considerably in 1860 by the abutment of the bridge connecting the old hospital with the new West block. This has destroyed any symmetry which originally existed.

The east side was partially hidden by the Bear Inn which occupied the site of Union Street. The Bear Inn was demolished in the 1790's. The east elevation, originally faced with plaster, was refaced with Bath stone in 1837. The present inscription dates from 1964 when the hospital was refurbished after the last war but an earlier inscription was painted on this side in 1810 and read:

(*below*) William Pulteney, Earl of Bath.

The Bath Hospital, or Infirmary, appropriated for the reception of poor strangers whose cases require the use of the Bath waters, established by Act of Parliament and supported by voluntary contribution.

THE FIRST STONE

The hospital took over three years to be built. The foundations were dug during the summer months of 1738 by one Joseph Williams who received sixteen shillings and fourpence for his labours.[8] The first stone was laid ceremoniously at the north-east corner by the Right Honourable William Pulteney, Earl of Bath, on July 6th and simply inscribed: "This stone is the first which was laid in the foundation of the General Hospital. July the sixth AD 1738. God prosper this charitable undertaking." All the stone for the hospital, together with paving slabs and lime, were donated by Ralph Allen who provided the materials from his stone quarries in Combe Down. All other materials were purchased. Lead was ordered from Messrs Jacob Elton and Son at Bristol while all the glass, cut to the required size for the window panes, was obtained from a firm of London glaziers called Cookson and Jefferies. These panes were packed into crates and transported in waggons belonging to a Bath haulier called John Willshire whose family business was still flourishing forty years later when Thomas Gainsborough employed them to move his paintings between the two cities.

A vaulted ceiling in the basement of the hospital. This is the only room in the building to retain the Georgian sash windows.

BUGS BELOW STAIRS

Many hospitals designed in the Georgian period have a striking resemblance to English country mansions and their interiors are not so far removed from the arrangements of domestic architecture. The servants offices are generally "below stairs" and the front entrance on the principal storey is frequently elevated up a short flight of steps. This was the general plan adopted by Wood at Bath.

The interior of the hospital today bears scarcely any resemblance to the original. In 1742 when the hospital first admitted patients, they entered by the door-way in the centre of the building, now blocked off. Beyond the entrance vestibule, they would have been greeted by the porter who occupied a small room near the staircase. The resident apothecary and matron each had a bedroom and a sitting room on this floor and the apothecary's shop, later renamed the dispensary, was also here. There were separate rooms for the physicians and surgeons but, in view of their rather infrequent visits, their rooms were converted to other uses quite early on. Most of the women patients were accommodated on the ground floor in Queen's and Princesses' wards.

The original staircase ascended in an apse overlooking the rear courtyard, but all trace of this has disappeared and the present concrete staircase on the east side is of recent construction.[9] Upstairs, there were four more wards[10] and a large storeroom which was converted into a ward in 1754.[11]

The basement provided accommodation for the maids and other servants of the hospital as well as a kitchen, a bakehouse and brewhouse, a pantry, wash-houses for the patients, a laundry and a laboratory for compounding and refining medicines. There was probably a mortuary on this level. Access to the basement was gained either via the main staircase or through a side door in Vicarage Lane. This was the entry for delivery of provisions and fuel. The lavatories, known variously as the houses of offices, necessary houses and privies were also on this level[12] and there were frequent complaints that they stank, hardly surprising when one considers that all the hospital waste was swilled away along a drain which terminated in the ditch beyond the city wall. The hospital's drains were not connected to the city's common sewer until 1764,[13] and, even then, nobody had yet considered the idea of using S-bends in plumbing. The stench continued to provoke complaints until, in 1792, a plumber called Edward Mullins installed traps in the privies called "stop troughs."[14] At least the waste was conveyed in the opposite direction from the well in the back yard where water was obtained through a hand pump.

(*above*) Portrait of Dr Stephen Hales.
Courtesy of the National Portrait Gallery, London.

(*below*) Stothert and Pitt steam engine, now at Bath University. Installed in the hospital in 1895 to pump mineral water from the King's spring, it replaced an earlier engine dating from 1830.

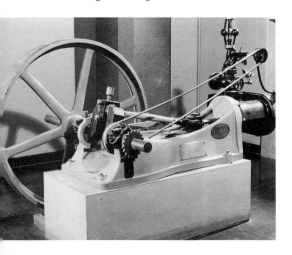

More water closets were added when the mineral baths were built at the rear of the hospital in 1830. Privacy was considered a low priority because the lavatories were designed without any partitions. When this was queried by one of the Governors, he was told that "in view of the general habits of the patients", there was no need to waste money on such delicacies.[15]

The upper floors were kept relatively free of noxious odours by the installation of a bellows ventilator, a piece of up-to-the-minute technology "erected in the most commodious place in the house"[16] and invented by an ingenious country parson, Dr Stephen Hales (1677-1761), whose interests lay in as diverse subjects as measurement of horses' blood pressure and clearing mud from harbours. The terrible scourge of typhus which earned itself the name hospital fever because of its predeliction for these institutions was almost entirely eliminated by Hales' inventions. It was never a problem in the Bath Mineral Water Hospital and apart from several outbreaks of smallpox the hospital seems to have been a reasonably healthy place. There were no cases of cholera in the building when the disease broke out in Bath in 1832 even though 74 people died of the disease in the lower parts of the town.[17] The hospital was less fortunate with blood-sucking insects: in May 1751 a committee was convened to consider "the most proper method to destroy and prevent bugs in the hospital."[18] Their deliberations do not seem to have stemmed the flood of these small but voracious parasites for three years later the apothecary, Mr Morris was asked to investigate how the nurses' room might be altered "in such a manner as may best prevent bugs from harming them."[19] In 1826, Nathaniel Gundry presented a bug-destroying machine to the hospital[20] and we hear no more about the matter. But bugs were not the only parasite causing consternation and both staff and patients were frequently afflicted with the *Itch*, caused either by scabies or body lice.

LIGHT AND HEAT

In its early days the building was heated by open coal fires. The coal, which was mined at the nearby village of Timsbury, was delivered by a coalmerchant called Joseph Cox who charged six pence a bushel. The house steward had the duty of measuring the quantity delivered to guard against fraud. Light in the hospital was provided by oil lamps and candles. In 1749 a total of 149 gallons of rape seed oil was used in lighting the building at cost of nineteen pounds, seven shillings and threepence farthing.[21] The ubiquity of candles and open fires constituted a considerable fire risk. The building was insured with the Sun Fire Office for £3000 and its contents for £1000. Just before Christmas 1784, a fire broke out which was fortunately brought under control by the chairmen.[22]

Gas was first introduced in Bath in 1818.[23] The hospital was connected to the supply 11 years later.[24] At first, gas was only used to provide light and it was not until 1859 that gas cooking was introduced into the kitchen.[25] The hospital continued to be heated by coal fires though a primitive form of central heating was installed around 1830. This was powered by a furnace which sent hot air through ducts built into the walls. A steam engine was installed at the same time, made by the local engineering firm of Stothert and Pitt and was primarily intended to pump mineral water into the hospital's reservoir from the conduit connected to the King's spring at the Roman Baths. The original engine was replaced in 1895[26] and this second engine has since been removed and is now preserved at Bath University.

ENGINEER

It was a requirement of the city council, even in the nineteenth century, that furnaces should produce no appreciable smoke[27] and there were complaints that the hospital's boiler flue was one of the principle sources of pollution.[28] The problem was solved in 1853 by George Wheeler, who devised a "scrubber" which literally washed the smoke away as it ascended the flue.[29] George Wheeler was appointed first engineer to the hospital in 1829 when he was thirty and remained in office for 42 years.[30] He was a man of considerable engineering ability and worked closely with Stothert and Pitt, a Bath firm famous for their dockside cranes, who manufactured and installed the various plant in the hospital during the nineteenth century. (The baths and vapour baths, the steam plant and engine, and the hydraulic lift). By the mid century, the complexities of the system were sufficiently mysterious for the Committee to request Wheeler to "make such plan or model as will render intelligible all pipes and apparatus connected with the engine, steam boiler, hot and cold water and ventilating flues."[31]

AS MANY AS THE HOUSE WILL CONTAIN

As the wealth of the hospital increased and its reputation grew, the number of patients accepted for admission began to overflow the space available. In 1754, the Governors considered purchasing the Swan Inn at the rear of the hospital,[32] now the site of Owen Owen's store. In the following year, an epidemic of smallpox caused more problems of space and Prince ward had to be turned into an isolation ward so that patients with the disease could be nursed separately.[33] Meanwhile the Committee continued to deliberate over the purchase of additional property but failed to find anything suitable before the epidemic had subsided. Ensuing financial difficulties relinquished any further thoughts of expansion and the Committee were forced to close two wards, dismiss half the nursing staff and drastically reduce the number of patients admitted. They even considered letting out one of the vacant wards to bring in extra money but the Governors were not prepared to go this far.[34] A few years later the Committee were happy to report that the stringences were over and the number of patients admitted would be "as many as the house will contain."[35]

EXPANSION

The idea of rebuilding the hospital on an entirely new site was first proposed in 1791 and has been repeatedly suggested ever since. At the end of the eighteenth century, the main reason for moving was to get a site near enough to the hot springs to make it feasable for the hospital to have its own hot bath. It was mainly due to opposition from the medical staff that the move was not then made as the present situation was "in every respect convenient for those who have the care of the patients, as well as the patients themselves".[36] They also considered a hot bath in the hospital would make the air damp and such moisture would be bound to spread infection of every kind. All were agreed, however, that more room was desirable and one of the Committee, architect Thomas Baldwin, offered to submit designs for enlarging the building. Baldwin had a successful record as city architect and his work included the new Guildhall and Great Pulteney Street. Baldwin was also Deputy Chamberlain for Bath but failed to be re-elected to the post in 1791.

The city council were at this time considering Baldwin's proposals for the new Union Street which would link Upper Borough Walls with the lower part of the town. The new street cut right through the Bear Inn which was adjacent to the east side of the hospital. As compensation, the landlord, Henry Phillott, was to be granted the whole of the west side of Union Street to rebuild his hotel, provided he did so within two years.[37] This meant that the hospital, hitherto enjoying an open aspect on its south side, would have its central court yard totally enclosed.

In January 1792, Henry Phillott offered the Governors some ground on which they might enlarge the hospital and in the same week, the Alfred Hotel came on the market. This was a large elegant building close to the newly built Royal Baths (previously the Hot Bath) which had once been the residence of Charles Bave, a physician whose practice devolved upon William Oliver.

The Alfred Hotel was such an attractive property, both in terms of size and site, that some of the Governors were keen to resite the Mineral Water Hospital there,[38] despite previous reservations from the medical staff who said it was too prone to flooding. But in the characteristic way that hospital management committees have always conducted their business, the affair dragged on while the public was kept in a state of confusion as various letters appeared in the press arguing for and against the resiting of the hospital. Eventually, the Alfred Hotel was purchased by several of the Governors who were confident their colleagues would agree to the hospital buying them out. But the other Governors were less enthusiastic about the move and resolved to keep the hospital where it was.[39] Ironically, the Alfred Hotel did become a hospital, but it was not the one the purchasers had intended. In the end, they let the building to the Bath Pauper Charity[40] which provided a free medical service to the poor people in the city. As a result, the building became the Bath City Infirmary and Dispensary and, ultimately, the Royal United Hospital.

Watercolour painting of the Alfred Hotel, later the Bath City Infirmary and Dispensary. The building was demolished in the early 19th century.
Courtesy of Christopher Wood.

The hospital after the addition of John Palmer's top storey. Old Blue Coat School is seen in the foreground.
Courtesy of Prof. P. Maddison.

Meanwhile, the Governors of the Mineral Water Hospital, frustrated in their attempts to find a nearby house for extra patients, reconsidered Thomas Baldwin's plans to enlarge the existing building. Unfortunately, Baldwin was in trouble with the city council after failing to make proper accounts of his building work[41] and, as many of the hospital's management Committee were also councillors, they thought it prudent to involve another architect, John Palmer, who was asked to take on the project. Palmer shortly replaced Baldwin as city architect and was ultimately responsible for the cumbersome attic storey which rests uneasily on top of Wood's building and was added in 1793 at a cost of £900.[42]

TEMPTATIONS OF THE CITY

There have been two further attempts to resite the hospital and ironically both failed for the same reason – war. The first was made in the mid nineteenth century, a time when the Governors were becoming increasingly concerned by the lack of discipline amongst patients, particularly with regard to their behaviour when they left the precincts of the hospital to take exercise. This was far less of a headache to the Governors in the early days because the land, at least on the north side of the hospital, had not been developed and open fields provided a place for the patients to "take the air" – a necessary performance in the course of their convalescence. But by 1850, the hospital was no longer on the edge of the town, and the advantages of an open aspect had been lost. In place of fields was the bustling thoroughfare of Milsom Street, thronging with shoppers. But it was not just the architecture of the town which was changing: the whole tone of Bath society had metamorphosed since the rumbustuous and frivolous days of Beau Nash into one of genteel and smug moralising. Bath had ceased to be the resort of hedonists and gamblers and was increasingly populated by half-pay army officers, retired parsons and ageing spinsters, just the sort of person to be outraged and affronted by the sight of drunken and brawling patients shambling around the streets. The Governors and

27

medical staff, for the most part represented by the same strata of Bath society, were obliged to put their house in order. In any case, would not "the convalescence of the patients be materially accelerated if they had a convenient and private place of exercise which would effectively remove them from the temptations to which they are daily exposed in the city?"[43] The "temptations" were principally to be found in ale-houses and so many patients seemed to find their way into licenced premises that the Governors voted in 1850 to contribute one pound per year of the hospital's income to the Bath police sick fund on the understanding that constables informed the hospital whenever they observed a patient entering a public house.[44]

What was needed was a larger site on which to build a new hospital in grounds of sufficient area to make it unnecessary for patients to venture beyond the perimeter walls. Various sites were considered by the Governors[45] and of these, Sydney Gardens seemed the most promising. The proposal was made to convert Sydney Hotel (now the Holburne of Menstrie Museum) into the new hospital, adding an extension to the rear of the building. The share-holders of the land agreed to sell for £1540, but planning permission had to be agreed by Lord Powlett who at the time was the trustee of the Cleveland Estate in which the building stood. On requesting Lord Powlett's permission to go ahead with the scheme, the Governors were dismayed to meet with his refusal. Residents living in nearby Sydney Place had quickly lobbied Powlett and objected to the proposals in the strongest terms. "I confess I entirely sympathise with their feelings", wrote Lord Powlett in his letter to the Governors,[46] "I must think it will entail a great nuisance in that locality... I should have thought a much more airy situation than Sydney Gardens could be obtained in the neighbourhood of Bath." What was not said was that the hotel was already in use as a private Water Cure Establishment and seems to have been considered "airy" enough for Prince Napoleon when he stayed there for hydropathic treatment.[47]

The Sydney Hotel, one of the proposed sites for the hospital in 1850. The building now houses the Holburne of Menstrie Museum.

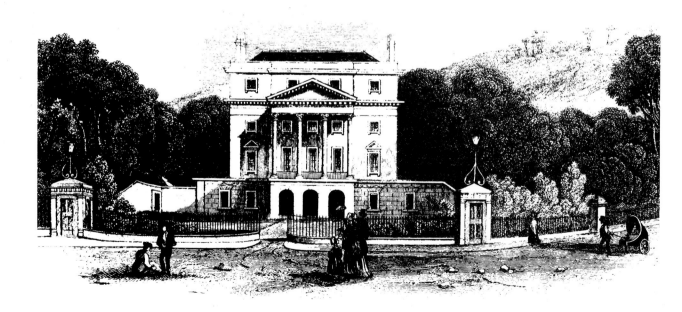

The next site to be recommended by the medical staff was in the lower part of the town and part of the Manvers Estate. Lord Manvers was approached as it had been rumoured that he was willing to sell but he demurred, giving no reason[48] to the Governors but intimating that if an equal or more eligible site presented itself, he would not be upset if the Governors chose to go for it. When Manvers finally agreed to sell, his price was too high and other more attractive sites were being offered. The ground finally chosen was in the corner of Victoria Park, to the west of the city. Despite its being over half a mile away from the hot springs, the Governors were assured by Professor Maskelyne, reader of mineralogy at Oxford University, that the Bath waters could be safely piped to a distance of 1200 yards without diminishing their ''important properties.''[49]

The move was never made. England was suddenly engaged in a war ''on a magnitude and duration of which no-one can calculate.''[50] The Governors feared the catastrophic effect of the Crimea war on government stocks, the main source of the hospital's income, and were also worried by the rising cost of building materials. By the time the war was over (1856), Bath Abbey Rectory, immediately to the west of the hospital in Upper Borough Walls, became available[51] and after some haggling over the price, the Governors purchased the land, demolished the rectory house and built a large new block connected with the old building by a bridge over Vicarage Lane.

Rectory House, demolished in 1858 to make way for the West Wing of the hospital.

Laying the foundation stone of the new wing which opened in 1861. RNHRD.

EVERYBODY IN

Designed by George Manners and John Elkington Gill, the building provided the hospital with a chapel, an ''airing'' ground in the former rectory garden, and two capacious day rooms which obviated the need to have patients languishing by their bedsides in the old wards. Perhaps what satisfied the Governors the most was the their ability to confine the patients within the hospital, seven days a week. Whereas it had been formerly possible for patients to leave the hospital on Sundays on the pretext of attending a service in the Abbey, they were henceforth obliged to attend the hospital chapel: there would no longer be any danger of stragglers losing themselves in an ale-house along the way. Only dissenting patients were now allowed to leave the hospital on the Sabbath and only if issued with a special ticket, printed with a reminder that anyone neglecting to attend the chapel of the persuasion to which he belonged would be immediately dismissed.[52]

The foundation stone of the new building was laid by Lord Portman on 4th June 1859, using the same trowel that spread the mortar beneath the first foundation stone over a century earlier. The town on that day was awash with pomp, ceremony and sickly speeches which the Governors took great pride in publishing. Hymns were sung and psalms chanted: children from the Blue Coat School lined up in their best Sunday uniform and led the procession of worthies around the streets. The whole performance seems to have been replayed two years later when the building was opened: Blue Coat boys, clergy, aldermen, city and county dignitories, all marching along to the strains of a Hanoverian Band. The Bishop of Bath and Wells preached in the hospital chapel and luncheon was taken in the new Board Room following a spate of mutual congratulations.[53]

With the extra room available, substantial alterations were made to the old building. The old board room and ground floor staff quarters were opened out as a new night ward, named after a benefactor called Dr William Perry. Additional hydrotherapy facilities, reclining and vapour baths, were installed by Stothert and Pitt. In 1866, a further addition to Palmer's attic storey was made, creating two wards, but despite so much new building, the number of patients accommodated only rose by 30 beds.

RESURRECTION FROM RUIN

Just over eighty years after its completion, the West Wing was almost entirely destroyed in the space of one night. As part of the retaliatory measures by the Nazis which became known as the Baedecker Raids, German bombers dropped their deadly cargo on the night of the 26th April 1942. Miraculously, none of the patients huddling in the hospital cellars was injured despite the damage going on above. The explosion ripped out the midst of the West Wing and left the chapel filled with rubble and smashed glass.

Ten years later, the west half of the hospital was still in ruins though patients continued to receive treatment in the older part of the building which had escaped destruction. But a new enemy threatened the hospital. A nationalised health service meant a rationalised one. District General Hospitals, huge all-purpose institutions, were poised to sweep away specialist hospitals which were seen as uneconomical anachronisms. Despite the fact that a large number of its patients came from all over the country, the Mineral Water Hospital was financed from a regional budget, an arrangement that remains a bone of contention to this day. With so little support for specialist hospitals in the 1950s, particularly from many of the local medical profession who were advising the South West Regional Hospital Board, closure of the hospital seemed imminent.

One doctor stood resolute against this decision. Dr George Kersley, who had been physician to the hospital since 1935, set out to wage a one-man

The West Wing after receiving bomb damage. RNHRD.

crusade to martial public and political opinion to retain and rebuild the Mineral Water Hospital. Aided by the Times newspaper and the opportunity to address a large assembly of MPs at a dinner in the House of Lords, George Kersley gained enough support to win his case, though he made himself unpopular amongst several of his own profession in the process. Between 1962 and 1965, when the building was reconstructed under the architectural direction of Mollie Gerrard, a local architect, the patients were transferred to a 50-bedded ward at Combe Park, an arrangement which could have become permanent had it not been for the diligence of Dr Kersley. The Mineral Water Hospital was reopened in October 1965 by H.R.H. Princess Marina, Duchess of Kent who was then Patron of the hospital. A new storey had been added to the West Wing to house a minor operating theatre plaster room and clinical research laboratory. The accommodation for the 100 patients was much brighter and spacious and the staff were given better facilities than before.

ERASING THE GHOSTS

One of the attractions of the hospital today is that, despite the many further alterations it has undergone to enable patients to enjoy the fruits of modern medical research, there is still a comforting human scale about its dimensions which is often sadly lacking in the factory semblance of so many modern hospitals. But despite its link with the past, virtually all trace of the hospital's Georgian interior has vanished. The enthusiasm for modernisation in the nineteen-sixties, coupled with the desperate struggle to finance the bid of rescuing the institution from the ignominious end which the Ministry of Health had in store for it, has resulted in a decided triumph for concrete. Only one room, now the rest place for the porters, still retains its ancient appearance. Its original purpose must remain a mystery, for no early plan of the hospital's basement has survived, but for years its curious barrel-vaulted ceiling lay hidden beneath a plaster covering until it was rediscovered in 1914. The kitchen is still in its original position but very much modernised and enlarged. The wash-house has long since been replaced by the boiler-room and there is now an ugly gap leading from the yard where once John Wood's oak staircase ascended in its apse. But just occasionally, below stairs in the narrow vaulted corridors of the old building, one can fancy hearing the sound of the housemaid's footsteps as she hurries towards the wash-house with her basket-full of linen, or the muffled cursing of the chairmen on the stairs as they carry another paralysed patient to the top of the house.

Two views of the Mineral Water
Hospital.
(Top) : 1742

(Bottom) : 1861.
Courtesy of Dr G.D.Kersley.

CHAPTER THREE
Subscription for Health

Every Thursday evening at the Rummer Tavern, the newly founded committee of thirteen met to execute the final plans of the hospital. After years of planning and procrastination, the trustees were able to look forward to the fruits of their labours. With £2000 already donated to the project, they were in a position to acquire the chosen site on the north edge of the city and begin building.

The funds swelled rapidly. By 1739, the previous year's sum had more than doubled and by the time the first patients were admitted in 1742, the funds stood at over £9000. Nearly a fifth of this was collected by one man, Beau Nash.

Nash had a way of extracting money from rich ladies which fascinated his biographer, Oliver Goldsmith:

I am told he was once collecting money in Wiltshire's (assembly) Room when a lady entered, who is more remarkable for her wit than her charity, and not being able to pass him unobserved, she gave him a pat with her fan and said:

"You must put down a trifle for me, Nash. I have no money in my pocket."

"Yes, Madam, that I will with pleasure, if your Grace will tell me when to stop."

Then taking a handful of guineas out of his pocket, he began to tell them into his white hat, one, two, three, four, five.

"Hold!", says the Duchess, "consider what you are about."

"Consider your rank and fortune, Madame. Six, seven, eight, nine, ten..."

Here the Duchess stormed and caught hold of his hand.

"Peace, Madam, you shall have your name written in letters of gold, Madam, and upon the front of the building, Madam... sixteen, seventeen, eighteen, nineteen, twenty..."

"I won't pay a farthing more"

"Charity hides a multitude of sins... twenty-one, twenty-two, twenty-three..."

"Nash, I protest; you frighten me out of my wits; I shall die!"

"Madam, you will never die with doing good; and if you do it will be the better for you,"

"Come," says she, "I will be friends with you though you are a fool, and to let you see I am not angry, there is ten guineas more for your charity. But this I insist on, that neither my name nor the sum shall be mentioned"[1]

Donations from "an unknown hand" are frequently mentioned in the early minute books, usually in guineas but on one occasion, the sum of £1-3-7¾d appears, presumably from someone wanting to rid his pockets of loose change. Not all donations were given out of pure charity. In 1800,

(opposite) Portrait of Thomas Carew, first president of the hospital, 1739-41. By Thomas Hudson. Courtesy of the owner.

(below) Signatures of the Committee members from the first Minute Book.

(below) List of subscribers to the hospital. RNHRD.

LIST of the CONTRIBUTORS

	l.	s.	d.
Brought over	8910	0	8¼

The following Sums collected on Sunday 24th of Octob. viz.

	l.	s.	d.	
Abbey Church	104	4	0	⎤
St. James	18	12	0	⎟
Chapel in the Square	49	11	0½	⎬ 212 15 3
St. John's Chapel	16	15	1¼	⎟
Dr. Stevenson's	23	13	1¼	⎦
Messrs. Hall *and Company, by Mr.* Morris	5	5	0	
Parish of Leominster, *per Dr.* Oliver	2	2	0	

	9130	2	11½

Annual SUBSCRIBERS.

	l.	s.	d.
Richard Nash, *Esq;* –	10	10	0
Ralph Allen, *Esq;* –	21	0	0
Lord Palmerston – –	5	5	0
Col. Harbord Harbord –	10	0	0
Francis Fauquier, *Esq;* –	10	10	0
Dr. Oliver – – –	5	5	0
Mr. John Wood – –	5	5	0
Richard Roberts, *Esq;* –	3	3	0
Mr. Paul Bertrand – –	2	2	0
Mr. Jerry Pierce – –	5	5	0
Mr. John Stagg – –	2	2	0
Mr. Samuel Bush – –	2	2	0
Mr. John Morris – –	2	2	0
Mr. James Leake – –	2	2	0
Dr. Bennet Stevenson – –	2	2	0
Mr. James Grist – –	2	2	0
Rev. Mr. James Sparrow –	2	2	0
Mr. John Hartford –	2	2	0
Rev. Mr. Walter Chapman –	2	2	0

Carried forward	97	3	0

(bottom) A Bath Ball by Thomas Rowlandson. From his series "The Comforts of Bath."
Courtesy Bath Museums Service.

the hospital's capital fund was increased by the sum of £2-12-6d, "being a forfeiture from a postillion for damaging a gentleman's coach."[2] Fines for gambling were also paid over to the hospital on occasions. In 1787, the Mayor sent £298-5-11d to the hospital, part of a penalty levied against two gentlemen for playing "diverse and unlawful games of chance at a house in Alfred Street, contrary to the statute."[3]

BALLS AND SERMONS

No opportunities were lost in collecting money. Sometimes it was by pricking the consciences of affluent visitors enjoying the frivolities of Bath society - balls and breakfast parties. "We have music in the pump-room every morning, cottilions every forenoon in the rooms, balls twice a week, and concerts every other night, besides private assemblies and parties without number," wrote Smollett whose description of the balls at this time must make us wonder how anyone managed to enjoy them.

Imagine to yourself a high exalted essence of mingled odours arising from putrid gums, impostumated lungs, sour flatulencies, rank arm-pits, sweating feet, running sores and issues; plasters, ointments and embrocations, Hungary water, spirit of lavender, assafoetida drops, musk, hartshorn, and sal volatile; besides a thousand frowzy steams I could not analyse. Such is the fragrant ether we breath in the polite assemblies of Bath.[4]

Another effective situation in which to tap people's pockets was in church. Beau Nash was not above standing in the Abbey with a basin, arousing the Christian principles of visitors to offer their financial support for the hospital.[5] There was also a lot of support from some of the clergy, particularly the rector of the Abbey and a dissenting minister called Bennett Stevenson, both of whom sat on the hospital Committee. Every year, visiting clergy were invited to preach in the Abbey in the hope of persuading their congregations to perform charitable deeds and give generously towards the hospital. The sermons were not exactly exciting. In 1766, the Rev. Dr Goodall, a gentleman "possesed of several Ecclesiastical Dignities" preached on "the Character of the Centurion, both in public and private behaviour, his goodness to his servants, the regularity of his family and the zeal of his religion."[6] Whatever this particular reverend gentleman said, it induced his congregation to part with £65. Some of the sermons were published by request of the hospital Governors, not because they represented any particular brilliance on the part of the preacher but rather to provide an opportunity of informing the sort of persons whose libraries bulged with religious tomes that the hospital needed their support.

Being a national hospital, the Governors were anxious to spread information to as many parishes as possible throughout Britain. Initially, advertisements were placed in the London newspapers by courtesy of Samuel Richardson, the novelist.[7] Unfortunately, London newspapers seem to have had little impact on rural charity and the Governors had to resort to more direct methods. In 1741, they sent out thousands of printed sheets giving details about the terms of admission and suchlike, enough to pin up in every parish church in the land. They sent them to the bishops of each diocese, who were requested to distribute them. But a lot of the sheets never reached the parishes for which they were intended. Some of those who were given the task of delivering the broadsides thought themselves entitled to charge for their services and informed the parish officers that they would have to pay for each sheet.[8] Not surprisingly, the parish officers told the distributors where they could put their broadsides. As a result, these parishes remained ignorant of the terms of hospital admission and often sent patients on a long and fruitless journey to Bath, only to find them back on their doorstep a week later having been refused entry to the hospital. Such apparently callous treatment did little to engender charitable feeling towards the Bath Mineral Water Hospital.[9]

It was some years before a sizeable number of parishes subscribed to the funds and even then the hospital had to frequently remind them that their subscriptions were overdue. Every subscriber in arrears was politely reminded of the fact by post.[10] At one point, the Governors became so exasperated by defaulters that they tried to shame them into paying by printing the number of years they were in arrears against their name on the annual subscription list. The practice was abandoned in 1769, "having given great offence to many well-wishers of the charity."[11]

Donations and subscriptions poured in from all levels of society: parish clerks, clergymen, businessmen, landed gentry, aristocracy, and royalty. At the opening of the hospital, King George II donated £200, the Prince of Wales £100 and further sums were donated by the princesses. As a result of this royal beneficence, the Governors named six of the wards with regal titles. A few years later, the Prince of Wales was amongst the principal donors of £1000 collected for the hospital during the 1745 rebellion when many wounded soldiers were rehabilitated in the hospital.[12] This was a particularly substantial sum in those days and one wonders how the Governors managed to spend it. At Aberdeen, where the whole place had

A
SERMON
Preached at the
Abbey-Church *at* B A T H,
For Promoting the
CHARITY *and* SUBSCRIPTION
Towards the
GENERAL HOSPITAL or INFIRMARY
in that CITY;
On SUNDAY, *October* 24. 1742.

Publifh'd at the Requeft of the *Governors* of the faid HOSPITAL.

By Mr. WARBURTON.

To which is added,
A fhort ACCOUNT of the NATURE, RISE, and PROGRESS, of the GENERAL INFIRMARY at *BATH*.

LONDON:
Printed for J. LEAKE, at *Bath*; And fold by J. and P. KNAPTON, near *St. Paul's.* 1742.

[Price Six-pence.]

(above) Frontispiece to a sermon delivered for the benefit of the hospital. RNHRD.

(below) Engraving of Bath Abbey. Courtesy of Avon County Libraries

been taken over for several months as a barracks as well as an army hospital, the total expense involved was only £300.[13]

MEN OF QUALITY

Any person subscribing or donating £40 or more was invited to become a Governor. This was intended to ensure that Governors were always "persons of note and property," the sort of people who could be depended on to manage the hospital's affairs. It also meant there was no restriction on the number of Governors, though in practice only thirty-two Governors actually administered the charity. These were elected each year and were usually persons who lived locally.

Many famous people became Governors, including the actor David Garrick (1775); two governors of Virginia, Francis Fauquier (1738) and Robert Dinwiddie (1768); Lord Clive of Plassey (1762) and artist William Hoare. On the arrival of eminent men in Bath, it was customary for them to give a guinea to bellringers to peal the Abbey bells so announcing their presence. Both Smollett and Goldsmith objected strongly to this practice. "One of the principal grievances of this city is the bells which are continually ringing for joy, sorrow or a parcel of idle fellows." It must have been a considerable relief to such men when the Earl of Orrery and the Duke of Bedford arrived in silence, preferring to give their guineas to the hospital. Both these gentlemen donated handsomely to the hospital and the Duke of Bedford was eventually elected one of the Presidents.

Portrait of Francis Fauquier, treasurer to the hospital, 1739-45. Courtesy of the Thomas Coram Foundation.

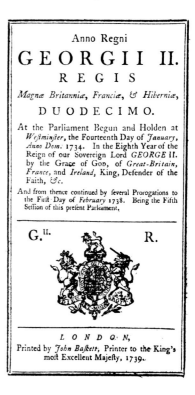

(left) Portrait of Marshall George Wade, President of the Hospital in 1741. Courtesy of the National Portrait Gallery, London.

(right) Schedule of the Act of Parliament for establishing the hospital. RNHRD.

The first president, elected on July 16, 1739, was Thomas Carew of Crowcombe. The Carew family took a keen interest in the hospital's foundation. Thomas Carew's brother, John, who lived more locally at Camerton, provided workmen from his estate to help with the preparation and transport of timber for the new building.[14] Thomas Carew, through his political influence as an MP,[15] facilitated the passage of the Act of Parliament necessary for the hospital to be established.

During the next fifty years, the list of presidents reads like a roll-call for a state banquet. Frederick, Prince of Wales, re-elected several times (1745-1747), the Duke of York (1767), Earl Spencer (1780), the Archbishop of Canterbury (1760), Lord Palmerston (1750) are just a few. Some took more interest in the affairs of the institution than others, judging by their attendance at Governors' meetings. Ralph Allen, president in 1742, did as much as anyone in giving both time and money to the hospital. In the eighteenth century, most presidents were elected on account of their social standing; theirs were names which looked good at the head of annual reports, adding importance to the charity and reassuring subscribers that their donations would not be squandered. It was only when a lesser mortal had been particularly generous towards the institution that the Governors considered departing from this arrangement. Throughout the whole century, only seven presidents were untitled.

In 1750, the Governors offered the presidency to an Oxford physician, Dr Richard Frewin (1681-1761), who had been a generously regular subscriber since the foundation. Frewin had been a partner in a lucrative Oxford practice as well as Praelector in Chemistry, Rhetoric Reader, and ultimately Camden Professor of History at the university. So far as is known, Dr Frewin never delivered a single lecture during his thirty-four years tenure in this chair though he is supposed to have had a library of some four-hundred historical tomes. Such was his success in practice that he enjoyed the luxury of four coaches and two coachmen.[16]

His first wife, Lady Dorothy Tyrrell, was a young widow of thirty-six whose previous husband had died in Ireland in 1714 leaving her with a small estate and three lively daughters. She married Richard Frewin in the following year and bore three more children, all of whom died in childhood. In her youth, Lady Dorothy (who was the daughter of a Wiltshire justice, Sir Giles Eyre), gained a dubious reputation by associating with a restoration rake whose nudist antics made him notorious. But as the wife of the respected Oxford physician she was described as a very good woman, and very charitable.[17] Unhappily the duration of her marriage to Richard was relatively short, her health being "afflicted for a great while mightily with the Gout and Rheumatism." She died in 1725. It was perhaps the nature of his wife's illness which prompted Dr Frewin's benevolent interest in the hospital at Bath. Certainly, he recommended many of his patients to go to Bath for treatment and in 1744, he purchased a house in Queen Square where he lodged during the bathing season. By this time, he was into his third marriage. But tragedy struck again: his youngest son died of "the gout" – most probably rheumatic fever. Neither parent recovered from this bereavement though Richard remained in practice at Oxford for at least another decade.

Sir George Jackson wrote of him, "his abilities in physic and his character as a polite scholar are too well-known to need any Encomium. The former were remarkably visible in the extension of his own life greatly beyond the limits apparently adapted to his constitution – a life not only spent in the service of the public, but in the compassionate relief of private indulgence and distress." He was also a modest man for he refused to accept the presidency of the hospital and suggested the Governors should elect instead a "man of quality who has interest and ability to serve the infirmary."

Portrait of Dr Richard Frewin.
RNHRD.

FESTIVAL OF MUSIC

Entertainment has always been a popular way of fund raising and the hospital has benefitted in this manner throughout its history. Just before Christmas 1783, an advertisement appeared in the Bath Chronicle informing the public that Master Crotch, the celebrated self-taught musician, would shortly delight the populace of Bath with a performance of organ music for the benefit of the hospital. The concert by this remarkable seven-year-old who, in later years became professor of music at Oxford, was a resounding success and benefit concerts for the hospital became a regular feature in Georgian Bath.[18] In 1758, they established themselves in a grand manner; works by Handel in the Abbey, Oratorios in the Assembly Rooms; performances acclaimed as excelling any within living memory.[19] The idea of this musical extravaganza was hatched by several leading musicians who were living in Bath at this time. They approached the Governors, offering to give performances of sacred music gratis for the benefit of the hospital.[20] The Governors, having graciously accepted the offer, must have been rather dismayed to learn that some of the musicians, including Thomas Chilcott, organist of Bath Abbey, and Thomas Linley, had had a change of heart over providing free entertainment and would only perform gratis if there was insufficient money from the sale of tickets to pay their fees. The musicians were not to be disappointed; the tickets, at five shillings each, sold extremely well. The hospital was not disappointed either for they collected £161-14-1d after deducting expenses[21] and were resolved to make the occasion an annual event.

In the following spring, the event blossomed into a veritable festival of music, with Professor Hayes from Oxford conducting Handel's Te Deum at the Abbey in the mornings and the Messiah and Judas Maccabeus in the Assembly Rooms in the evenings. No expense was spared in engaging the best voices from Salisbury, Gloucester, Bristol and Worcester and importing "eminent performers in instrumental musick and voices" from London.[22] Scaffolding was erected in the Abbey to give the audience a better view. The Bath Journal, reviewing the event, reported that the performances "gave universal satisfaction to the vast number of Gentlemen and Ladies present." Unfortunately, with expenses running in excess of £200, the profit proved less than satisfactory and benefit concerts on such a lavish scale were never repeated. Future performances were more modest, confining themselves to one man organ recitals or offers from amateur musicians.

THEATRE

Music was not the only entertainment benefitting the hospital. The management of the Bath Theatre were equally beneficent in their support of the charity. In 1752, when the Theatre was in Orchard Street, the profit from a performance of Vanburgh's "Beaux Stratagem" was donated to the Governors[23] and a year later the managers of a rival theatre at Simpson's Assembly Rooms gave a benefit performance of Hamlet which produced a profit of £41-7-6d[24] Amateur performers also helped raise money for the hospital, particularly in the nineteenth century. More recently, a premiere of the Boulting brothers' film "80,000 Suspects" was shown in Bath to help raise money for a research laboratory.

CHARITY IN COMPETITION

After the eighteenth century, the hospital had to compete with a growing number of other medical and social institutions in the city all relying

Scene from the play "Beaux Stratagem".

Bath Humane Society, one of the many medical charities founded in the early 19th century, ran an emergency service to treat cases of drowning.
Courtesy of Bath Clinical Society.

on the generosity of benefactors. By 1820, there were at least eleven other such charities hoping for a slice of the cake. The Casualty Hospital had been founded in 1788 in response to the large number of injuries suffered by drunken building workers falling off scaffolding or crushing their limbs under freestone blocks. The City Infirmary and Dispensary was providing hospital facilities for Bath citizens, themselves excluded from admission to the Mineral Water Hospital. (These two institutions amalgamated in 1826 to become the United Hospital). There was also growing public concern for the plight of soldiers returning from foreign campaigns whose sight had been damaged by injury and disease and Bath was one of the earliest provincial towns to establish an Eye Infirmary (1811).

In the dawn of the nineteenth century, medical charities sprouted like mushrooms along the streets of Bath: a Lock Hospital for Fallen Women, a Childbed Charity, a Lying-in Hospital and a Humane Society for the Resuscitation of the Apparently Drowned, all of which depended upon the goodwill of the public. This had dire consequences for the Mineral Water Hospital's income, particularly that derived from money collected at local church services where the collections began to dwindle year by year. Had it not been for the simultaneous increase in collections from remote parishes and new subscribers wooed from distant places, the expansion which took place in the mid-century could have never been entertained. Even in the heady days of the eighteenth century, the hospital ran on an exceedingly tight budget which often required the temporary closure of beds or the enforced redundancy of staff. But in the austere Napoleonic years, when viewed against the other medical charities of the city, the Mineral Water Hospital must have presented the semblance of a palace where patient care was proferred on an unnecessarily lavish and extravagant scale.

This view was expressed by the anonymous author of a pamphlet which appeared in 1818 and so incensed the Governors that they felt obliged to publish their own statement vindicating their management.[25] The author proved to be a retired businessman from Hamburg called John Parish who had taken up residence in Bath at the age of 67. Parish lived in grand style at the end of Great Pulteney Street and delighted in taking a daily ride around the town in a barouche drawn by four grey horses accompanied by two postillions sporting blue jackets with silver buttons, buckskin breeches and black velvet huntsman's caps with gold bands and tassels. Parish delighted in ostentatiousness, promenading up and down Pulteney Street in a dressing gown, richly ornamented slippers and a white hat distinguished by an enormous brim.

If Parish was something of an eccentric, he was certainly a generous one, both in his private life and towards public charity. He probably donated handsomely to every one of the charitable institutions in Bath. His beneficence towards the Mineral Water Hospital was on a sufficient scale to incline the Governors to elect him President in 1817. It remains a mystery why, three years later, Parish published such vitriolic criticism of the institution over which he had formerly presided, insinuating imprudence and gross extravagance as he informed the public of the forty staff employed to attend upon a mere 106 patients![26] However, the hospital governors had the final word when they revealed that Mr Parish had only attended two meetings during his entire term as president. How could he possibly be familiar with the hospital's affairs?

Nothing more was heard from Mr Parish but enough damage had been done. Competition from other charities began to seriously erode the level of income from local donations. One of Parish's criticisms had been that, although Bath citizens were asked to donate money to the hospital, residents of Bath were barred admission. It was probably in the hope of restoring local financial support that the Governors rescinded this rule in 1835.

Cartoon drawing of John Parish, an eccentric businessman who was elected President in 1817.
Courtesy of Avon County Libraries.

43

(opposite) Hygeiea. A painting presented to the Mineral Water Hospital by William Hoare. RNHRD.

(below) 18th century strong box kept at the hospital. RNHRD.

BEDS AND BEQUESTS

Fortunately the income from sources beyond Bath remained buoyant during the Victorian era, particularly from bequests. The London Hospital Saturday Fund became a regular contributor in acknowledgement of the service offered to patients from the metropolis. Many more parishes in England and Wales began subscribing. Miners from the South Wales collieries were particularly grateful that their colleagues could receive free treatment in Bath and sent sizeable donations, including money raised from benefit concerts held at Porth Town Hall (near Pontypridd) in 1892.[27] Enough money was donated by miners in 1906 to endow a *South Wales bed*.

Beds were periodically named after benefactors. The two *Primate of all Ireland* beds were the result of a benefaction by Lord Rokeby in 1795 and were marked as such by brass plates on the adjacent walls. The benefaction, four shares in the newly built Assembly Rooms, produced an excellent annual return until 1931 when the Rooms were sold to the City Council. Besides Lord Rokeby's gift of Assembly Room shares, the hospital has at various times received shares in the Theatre Royal, bonds for the Southampton Turnpike, a diamond (1843), a cannon ball, a basin and ewer thought to have belonged to Oliver Cromwell (1868) and one thousand oranges (1914). Quite what possessed Mr Nelmeth Walters to donate a cannon ball will always remain a mystery but the oranges were certainly appreciated by the patients who consumed them.

The hospital has also been the recipient of several fine paintings. In the eighteenth century, artists were keen to donate their own paintings, hopeful that their work might fall on the eyes of potential patrons amongst the many Governors visiting the hospital. There are paintings by William Hoare, Thomas Barker, and Benjamin Morris. Unfortunately, a number of paintings mentioned as bequests in the Minute Books have disappeared.

Ready cash was kept in a strong-box and was the responsibility of the treasurer. Treasurers were elected from amongst the Governors. Until 1841, when an account was opened at Tugwell's Bank (now the National Westminster), this was the only way of securing the running cash and important deeds and documents. After that time, the local bankers handled an increasing proportion of the hospital's money, though the original account with Hoare's Bank was still maintained until 1948.

The names of wards acknowledge particularly generous benefactors. Dr William Perry, a Gloucestershire practitioner who left the hospital £26,000 in 1825 had his name immortalised in this way. Bequests sometimes had onerous strings attached. The sculptor, Prince Hoare, left £600 to the hospital on condition that his family's monuments in the Abbey and St Swithin's Church, Walcot, were annually inspected and maintained by the Governors.[28] Even in recent years the hospital secretary had the dubious privilege of examining the Hoare memorials though the practice seems to have now lapsed. In 1829, a certain Col. Frederick Sackville, late of the Bengal Army, left £700 to the hospital provided the Committee could find 12 poor widows with more than two children, and give £50 to each. This of course left only £100 to the hospital and the onus was on the Committee to track down poor widows, a task that its members were reluctant to take up. They suggested that the benevolent intentions of the testator might be better supervised by the Bath Society for the Relief of Occasional Distress and Suppression of Mendicity.[29]

(above right) Self portrait by
William Hoare. RNHRD.

(above left) Miniature self-portrait
by Benjamin Morris. RNHRD.

(below left) Miniature portrait of
Richard ''Beau'' Nash. Holburne of
Menstrie Museum.

(below right) Portrait of Ralph
Allen. Attributed to J. Richardson.
RNHRD.

The Governors sometimes had to involve themselves in legal disputes over bequests as it was not always clear which Bath hospital was the intended beneficiary. The fact that the hospital was known at various times by totally different names merely compounded the confusion.

CUTS AND ECONOMIES

Constrained budgets have always been a feature of hospital management and are certainly not unique to the present age. A mere three years after the Mineral Water Hospital opened, the Governors announced that the number of beds would have to be cut from 70 to 40, wards closed and over half the nurses made redundant.[30] There has been much the same scenario in recent times though the resident medical staff are no longer expected to take a 33% cut in salary as the house apothecary did in 1744. (His initial salary was well above average for the time so he could hardly object). Indeed, the Governors seem to have pitched expenditure at an optimistically lavish level during the institution's infancy. As the reality of financial stringencies began to bite during the first decade, so came the cuts:

June 1746. Resolved that, in future, chairmen shall have a greatcoat provided every other year instead of annually and that lace trimmings shall be omitted from their hats.[31]

The Governors could hardly expect would-be donors to bail out an ailing charity when its staff were parading about town like the servants of nobility. Lace trimmings had to go.

For most of its history, the hospital was financially solvent though there were several periods of stringency. After the first world war, it proved difficult to balance the books. The Governors of the time suggested various reasons for the fall in income. Unlike other voluntary hospitals, subscribers to the Mineral Water Hospital could not nominate patients of their choice, and so they were deprived of any personal advantage which subscription usually accrued. Furthermore, because the hospital had attained the reputation as a centre of excellence in rheumatology, there was a growing number of patients in the hospital who were far from being indigent and for whom middle class subscribers saw no justification in supplying charity.[32]

One solution would have been to charge patients of moderate means but this was contrary to the statutes of the hospital and would have required an Act of Parliament to change, though the Governors did approach the Charity Commissioners with such a request. A number of the patients did pay, indirectly, via their weekly contributions to Friendly Societies which in turn donated some of their funds to the hospital. In 1931, there was some consternation amongst the Governors when these patients refused to help clean the wards, a task that was traditionally expected of the more able-bodied.[33]

INVESTMENT

Before the advent of the National Health Service, the hospital derived a considerable portion of its income from investment in stocks and shares. The earliest investment of this nature, £2000 of Old South Sea Annuity stock, was purchased through Hoare's bank in 1739 and remained a dependable source of interest for most of the eighteenth century. Until 1873, investment seems to have been limited to Government stocks, mainly consolidated annuities. Interest was then two and a half percent and the

Daniel Danvers, treasurer to the
hospital, painted in 1760 by William
Hoare. RNHRD.

Governors were casting their eyes at a more attractive investment - railways. By reinvesting its capital, the hospital's income from stocks rose from £640 to £950 per annum. [34] The capital was invested in various English railway companies as well as those in India and Russia. From then on, investments were manipulated to provide an optimum yield while retaining a good margin of security.

The hospital's securities in 1948, at the time of the hand-over to the NHS, amounted to £160,000, well over half of which was earmarked for building a new hospital. [35] The Ministry of Health commandeered the entire sum and left the hospital in a semi-ruinous state for over a decade.

LANDLORDS

The stock market was not the only repository for capital. In 1750, a large estate situated at Charmy Down about four miles north of Bath, came up for sale and was purchased by the hospital for just over £5,500. [36] The rent from tenant farmers provided a continuous source of income for almost two centuries. The estate required considerable administration and the Governors appointed a sub-committee from their members to supervise its management. Tenants, particularly in the 18th century, often fell behind with their rents and needed constant reminders. An unexpected bonus came in 1860 when the city council required part of the land for a reservoir and arrangement was made to obtain a free supply of water for the hospital in perpetuity. [37] The estate remained the property of the hospital until 1925 when it was sold to the city council. [38]

COMMITTEES AND REGISTERS

The hospital has always been run by committees. In the early days, there was only one – simply known as The Committee – which was made up of the thirty-two elected Governors responsible for managing the institution's affairs though all Governors were invited to attend a quarterly meeting known as the Court. Since that time, sub-committees have sprung up like mushrooms so that hospital administration is now bedevilled with so many committees that there are even committees to coordinate committees. But the NHS is merely perpetuating a legacy from the past.

The key figure in many of these committees is the Hospital Administrator, known at various times as Hospital Manager, Hospital Secretary and Registrar. In the 18th century, the Registrar, or *Register* as he was then known, was the highest paid member of staff after the apothecary, earning £30 a year. The first Register, Edward Brett, held office for 33 years. He must have spent most of his time with a quill in hand transcribing names and addresses in the many record books kept by the hospital. He had several responsibilities including the care of the ready cash, writing admission and discharge notes and all other letters, and preparing advertisements. He also had to supervise the weighing of provisions on delivery at the hospital, although this job was originally entrusted to a house steward until 1774.

The Registers attended the weekly Committee meetings and recorded the minutes with a stylish and flourishing hand. The hospital got its first typewriter in 1916 but the hand written minute books continued for some years afterwards. Nowadays, the minutes are prepared on word-processors and electronic data retrieval has revolutionised the storage of patient records, though the actual case notes are still written by hand, albeit without the calligraphic niceties of 250 years ago.

The early Committees met on Thursdays and discussed any matters involving the hospital. A list of donations would be announced, resolutions passed and complaints investigated. The Committee were also concerned with selecting patients for admission. Indeed, it was the Committee, albeit with the approval of the medical staff, which was the ultimate arbiter of both patients' admission and their discharge from hospital. At the end of their course of treatment, patients were paraded before the entire committee to determine how effectively they had been cured though one assumes that those patients who had the misfortune to die in hospital were not subject to this routine.

Nowadays, the suggestion that patients are being selected or rejected for admission by non-medical administrators brings a flurry of angry disapproval from the general public and doctors get particularly incensed by the possibility that they have lost "clinical control." In the 18th century, the honorary medical staff nearly always sat on the Committee and their presence helped to prevent any gulf occurring between the medical and lay representatives of the charity. By the end of the 19th century, few if any of the medical staff attended meetings and the relationship between the two groups underwent a disastrous deterioration. The honorary physicians became upset by the way the Committee, without consulting the doctors, were selecting and admitting patients who were medically unsuitable for treatment. Dr Preston King, one of the physicians, also criticised the hospital management in public by writing to the local paper[39] to complain of the large number of empty beds in the hospital. Matters came to a head in 1905 when a resident medical officer was selected by the lay committee without canvassing the opinion of the medical staff about his suitability. It transpired that the lay members of the Committee preferred the opinion of a retired medical practitioner rather than rely on their own honorary staff. The senior surgeon, Mr Green, was so incensed by this revelation that he tendered his resignation. "I have heard," he wrote, "of such proceedings before in irregularly managed hospitals, but I am surprised that a retired medical man should allow himself to act on your sub-committee with full knowledge that that body is usurping the functions of the staff."[40]

The rift was eventually healed and the Committee resolved to always appoint three of the honorary medical staff amongst their number, making them Governors if they were not already so. Involvement of medical staff in the management of the hospital's affairs is seen as a desirable feature by both doctors and patients but the profusion of committees and bureaucratic jungle which has developed in the recent years of NHS administration has periodically rekindled the sort of feeling that was prevalent in 1905.

The GENERAL ACCOUNT *of the*

DISBURSEMENTS

Made on Account of the Hospital at BATH,
to 31 October 1742, *inclusive,*

Cr.

	l.	*s.*	*d.*
BY the General Hospital, paid for the Purchase of Ground whereon the Hospital stands - -	892	10	0
By *ditto*, paid the Expences of the Building - -	4544	2	9
By *ditto*, paid for Furniture of *ditto*	662	7	2
By *ditto*, paid Officers and menial Servants Salaries - - -	327	13	7
By *ditto*, paid House-Expences, Apothecary's Shop, Surgery; &c.	421	10	$5\frac{1}{2}$
By *ditto*, paid the Expences of the Act of Parliament, Printing, Advertisements, and other incident Charges	471	18	11
By *ditto*, paid the Hospital annual Ground-rent - -	10	6	3
	7330	9	$1\frac{1}{2}$
By Old S. S. Annuity Stock 150 *l.* at 112 *per Cent.* - -	168	0	0
By *ditto*, 1500 *l.* valued at $112\frac{1}{4}$ *per Cent.* Brokerage $\frac{1}{8}$ -	1685	12	6
Cash in Mr. *Hoare's* Hands -	179	1	$1\frac{3}{4}$
Running Cash in Hand -	8	12	$1\frac{1}{2}$
In Dr. *Oliver's* Hands -	0	10	6
	9372	5	$4\frac{3}{4}$

Engraving of the Mineral Water
Hospital in the early 19th century.

CHAPTER FOUR
Life in the Wards

In the spring of 1754, the same year in which John Wood started building the Circus at Bath, a soldier called John Guy was billeted on the tiny Mediterranean island of Minorca where his regiment occupied the British garrison at St Philip's Castle, a square fort of four bastions overlooking the harbour. Unfortunately for Guy, his days on the island were numbered. Within a few months of his arrival, he developed an insidious weakness of his legs and had to be relieved of his duties. He was diagnosed as having rheumatism and sent back to England, back home to the tiny Somerset village of Marston Bigot. Inevitably there was no work available for this twenty-three year old cripple whose legs were perpetually bent in painful contractures. This was a double tragedy for the Guy family as John's twin sister had just died.[1] With his prospects of employment ruined, John was obliged to turn to his parish for relief.[2]

A local doctor called Samuel Bowden, who practised in the nearby town of Frome, was consulted. He thought that bathing might "be of service to relax the fibres and restore them to their proper function." The parish overseers were aware that persons like John Guy "who by loss of their limbs are become a burden to themselves" were often successfully treated at the Mineral Water Hospital in Bath and their parishes were thereby "eased of the burden of their useless poor cripples." The Hospital took great trouble to advertise its services and admission rules. Literally thousands of leaflets were printed and distributed to parishes throughout the realm.

No person could be admitted unless the local doctor first sent a referral letter describing the patient's case. A minister or churchwarden of the parish was required to vouch that the person was deserving of charity. Each referral was vetted by the physicians at the Hospital so that they might decide if the person was a "proper object of the charity." Their judgement was notified to the parish and a further letter sent when a vacancy occurred. The medical staff relied entirely on the clinical information given in the referral letters to make a decision on the suitability of each case. Because of the variable abilities of the patients' practitioners to accurately describe cases, a significant number of patients had to be prematurely discharged as "improper." Some practitioners had a particularly black reputation. In 1854, the Committee complained about a Trowbridge surgeon called Stapleton of whom it was stated that there was "invariably much difficulty in obtaining from that gentleman fair and satisfactory reports of the numerous cases which he sends to the hospital."[3]

WAITING LIST

There has always been a waiting list for admissions since the earliest days of the hospital. In 1818 it was 42. The Committee were always anxious to keep it to a minimum but, like the present day waiting list, it reflected

(*right*) Invalid on the way to Bath. Detail from Thomas Rowlandson's "Comforts of Bath".

(*below*) Letter sent by the hospital relating to a patient on the waiting list. 1785. RNHRD.

Sir John Davis — is minuted to be admitted into the Bath Infirmary; and as soon as a Vacancy happens, I shall write for his coming, and enclose a Blank Certificate, to be fill'd up and return'd with Three Pounds Caution-Money, &c. as the Act of Parliament (relating to the Admission of Patients) directs.

I am,
Your humble Servant,

R. Price Regifter.

BATH,
10th March
1785

N.B. The Certificate must be sign'd by the Two Justices for the County, but you will have no occasion to go your self, only send a person, and let the Certificate be attested by the same R.P.

the state of the hospital's finances. The rules forebade queue jumping:- "Every person minuted (for admission shall absolutely succeed in his turn, any interest or application from anybody whatsoever notwithstanding."[4]

In 1868, the Committee, disturbed by the length of the male waiting list, suggested several novel ways of reducing it. One was to reduce the time allowed for people to arrive at the hospital after they had been summoned. It was suggested that patients coming from neighbouring counties should arrive within two days, while those coming from further afield could take five.[5] But even allowing for the increased speed of travel after the advent of the railways, these limits proved totally impractical. Finding this proposal unworkable, the Committee then asked the medical staff to tighten their criteria on what constituted a "proper" case. This certainly weeded out a considerable proportion of patients waiting for admission who were sent a circular telling them that their cases were no longer appropriate for Bath water treatment. Unfortunately, the Marquis of Westminster was most displeased by this ploy as his agent had applied for the admission of a patient subsequently removed from the waiting list in this way.

ARRIVAL

Climbing the short flight of steps to the front door, the new arrivals must have sometimes wondered what terrible deformities and disfigurements they were about to witness within. Compared with todays's patients, the scene on the wards would have presented a lurid spectacle. Skin disease was much more florid in its appearance and the term leprosy, though a misnomer as far as the actual diagnosis is concerned, was an understandable description for the disfiguringly severe skin disorders then prevalent. Jemima Scott, a patient from Essex, was admitted in 1754 with a "scurfy humour all over her body"[6] while nine year old Ann Gunstone from Bathford came in with scald-head, a disease due to staphylococcal infection which caused the hair to fall out and the skin to swell into a mass of red blisters, hence the name.

It was not unusual to find children in the hospital during the eighteenth century: about 5% of admissions in 1752 were under ten years old. Like the adults, they often had to stay in the hospital for several months. Eight year-old Alex Knapman from Crediton in Devon was in for three months after injuring his spine. Seven year-old Sarah Sandford from Exeter stayed for seven months and four year-old John Sartain from Trowbridge was in for even longer. Children were accommodated on the women's wards. In an age when the young were treated at best like adults-in-minature and at worst like animals, life in the women's wards was probably a pleasant release from the drudgery, harshness and poverty of outside. A century passed before child patients received regular education during their admission.[7] Even then tuition was sporadic,[8] probably because there were seldom more than a handful of children in the hospital and it was not felt worthwhile engaging an infant teacher as a permanent member of staff. Sometimes, female patients took it upon themselves to teach the children. In 1857, the chaplain suggested that the committee reward such women with 6d a week and engage the infant teacher of St Michael's parish to attend regularly on Saturdays.[9]

Poverty was the one common denominator in all patients admitted to the Hospital in its early days. Some patients arrived in such a ragged state that they had to be given clothes by the Hospital merely for the sake of decency.[10] Others were filthy and it was the Matron's job to inspect and to "cause new patients to be made clean."[11] There was a bath tub in the basement for this purpose, and the hospital seems to have ordered a liberal supply of Best Bristol Soap in its earlier years as well as plenty of "flesh" brushes for scrubbing the skin, though both of these may have been intended primarily for therapeutic use; the soap to make linaments and enemas and the flesh brushes as instruments of massage. The frequent immersion in the hot baths during their stay would have ensured that patients in the Hospital were a good deal more savoury than many a person of quality lodging in easier circumstances a few streets away.

(*above*) Child patient with skin disease, wearing a brass identity medallion on his lapel. Detail from a painting by William Hoare. RNHRD.

(*left*) Page from the '*Case Book*,' giving examples of doctors referral letters in the 18th century. RNHRD.

55

Making tin plates. Many of the patients admitted in the early days of the hospital handled lead in their work.

ARTISANS

The case book of referral letters for the 1750 decade gives some indication of patients' social circumstances. The age distribution reflects that of the general population at this time and there are relatively few patients over sixty. The patients' occupations are infrequently recorded in the letters but the information available suggests that many of the male patients were agricultural workers and domestic traders – eg: farm hands, gardeners, barbers, butchers, tailors, carpenters. Some patients were involved in manufacturing industries – eg: brass-founders, glaziers and glass-grinders, pewterers, shoemakers, potters. Of the latter group, exposure to lead and other heavy metals was often the precipitating cause of their illness. Painters and plumbers frequently appear for the same reason (see chapter 5). Only a third of all admissions were female. Those women who were single were mostly in service but many were married women who, as a result of physical disability, were incapable of looking after their families.

Not infrequently, the patient's illness was itself the cause of impoverished circumstances and some of the referral letters dwell as much on the patient's financial misfortunes as on their medical details. James Ward, a 50 year old surgeon, had once enjoyed a thriving practice at Bodmin but years of ill health had greatly reduced his circumstances. He was struggling to maintain his practice when he fell from his horse and broke his leg. After that, he could no longer walk unaided and, with meagre savings and no work, he could not even entertain the prospect of a trip to Bath where he might find the most efficacious treatment. Fortunately, he was accepted for admission by the Mineral Water Hospital and was able to scrape enough together for the journey.[12]

Soldiers also appear quite frequently amongst the early records, particularly when the British army was engaged in military action. Large numbers were admitted in 1745 after receiving injuries in the Jacobite uprising. In the following century, the hospital played its part in rehabilitating soldiers wounded in foreign campaigns, notably in the Crimean and Boer wars. During both world wars, the hospital was commandeered by the military services to provide treatment for the many service men whose injuries had left them with chronic physical disabilities.

(left) Map showing origin of patients admitted in the 1750's.

FROM FAR FLUNG CORNERS

Although the majority of patients admitted in the eighteenth century lived within a day's journey of Bath, some came from the far flung corners of the British Isles. Sometimes a request to retain a bed was sent on ahead of a patient delayed on the road.[13] The cost of transporting poor patients frequently had to be borne by their parishes and the hospital demanded three pounds "caution money" for each patient admitted.[14a] This was retained until the patient was discharged and it indemnified the hospital against the cost of providing transport home. When an Irishman, John Commerford was discharged in June 1743, it cost £2-9-6d for his passage to Cork.[14] The higher cost of long journeys determined the Governors to recommend an increased rate of £5 caution money for patients coming from Ireland and Scotland. In the nineteenth century, the railways transformed travel, making it easier and cheaper to get to Bath from distant areas of Britain but in earlier years the colossal expense of long distance travel probably deterred many patients from coming to the hospital. A Leicester doctor, referring a poor patient for admission in 1754, wrote that the man's equally poverty-stricken friends were desirous that the patient should go to Bath to take the waters and were trying to raise money to convey him to the hospital "with great difficulty – even that of begging."[15]

We forget, living in an age of helicopter rescues and escorted ambulances, that patients in the eighteenth century had to accept life on an entirely different time scale. This is well illustrated by the case of one Thomas Francis who was admitted to the hospital in February, 1785. The man was a sailor, apprenticed to the captain of a merchant ship which was on a trading voyage to Gibraltar bay where he arrived in April 1784. On the night of the 16th, whilst the ship was lying at anchor, Francis was about to climb the rigging when a flash of lightning dashed him to the deck. He was carried senseless to the captain's cabin where he remained unconscious for a further three hours. His arm was badly scorched where he had gripped hold of the rope. His neck was wounded and a hole had burnt through his woollen hat, singeing his hair.

He recovered consciousness but was found to have lost all use of his limbs. The day after the accident, the ship resumed its planned itinerary, first to Russia and then back to Dublin with a further cargo. During the four months of this voyage, the injured sailor remained on board and it was not until autumn that he was able to get back to his home in Glamorgan. By this time he had recovered some use to his arms but was still unable to walk. He was referred to the Mineral Water Hospital for treatment, nine months after his injury. [16]

In recent times, with the growth of rheumatological departments in district general hospitals, far fewer patients come from remote parts of the British Isles, but the catchment area extends well beyond the limits of the Bath health district and the hospital can still claim to live up to its "national" title. Nobody pays caution money now: the last collection was made in 1937. [17]

Early photograph of the hospital. RNHRD.

TURNED AWAY

Caution money was used to defray other expenses such as extra wages paid to nurses who looked after patients with smallpox.[18] Those who arrived suffering from infectious diseases were turned away, as was anyone whose case was thought to be venereal. Expectant mothers were also barred from admission though women recently confined were accepted. In such cases, a nurse was sometimes employed at extra expense to "draw the breasts."[19] Occasionally, women patients were accepted for admission and subsequently found to be pregnant. The medical staff sometimes missed quite obvious symptoms of early pregnancy. It took them over a month to realise that a patient admitted in 1754 with abdominal discomfort, vomiting and missed periods was becoming "big with child."[20]

The only other bar to admission was against patients resident in Bath itself. This rule, which was rescinded in 1835, was introduced because it was thought that local people would not require accommodation and yet could still avail themselves of the Corporation's baths. In fact, this rule only applied to persons resident within the old city walls: those living in areas like Walcot and Widcombe, now very much part of Bath, were eligable for admission.

TEN SHILLINGS A COFFIN

If a patient had the misfortune to die in hospital, caution money provided a means of defraying the funeral expenses. Eighteenth century funerals, like those of today, were not cheap. When a patient died in 1756, it cost thirteen shillings "for breaking the ground," five shillings for a shroud and ten shillings for a coffin.[21] Deaths were uncommon – out of 500 cases admitted between 1752 and 1754, only 24 died in hospital. This is all the more remarkable, bearing in mind that Bath was often the last resort for the chronically ill and injured. Quite a few patients had already received treatment without any benefit in other voluntary hospitals, particularly in London.[22]

The hospital had its own burial ground situated across the street on the far side of the city wall. It is first mentioned in 1743[23] when Mr Emes, the hospital's builder, was employed to "make a passage through the town wall and a staircase down to the burying ground" though the city council did not officially grant use of the land for burial until 1767.[24] Only then would the Bishop of Bath and Wells agree to consecrate the ground. There seems to have been some trouble getting coffins through Mr Emes' doorway and in 1783 a Mr West offered to widen it at his own expense.[25]

By the mid-nineteenth century, the ground could accommodate no further bodies and was closed.[26] For a while it was used as a refuse tip for a nearby shop then, in 1887, a Mr Taylor of Trim Street requested permission to keep his ducks there.[27] In 1954, the hospital proposed turning it into a car park but was declined planning permission.[28]

NO DICE

The wards were furnished in much the same manner as we are accustomed to seeing in the more traditional hospitals of the present day: beds at intervals along the two long walls and a long table down the middle. The first bedsteads were wooden and made by a local cabinet maker, Gracious Stride, at a cost of thirty shillings each.[29] The design was copied from those used in London hospitals[30] and each bed was draped around with

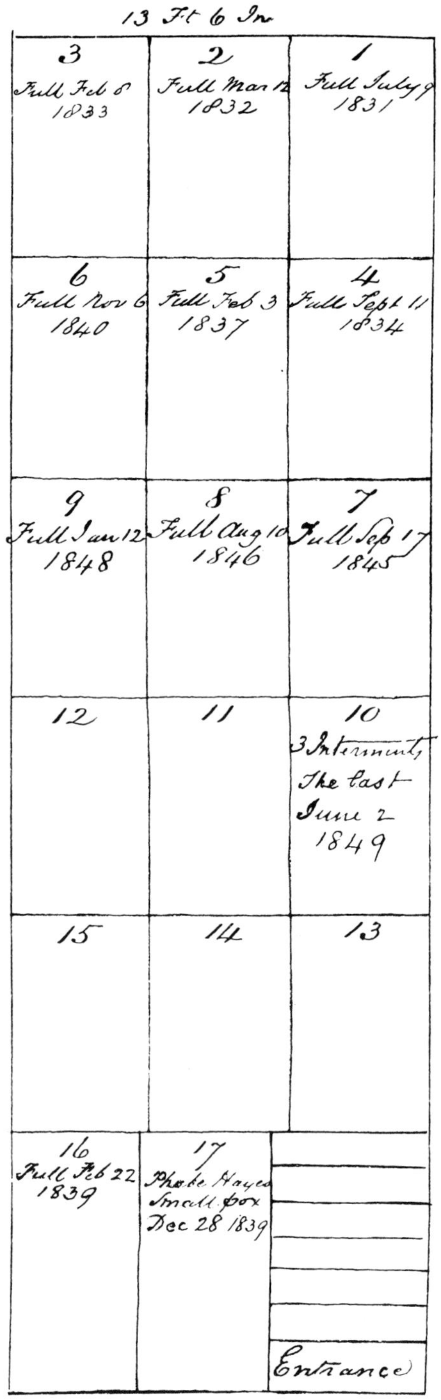

```
                    13 Ft 6 In
   ┌──────────┬──────────┬──────────┐
   │    3     │    2     │    1     │
   │ Full Feb 8│Full Mar 12│Full July 9│
   │   1833   │   1832   │   1831   │
   ├──────────┼──────────┼──────────┤
   │    6     │    5     │    4     │
   │Full Nov 6│Full Feb 3│Full Sept 11│
   │   1840   │   1837   │   1834   │
   ├──────────┼──────────┼──────────┤
   │    9     │    8     │    7     │
   │Full Jan 12│Full Aug 10│Full Sep 17│
   │   1848   │   1846   │   1845   │
   ├──────────┼──────────┼──────────┤
   │    12    │    11    │    10    │
   │          │          │3 Interments,│
   │          │          │ The last │
   │          │          │  June 2  │
   │          │          │   1849   │
   ├──────────┼──────────┼──────────┤
   │    15    │    14    │    13    │
   │          │          │          │
   ├──────────┼──────────┼──────────┤
   │    16    │    17    │          │
   │Full Feb 22│Phobe Hayes│          │
   │   1839   │ Small pox│          │
   │          │Dec 28 1839│         │
   │          │          ├──────────┤
   │          │          │          │
   │          │          ├──────────┤
   │          │          │          │
   │          │          │ Entrance │
   └──────────┴──────────┴──────────┘
50 Ft (left margin)
```

(*above*) Plan of the burial ground showing grave sites.

(*above right*) Site of the hospital's burial ground. Part of the mediaeval city wall lies on the left.

(*right*) Inscribed tablet on the far wall of the burial ground.

[THIS PIECE OF GROUND WAS IN THE YEAR 1738 SET APART FOR THE BURIAL OF PATIENTS DYING IN THE BATH GENERAL HOSPITAL, AND AFTER RECEIVING 238 BODIES WAS CLOSED BY THE GOVERNORS OF THAT CHARITY IN THE YEAR 1849, FROM REGARD TO THE HEALTH OF THE LIVING.]

blue check curtains matching those at the windows.[31] The luxury of the inter-sprung mattress, indeed even bed springing itself, was not a feature of these eighteenth century beds; patients slept on mattresses supported on sack cloth. Pillows and bed linen were provided and Matron was expected to put clean sheets on the beds of new patients though the bed linen was only changed once a month.[32] From 1752 onwards, the wooden bedsteads were gradually replaced with iron ones.

In 1846, the hospital purchased a Dr Arnott's hydrostatic bed[33] designed to overcome bedsores in immobilised patients. The mattress was essentially a water-filled rubber bag, rather like a modern water bed.

Life on the wards has always stirred at an early hour, a tradition perpetuated since Georgian times when patients were aroused from their slumbers at the crack of dawn. The first task of the able-bodied patients was to help the nurses clear up the wards. The bare oak boards were cleaned by scattering sand and ashes about the floor and then sweeping them up. Matron visited the wards every day to supervise the nurses and make sure the patients were behaving in a proper manner. By modern standards, patients had to adhere to a relatively restrictive set of rules. They were not allowed to play cards or dice nor curse and swear. Nothing is mentioned about smoking until 1854 when a patient was caught smoking in the street and the medical staff were asked to inform the Governors "whether it be injurious to allow patients to smoke whilst under treatment."[34] Their decision is not recorded.

Men and women were not supposed to visit each other's wards without special permission from Matron, though this does not seem to have been rigorously enforced in the early days as at least two patients were recorded as having eloped.[35] In the Victorian era, the preoccupation with sexual segregation reached such obsessional heights that the corridor which connected the two wings of the hospital had to be divided along its length to prevent male and female patients catching sight of each other.

Photograph of one of the wards, circa 1910.

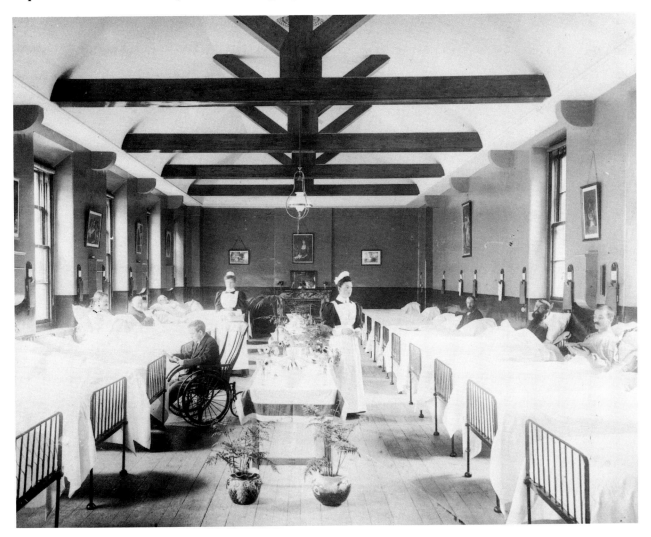

Brass identity medallions worn by patients in the 18th century.

IMPROPER CORRESPONDENCE

Patients who wrote letters were also viewed with suspicion. In 1742, the Committee exhorted "officers of the house (to be) diligent in discovering any correspondence that may be carried on between patients in the house or (with) any person of the house whatsoever, by letter or otherwise, and if any letter be suspected of holding an improper correspondence, such letter will be delivered to the House Visitors at their next visitation."[36] Patients were even forbidden to lend or borrow money, though this would not have bothered them much as there was nothing to spend it on except food and they were not allowed to have extra provisions.

Even today, admission to hospital is accompanied by a small loss of personal liberty, but this pales into insignificance compared to the no-nonsense attitudes of a century ago when patients were treated like irresponsible school-children. In this respect, the Victorians were far more pernickety than the Georgians who seem to have been quite tolerant of their fellow men's foibles. When no one owned up to a misdemeanour, the Victorian Committees would punish every patient in the hospital. In 1873, when obscene graffiti was discovered in one of the outside toilets, all patients were barred from leaving the hospital until the culprit had owned up.[37] Graffiti writers posed such a threat to the hospital that the Committee ordered the outside walls of the building to be rusticated.[38] Reprimands and expulsions were common. In the space of one week (August 1871), the porter nearly lost his job for lending his violin to a patient who played it in the ward and another patient was ordered to pay for damaging a door whilst racing his wheelchair around the hospital.

TEA ON PRESCRIPTION

Meals were eaten in the wards and all patients who could walk were expected to sit at the tables. The food was sent up from the kitchen and was not always as hot as the patients would have liked. The wards were supplied with saucepans and a kettle for boiling tea, a drink available only on prescription until the late 19th century when tea replaced gruel as the breakfast beverage. As connoisseurs of the drink will know, nobody ever makes a decent cup of tea using hard water and it is interesting to note that a small cistern of soft water was kept on each ward for making tea.[39]

Plenty of beer was available, brewed on the premises, and even some house wine, made from Malaga raisins obtained at Bristol.[40] The wine was supposedly drunk for its medicinal value. The Governors were only too aware of the problems of inebriation and publicans in Bath were forbidden to serve patients with intoxicating liquor on pain of losing their licence.[41] Patients were issued with brass identity badges when they were admitted and were not allowed out of the hospital unless they were wearing them.

The choice of patients' diet was the responsibility of the medical staff and the apothecary had to prepare a diet list for each ward. By modern standards, the diet was monotonous, though reasonably nutritious. Meals consisted principally of meat broth, bread, rice and cheese. No greengrocery was ordered until 1844 when the Matron was instructed to add a little oatmeal and vegetables to the broth "by way of experiment."[42] Preservation of food would have been a problem before the advent of refrigerators. The hospital kitchen was not equipped with a fridge until 1889.

During the eighteenth century, bread was made in the bakehouse below stairs. Towards the end of the eighteenth century, some experiments were made with different flour mixes in an attempt to cut costs. In 1796 the hospital purchased a milling machine so that the expense of paying a miller could be avoided,[43] though five years later it was cheaper to buy ready-ground flour imported from America.[44] After 1836, bread was bought from outside contractors and the hospital's baker was made redundant.[45]

The patients ate from wooden plates called trenchers and took their broth in elm bowls. China and earthenware were too fragile and expensive though drink was served in enamelled pint mugs.

COMPLAINTS

At nine o'clock each morning the apothecary commenced his ward rounds to check on the patients' condition and administer medicines. Once a fortnight, he recited the list of Hospital Rules for the benefit of patients who could not read and as a reminder for those who could.

Another daily round was done by two of the hospital Governors who were elected each week to be House Visitors. It was their job to investigate complaints from patients and staff and inspect the quality of the provisions and food. Major complaints were brought to the attention of the Committee. These mostly related to allegations of ill-treatment by the hospital staff. There were a whole spate of complaints lodged in the mid-nineteenth century, often made by a representative of the patient rather than the patient themselves. In 1844, the Committee received a letter from a woman in Bristol complaining about the treatment her servant had received while a patient in the hospital. The physician in charge of the case was questioned about his management and the Committee was pleased to find the allegations were totally unfounded and unreasonable.[46] Indeed this seems to have been the conclusion in virtually every case. When one Thomas Hammond died shortly after he was discharged, his friends complained that he had not received proper assistance. The Committee's verdict: complaint groundless.[47] If the patients complained while in the hospital, they risked expulsion and if they complained after their discharge, they could not expect to be re-admitted if their condition worsened. In 1855, notices were hung up in the wards warning patients that any complaints made after they had left Bath would automatically be considered groundless![48] This appears to have stayed the flood of complaints for two years until a patient tried to claim compensation for an injury he had received when a rope, which was being used to lower him into the bath, broke. Despite the fact that he subsequently developed an abscess, the hospital refused to pay him a single penny.[49]

INDECENT PRACTICE

Very few complaints were made against the medical staff but several incidents occurred a year after the hospital opened which eventually led to one of the surgeons being suspended. It was the sort of case which editor's of today's popular newspapers would have found totally irresistible, banner headlines blazing "SEX CASE SURGEON DISMISSED FROM HOSPITAL." But when Archibald Cleland was relieved of his post as assistant surgeon in 1743, the world had not experienced the phenomenon of sensational journalism. The only notice the public received was the appearance of a broadside in the Pump Room, announcing that an enquiry was about to be held to investigate charges of indecent practice brought against the surgeon by two women patients in Princess Ward; Mary

Hudson, afflicted with hysterical fits and Mary Hook, who was suffering from leprosy.

The enquiry took place on September 21st 1743 when Cleland appeared before a court of 18 Governors, amongst whom was the Mayor, Ralph Allen.

Cleland was accused of professional misconduct on account of performing repeated vaginal examinations on the two women.[50] Evidence was also brought against him in connection with another patient, Sarah Appleby, who had died at the hospital the month before. She had been admitted for treatment of hysterical fits and venereal disease. Witnesses told how Miss Appleby had been examined several times by Cleland who used a vaginal douche in an attempt to improve her fits, supposing them due to disease of her uterus. In the process he brought down blood and "pieces of placenta," suggesting that the woman had miscarried. Cleland did not deny making the examinations which he claimed were a necessary part of the treatment: he did not do so to procure a miscarriage. However, the Matron and nurses were suggesting that Cleland's douching had brought about the patient's death and they had observed her condition worsen after each treatment. A post-mortem examination proved not only had the woman never been pregnant (her womb was too small and the cervix tightly closed) but that her death was caused by a ruptured ovarian cyst.[51]

Mary Hudson's case was similar and Cleland's purpose for performing vaginal examinations "when she was in fits" was to discover if the uterus was the "seat and cause of this and her other complaints."[52]

In the case of Mary Hook, the examinations were more difficult to justify. Miss Hook was noted to have a large belly and complained of difficulty in passing water. Cleland examined her "taking oil on his hands whilst she was standing all the while"[53] because he suspected she might be pregnant. Certain Governors at the enquiry thought it unlikely that a woman who was pregnant would have consented to such an examination for fear of discovery and expulsion from the hospital and they questioned the need to do such an examination at all.

In reply to cross-examination, Cleland maintained that the complaints had been trumped up by women who were little more than common prostitutes.

He had evidence to prove this. One of the women, Mary Hook, was known to a physician in Cheltenham called Baptiste Smart who testified she was of ill-repute. Just before the trial, Dr Smart and Mary Hook's mother arrived in Bath. Cleland arranged for them to meet at the Carrier's Inn, but Mrs Hook failed to keep the appointment, claiming later she had forgotten the name of the inn. In fact she had visited her daughter in hospital and had been waylayed by the house apothecary who, Cleland claimed, had prevented her from meeting Dr Smart. A suggestion arose from the Governors that the meeting at the inn was contrived with the view of bribing Mrs Hook into persuading her daughter to retract the accusations against Cleland. Indeed the Governors later published an affidavit sworn by Hook's mother to this effect.[54] In his defence, Cleland insinuated that some of the physicians and surgeons, together with the house apothecary, had colluded to do all they could to get him suspended from the staff of the hospital. While he admitted examining the patients Hudson and Hook per vaginam on more than one occasion, he insisted that the examinations were necessary for clinical reasons. He denied that he had told a nurse to leave the room during examinations, or that he had bolted the door despite a sworn affidavit by the nurse.[55]

After considering all the evidence, the seventeen Governors present were unanimous. Cleland's actions amounted to "indecent practice," and the majority (13 to 4) voted for his dismissal from the staff of the hospital.[56] Cleland may well have been genuinely guilty of improper behaviour but many observers at the time, including the novelist Tobias Smollett, were convinced that the surgeon was victim of professional jealousy which had exaggerated some indiscrete yet well-intentioned examinations. Whatever the truth, the case illustrates the vulnerability of male doctors then, as now, to accusations levelled by female patients undergoing vaginal examinations. After the hearing, one of the Governors was heard to say that if he had been a surgeon he would be reluctant to examine any lady "above the shoestrings or below the necklace."

AN
APPEAL
TO THE
PUBLICK:
OR, A
Plain Narrative of Facts,
Relating to the Proceedings of a PARTY
OF THE
GOVERNORS
OF THE
New General-Hospital at BATH,
AGAINST
Mr. *Archibald Cleland,*
(One of the Surgeons of the said *Hospital*)
At an Extraordinary Meeting of the GOVERNORS,
held in their *General Committee-Room*, the 21st
of *September*, 1743.

Sold by A. DODD, without *Temple-Bar*, LONDON; and by
W. FREDERICK, Bookseller in BATH.

A SHORT
VINDICATION
OF THE
PROCEEDINGS
OF THE
GOVERNORS
OF THE
GENERAL HOSPITAL at BATH,
In Relation to
Mr. *Archibald Cleland,*
Late SURGEON to the said HOSPITAL;
WHEREIN
The several FACTS misrepresented in a PAMPHLET,
call'd, *An Appeal to the Publick*, by Mr. *Cleland,*
ARE FAIRLY STATED.
To which is prefix'd,
A short Narrative *of the* Proceedings.

By the GOVERNORS *of the* HOSPITAL, *who voted
for* Mr. Cleland's *Dismission*.

Printed for JAMES LEAKE, Bookseller, in *Bath*; and sold by
A. DODD, at the *Peacock*, near *Temple-Bar*, 1744.

(above) Tobias Smollett, novelist, who briefly practised in Bath as a surgeon.

(right) Two of a series of pamphlets vindicating the actions of the parties involved in the Cleland affair.
Courtesy of Avon County Libraries.

65

TAKING THE AIR

All able bodied patients were not only expected to help clean the wards but also lend a hand in the laundry and aid the nursing of their fellow patients whose infirmities confined them to wheelchairs or bed. The hospital provided crutches for those needing them and special chairs which were designed by the medical staff for paralysed patients.[57] The absence of nearby lavatories in the 18th century made provision of urinals and close stools a necessity on each ward for the convenience of those unable to get downstairs to the "Houses of Offices." It was therefore just as well that another of the apothecary's duties was to check that the wards were properly ventilated. When the philanthropist, John Howard visited the hospital in 1787 on one of his yearly investigative tours, his olfactory sensibilities were so offended that he was relieved to report in the following year that at least a few of the windows opened.[58] The physicians had always been in favour of keeping the windows closed for fear that the patients would risk catching cold after returning from the baths.

Throughout the week, the patients went to the baths for treatment. On Sundays they were able to go to one of the churches or chapels in the city, but only if they wore their badges. A visitor to Bath in 1766, the Rev. John Penrose, witnessed a party of patients attending a service at the Abbey.

"It was a very affecting sight to see all the patients ranged in two lines, men on one side, women on the other, making a lane from the outer door of the Abbey to the door of the inner part where the service is performed, for the Mayor and Magistrates and all the congregation to pass through. Eight beadles,[59] in a Uniform Dress (Brown Greatcoats with yellow capes and sleeves turned up with yellow) with a staff in hand with a brass knob on top, attended them. And when they went from church, they all walked two and two, very orderly, four beadles with staves preceding, then the men patients, then two more beadles, the women patients, then the two other beadles closing the procession."[60]

During the week, prayers were read on the wards. Before a chaplain was appointed (in 1755), this task fell upon any nurse who was literate enough to read the prayer book. Patients were also allowed out to "take the air" in the meadows beyond the town wall, presumably upwind from the ditch where the sewage discharged. All patients had to return in time for supper[61] and were not allowed out at night. There are several instances of patients being discharged for breaking this regulation.[62] Considering their long length of stay, on average ten months, it is not surprising to find patients' frustration venting itself. Fighting amongst persons was much more commonplace in those times; even medical staff sometimes settled disputes with their fists if they disagreed with each other.[63] Fighting and swearing by patients were frequently reported in the House Visitors' books.

Patients had little with which to amuse themselves in the early days. The whitewashed walls were devoid of pictures and the only reading material was a bible and a prayerbook. In the mid-nineteenth century, newspapers were allowed but the Registrar was ordered to withold the Weekly Despatch and other "notoriously objectional publications."[64] By this time, the need for more recreation was being recognised. "The medical board are unanimously of the opinion that if the hospital contained the means of placing patients through many hours of the day in well-ventilated room where they might be provided cheerful occupation such as a well-chosen library, they would derive far greater benefit than that obtained by general permission to leave the hospital which the closeness of the rooms they now occupy renders absolutely necessary."[65] Books were more easily obtainable than extra room. The "well-chosen" library was assembled and included such edifying tomes as "Bible Quadrupeds," "Jesse's Gleanings" and "The History of Common Salt."[66] Charles Empson donated a further 308 volumes in 1858[67] observing that "such an addition to the institution would while away many an hour that must otherwise drag heavily."[68] In a lighter vein, amateur dramatics and concerts were frequently performed for the patients' amusement.

With the library stocked, the Committee turned its attention to providing more room within the hospital precincts. Throughout the first half of the nineteenth century, there was increasing concern about the way patients might behave when let loose on the town. When the Committee wrote to The Duke of Cleveland in 1852, seeking permission to use Sydney Hotel as a new hospital site, they begged to assure his Lordship that the patients, being wholly confined to the hospital and gardens "under strict suveillance," would be rarely, if ever, seen by neighbours. Ironically, it was the hospital patients who, two years later, complained that their sleep was being disturbed by the foul language of drunkards roaming along Upper Borough Walls (a feature of the city's night life which still prevails!)

Some idea of what it was like to be a patient in the mid-nineteenth century is given in a lengthy rhyme by an anonymous lady. By this time the west wing of the hospital had been added and patients were able to use the spacious new day wards.

Its wondrous cures have gained a world-wide fame.
Bath Mineral Water Hospital is its name.
To all who feel an interest in my rhyme
I'll tell now how the inmates pass the time.
I can declare the truth of what I state,
To dwell amongst them it is now my fate.
For many months I lameness have endured
And by God's blessing hope to return home cured.

Seven wards there are all occupied by men.
Three for the fair sex which in all make ten.
To fifty only do the fair amount,
While twice that number do the men folk count.
But no description of them can I give
Though in the same house with them we live.
Each nurse takes care this lesson to impart
That from the men-folk we must keep apart.
'Tis true we sometimes catch a quick sly glance
But as for speaking, there's not half a chance.

Contented therefore I'll pursue my lay
And tell you how we females spend the day.
Soon after six our cosy beds we leave,
The drowsy ones wishing for a short reprieve.
At seven o'clock what a sight to behold
The young ones dressing the helpless and old.
And if it's not done, oh! then what a fuss
Nothing but grumbling all day by the nurse.
Next beds are made; some pains we then bestow
Upon ourselves and then upstairs we go
Into our day-ward, spacious, airy, lofty, light.
Gas from the ceiling lends its rays of light.
A spendid room that everyone confesses,
'Tis used by all three wards, Queen's, Colston's and Princess's

A bell is daily rung before each meal,
At eight o'clock for breakfast it does peal.
Towards the lift our footsteps now are bent,
By which our food is from the kitchen sent.
All cripples too do by this lift ascend,
Drawn by John Hall,[69] our sturdy constant friend.
Now by its aid the breakfast doth rise,
"'tis coming up!" some eager watcher cries.
"'Tis up, alright?" John from below doth call,
The nurse she answers "Yes-John Hall".

A Queen is chosen, one who is best able
To fill the post of honour at the table.
She cuts up and serves to all around,
One ounce of butter and of bread one pound.
She then entreats a blessing from high Heaven
Which if sincerely asked is always given.
New-comers with surprise their portion view
And wonder where the butter all goes to.
For Princess's ward, that honoured place I fill,
And strive my duties justly to fulfil.

The porter brings the letters and you'll trace
A look of expectation on each face.
The lucky ones now o'er their letters pore,
While those less fortunate their fate deplore.

When breakfast is over what hurrying to and fro,
For when the clock strikes nine downstairs we go.
Each by her bed doth sit with work or book
Awaiting the house physician Dr Cook.
And when he comes but little does he say,
Just asks of each "Well, how are you today?"
Should he be absent then Mr Keen attends,
'Tis he who from the dispensary sends
All medicines which by the Doctor's orders
We take to cure our various disorders.

The bathroom now with busy life is teeming,
The nurses calling and the Waters steaming.
The cripples in wheelchairs are brought along.
Those who can walk from every quarter throng.
To be amongst their line is no great treat
But what can you expect when fifty women meet.
They now by turns into the Waters dip,
Then back to bed and 'tween the blankets slip.
Some minutes there we are compelled to stay,
Then up and dress and to our work away.

At one o'clock we lay the dinner cloth.
Rice or potatoes and a pint of broth
Three days a week. The other four we've meat
Which is by one and all esteemed a treat.
At five we tea, at seven prayers are read,
At eight we go downstairs, at nine to bed.

On every bedstead a brass badge is hung,
On state occasions round our neck is slung.
Upon the surface are the numbers shown,
By which instead of names we are here known.

Part of a poem written by an anonymous patient, circa 1865.
(Boodle Collection, Bath Ref. Lib).

The practice of addressing patients as numbers seems to have arisen during Victorian times as there is no evidence of such anonymity in the early years of the hospital. The wholesale regimentation of patients in the nineteenth century, and even in the early part of the present, reflects a changing attitude in society towards the poor and underprivileged. Patients who accepted charity at this time were totally patronised by the governing structure of the hospital and, as such, could not expect many rights or privileges. Today's patients fortunately enjoy a rather more relaxed atmosphere.

NURSING

Today's image of the hospital nurse conjures up a busy, efficient and intelligent young woman, dressed in clean neat uniform, whose long training is terminated by exacting examinations. Not so in the eighteenth century. Nurses then were more like domestic servants and had a reputation for being rough and coarse as well as immoral and inebriate. Nursing has never been easy work and still requires great stamina and dedication. The *Hospital Rule Book* of 1782 instructed nurses to "behave with tenderness to the patients, submit to their superiors and show charity and respect for all strangers."[70] Moreover, they had to preside at the servants table, clean the wards by seven each morning and were not allowed to drink tea without consent of a physician.

The hospital now employs the equivalent of seventy full time nurses but there were only four when it first opened. They each received eight pounds a year with free board and lodging. Two of them, nurses Powell and Hubbard, worked in the hospital for two years and were then laid off. Nurse Hubbard seems to have been rather lacking in tender behaviour because several patients lodged complaints of *ill usage*. The other two nurses managed to remain in employment for seven years before being dismissed for stealing money from patients. New nurses were taken on and the total complement soon reached nine. The replacements were as motley a bunch of women as the first. One of them was so lame and disabled that the House Visitors mistook her for a patient and promptly admitted her.[71] Another two had to be dismissed after patients complained about their behaviour. Some were evidently of higher calibre; Nurse Marjoram and Nurse Dyke were on the staff for sixteen years.

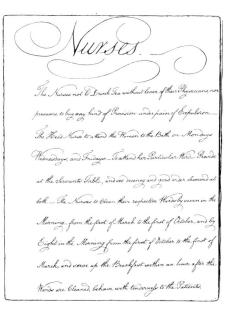

Page from Hospital Rule Book. 1782.

DECENCY AND GOOD ORDER

Each ward was staffed by one nurse whose duty was to look after the patients and ensure that "decency and good order prevailed." An hour after she finished her cleaning, the nurse would be busy serving breakfast sent up from the kitchen below stairs. Evidently the breakfasts did not always arrive very promptly so that patients on Duke's ward had cause to grumble that cook was abusing them by failing to provide their meal hot.[72]

Nurses slept at one end of their respective wards in a small apartment screened off by curtains. One can assume they must have been disturbed at night on occasions though the hospital's chairmen were employed to sit up with very ill patients and paid eight pence a night for their trouble.[73] Night nurses were not employed until 1891.[74] Before then, the hours of duty for nurses had been long and tedious and it is not surprising that these women became bad tempered and turned to the bottle. They could not even leave the hospital without permission from Matron. Even in 1931, the nurses were working more than the 56 hours per week recommended by the Royal College of Nursing.[75]

MATRON

The Matron was in a much more fortunate position. She was provided with two rooms of her own on the ground floor and paid an annual salary of £20, a sum exceeded only by the incomes of the Registrar (£30) and the resident apothecary (£60). The first matron, Mrs Whitlock was elected on Christmas Eve 1741 and remained in office for nineteen years. Her credentials are not recorded but she would have been chosen for a capability in efficient housekeeping and management, not for any special skill in nursing. Her duties were more akin to a matron of a boarding school than of a modern hospital. (Today's hospitals no longer have *matrons*: their modern equivalents are known as *clinical facilities managers*). The Matrons in the eighteenth century appear to be widows or spinsters, though at least two of them retired to get married. (Eliz. Whiting in 1777 and Martha Down in 1785). Elizabeth Morris, appointed in 1791, had been a housekeeper to a Mr Daniel of Belmont for twenty years. According to her testamonial,[76] she could "write in a good hand and do accounts."

Between them, the Matron and the house steward were responsible for running the hospital's domestic affairs. The Matron was given an allowance by the treasurer to purchase all the household linen, to order provisions for the kitchen and keep a stock of things like candles and soap in store. The Committee frequently exhorted Matron to be prudent and frugal. Linen was never thrown away until it was threadbare and even then it was cut up and used by the surgeons for dressings. A cloth-woman was paid two shillings and sixpence a week to mend linen and patients' clothes, though the patients themselves did a lot of this work.

MISDEMEANOURS

It was the Matron's job to supervise the staff and patients. She reported any misdemeanours to the House Visitors. There was a particularly troublesome patient called John Harpur who was one of the first patients to be admitted in 1742. Matron caught him "behaving indecently in the bath and quarrelling with his fellow patients."[77] In later years this would have resulted in immediate expulsion but as this was the very first complaint brought to the House Visitors notice, the man was merely given a

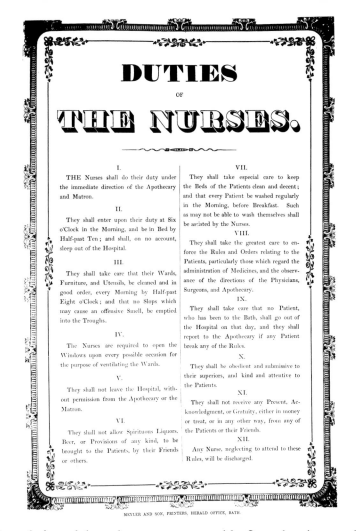

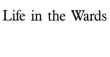

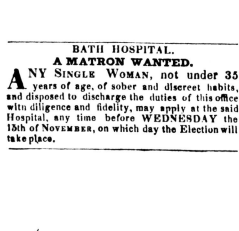

(above left) Duties of Nurses c 1835.

(above) Advert for a matron in the Bath Chronicle. 1826.

(below) Entries from the *House Visitors Book*. RNHRD.

reprimand. A week later there was more trouble. Several patients on King's ward "notwithstanding the orders of the house being read to them, insisted on going out and were with difficulty restrained by ye porter." Patients, like staff, were not allowed to leave the hospital without Matron's permission and she locked the outside doors at nine o'clock each evening to deter anyone slipping in and out under cover of darkness.

The patients in King's ward continued to be a thorn in Matron's flesh. She discovered that "Will Hagget did goe out to drink a pot of ale" and the errant Harpur was still making a nuisance of himself. Even the staff were in disgrace. When Matron sent one of the chairmen across the river to Bathwick mill for some oatmeal, he took five hours to get it. This so affronted the good lady that she had him dismissed by the Committee.[78]

During the eighteenth century the number of nurses varied from four to nine, depending on the state of hospital's funds. In 1773, a post of Head Nurse was created.[79] This woman was paid a higher salary of ten guineas a year. As well as attending to her own ward, she had to supervise the female patients when they visited the baths and "preside at the servants' table and see decency and order was preserved."[80] On the whole, the nurses during this time seem to have been dependable and remained in employment for an average of seven years, ranging from a few months to twenty years. Quite a few died in office. A minority was dismissed, primarily for drunkenness or insolence while in 1772 it was reported that Nurse Woodward would be replaced because she had eloped, though with whom is not recorded.[81] Occasionally there was a general reshuffle of staff so that a nurse became the cook, the cook became the house maid and so on. Not all indescretion led to dismissal. Despite Nurse Waters "obstructing ye charity of the house by advising a person not to put his benefaction into the (contributions) box but give it to the porter,"[82] she was retained on the staff for a further eighteen years.

LOW STANDARDS

The standard of nursing seems to have reached an all time low in the 1820's. Patients frequently had to pay nurses secret bribes to get attention. The medical staff regarded them as incompetent.[83] The Committee was also embarrassed to find the majority of nursing staff more aged and infirm than the patients.[84] They were rapidly pensioned off and a rule was introduced restricting the appointment of new nurses to single women aged between 30 and 45.[85] To encourage an improvement in standards, nurses had their wages increased by £1 a week after completing two years service to the satisfaction of the Committee.

The working conditions of the nurses changed little in the first hundred years. Until 1829 when they were provided with their own bedrooms, the nursing staff slept on the wards. There was no separate accommodation provided until 1883 when the hospital purchased the Sedan Chair Inn, to the rear of the west wing, for its first nurses home. Further properties were purchased in Trim Street, opposite the hospital, between 1913 and 1918, some of which still provide accommodation for nurses.

In the early part of the 19th century, the nurses had the most meagre food and beer allowance of all the staff (see table). Despite patients having mixed vegetables with their meals from 1830 onwards, nurses had to make do with potatoes alone until 1871.[86]

TABLE — **Daily food allowances for staff and patients. 1827. (excluding potatoes and rice.)**

	Bread	Meat	Cheese	Butter	Beer
Menservants	28 oz	14 oz	8 oz	?	4 pints
Chairmen	28 oz	14 oz	8 oz	?	8 pints
Washerwomen	21 oz	14 oz	4 oz	2 oz	6 pints
Maids	21 oz	14 oz	4 oz	1 oz	3 pints
Nurses	14 oz	14 oz	3 oz	1 oz	3 pints
Patients	14 oz	4 oz	½ oz	½ oz	1½ pints

TRAINING

Nurses pay remained at £8 per year between 1741 and 1828 whereas other staff saw an increase in income during this period. The Committee, conscious of the need to improve the standard of nursing, elected to increase nurses wages to £12 a year with biennial increments of £1, up to a maximum wage of £15. In return the Committee expected all prospective nurses to be able to read and write. For some reason married women whose husbands lived in Bath were ineligible to be appointed.[88] In 1898, the Committee reported difficulty in obtaining efficient nurses and reluctantly agreed to another wage increase, bringing the maximum wage to £30 a year. Probationers were also taken on at this time.[89] Though beer was no longer supplied by the hospital an allowance of "beer money" continued until 1903.[90] Properly trained, fully qualified nurses were first employed in 1910 as ward sisters but the only requirement for ordinary nurses was an ability to read and be fit enough to pass a medical.[91]

No formal training was given at this time apart from a course in sick-room cookery at the Bath Technical college but with the advent of the hospital's school of massage in 1912, nurses were encouraged to enroll on the six month course in massage, anatomy and physiology and sit the examination of the Incorporated Society of Masseurs. Though outsiders could also enroll on this course, the majority of these embryonic physiotherapists were nurses working in the hospital. Other skills like plastering, now performed by specialised technicians, were formerly carried out by nurses.[92] Conversely, some tasks previously carried out by the medical staff, like dressings and drug administration, have devolved onto nurses. No doubt their roles will continue to change.

(above) Nurse in uniform c 1910. RNHRD.

(below) Nurse applying a plaster splint c 1955. RNHRD.

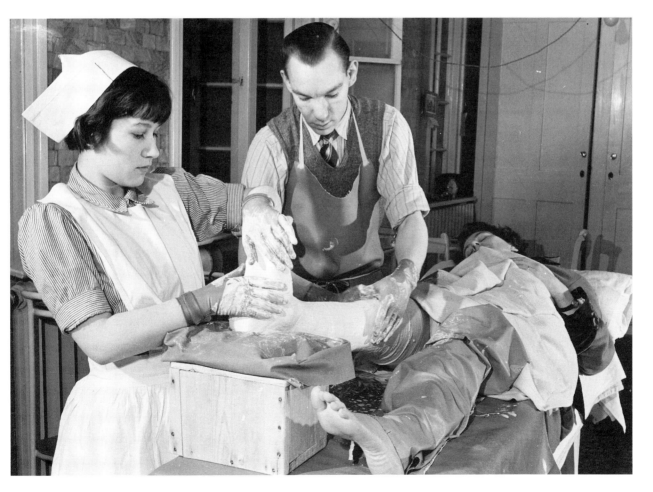

CHAPTER FIVE
Palsies, Rheums and Eruptions

Since its earliest days, the Mineral Water Hospital has been concerned with treatment of rheumatic disease. Everyone thinks they know what *rheumatic* means, yet few can agree on a definition. According to the Oxford Dictionary, the word was first used in English in 1398 when a certain John of Trevisa wrote about "rewmatyk humours." The words are synonymous, rheumatism deriving from the Greek word meaning humour. It should be explained that humour in this sense is not the basis of comedies but rather the bilious, sanguine, melancholic and phlegmatic fluids which our ancestors believed coursed around inside our bodies, causing ill-health whenever they became unbalanced. In the case of rheumatic diseases, they imagined it was the cold and moist humour, phlegm, which stagnated in the limbs and joints, causing the patient so much discomfort. Englishmen, being more inclined to excesses of phlegm on account of their country's atrocious climate, were the most likely of all Europeans to succumb to this disease. Indeed, Dr Oliver's teacher, the great Professor Boerhaave, was convinced that rheumatism was an exclusively English phenomenon.[1] It was therefore appropriate that an Englishman, Thomas Sydenham (1624-1689), was the first physician to try and make some sense of the subject.

Sydenham rejected the medical theorising of his time and based his practice on observation and experience. As a result he was able to make some meaningful classification of disease which remained a basis for defining illness throughout the eighteenth century. He divided rheumatism, a disease characterised by joint pains and swellings, into acute and chronic forms and added two other types, lumbago (pain in the lumbar region) and "scorbutical rheumatism" in which there was no joint swelling or fever, but the patient experienced pains occurring in various parts of the body.

(opposite) Detail from a painting by William Hoare depicting a woman with an arthritic hand, a man with wrist drop and a boy with skin disease. RNHRD.

(left) *'Compliments of the Season'*: A design for a Christmas card by Woodward illustrating rheumatic diseases and alluding to their relationship with inclement weather. Courtesy of the Wellcome Institute for the History of Medicine.

The *Compliments of the Season !!!*

SUITABLE CASE FOR TREATMENT

Rheumatic diagnoses repeatedly appear in the eighteenth century record books belonging to the hospital, together with sciatica, an ill-defined term which was applied to pain arising from a diseased hip-joint or femur, and to pain from irritation of the sciatic nerve. (In its modern sense, the word sciatica applies only to the latter). But rheumatic disorders were not the only illnesses to be treated at the hospital. Though it has become a specialist hospital in this particular field, it should be remembered that its specialist status in earlier times referred to the treatment it offered, rather than the type of disease treated. Any disease that was thought to benefit from mineral water therapy was considered appropriate for treatment. Palsies, skin disease, gynaecological disorders and disease of the digestive tract were given just as much consideration as rheumatism and, in the eighteenth century, these non-rheumatic diseases comprise the bulk of the cases. It was only during the nineteenth century that rheumatic diseases began to form the majority of admissions, which ultimately led to the renaming of the hospital in 1935 as the *Royal National Hospital for Rheumatic Diseases.*

Imprecise usage of diagnostic terms before the era of modern medicine means that, despite a huge record of illness treated in the hospital over the centuries, it is generally difficult to make any retrospective study of the incidence of rheumatic diseases as we now define them. However, the hospital had a policy of recording the referral letters of patients admitted. Often these gave detailed descriptions of the patient's illness in order to allow the hospital's physicians a means of judging whether the case was suitable for Bath water treatment. Unfortunately, only one book of referral letters survives but this alone contains notes of over 1500 cases admitted between 1752 and 1758 and, together with cases published by Oliver, Charleton and Falconer, provides invaluable information about eighteenth century patients and their diseases.

RANGE OF DISEASE TREATED 1752-56

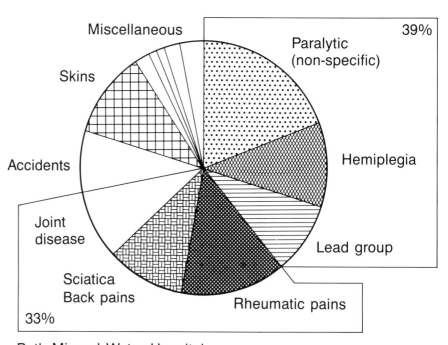

Bath Mineral Water Hospital

THE PALSY

There was an old man, and he kept an old cow,
And how for to keep her he didn't know how.
He built up a barn for us to keep his cow warm
And a drop or two of cider will do us no harm.
No harm, boys, no harm. No harm, boys, no harm.
And a drop or two of cider will do us no harm.

Traditional Somerset song.

At the end of every summer throughout the eighteenth century, country labourers spent long hard hours bringing in the harvest and haymaking. They were paid so poorly that West Country farmers offered free cider to attract the extra labour needed at this time. On hot days the cider flowed freely. It was not unknown for a man to drink several gallons in a day, though the usual allowance was two quarts.

William Bishop of Dunster in Somerset was one such labourer. He enjoyed his cider, drinking freely with his friends in the village. One by one, Bishop and his drinking companions began to suffer from a strange illness. At first, it was no more than stomach aches and indigestion. As the days passed, the pains became more excruciating. The men found themselves unable to relieve their bowels for days on end. Worse still they were no longer able to grip anything: cups, spoons, clothing, everyday objects simply slipped from their weakened hands. William Bishop's hands were so badly affected that his fingers contracted into his palms from where they could only be levered out with the utmost pain and difficulty. To add to their misery, large painful swellings developed on the backs of their hands.

The local medical man was at a loss to know how best to treat them and advised them to seek help at the Bristol Infirmary. The physicians there had seen many similar cases for the cider colic, as it was known, was a common disorder in the neighbouring county of Somerset. It was also well known in Devon. In 1724, there had been a particularly severe outbreak in that county which was described by the Plymouth physician, John Huxham. He called it the *Devonshire Colic* and wrote about it first in Latin and later in English.[2] The treatment, he considered, was to give emetics and purges. No doubt the physicians of Bristol followed Dr Huxham's advice but although they succeeded in moving their patients' bowels, the paralysis remained unremitting.

Bishop and his companions were advised to go on to Bath and arrangements were made for their admission to the Mineral Water Hospital. On arrival, Bishop was examined by Dr Charleton who found him in good health except for his hands which "fell pendulous from the wrists, the power of raising them being gone."[3] The other men were in much the same plight. After a few doses of medicine, they were sent to the King's Bath where their hands were douched and they immersed themselves for an hour or so in the hot water. In addition they were given mineral water to drink each day. Within a matter of weeks on this regimen, they recovered full use of their hands and were able to return home cured.

Bathers in the King's Bath. From Thomas Rowlandson's "Comforts of Bath."

WEST INDIAN GRIPES

About this time, a young sailor called Allen Lane was admitted with similar symptoms.[4] He had been working on a boat which had berthed in the West Indies. Rum was cheap and plentiful and Lane was determined to enjoy himself but, shortly after his arrival there, he became acutely ill and suffered griping belly ache and repeated fits. Nearly twelve months passed before he was well enough to return to England and pursue a course of treatment in the hospital. On admission, "his arms hung like flails from his body; his fingers were drawn into the palms of his hands, the backs of which were covered with large hard swellings and his legs were contracted close to his buttocks and so fixt there that no external force could displace them."[5] The contraction made it impossible for him to put his feet to the ground so that he had to move around by crawling on his knees and his elbows. His whole body was reduced to little more than a skeleton clothed in flesh and he was frequently tormented with violent stomach pains.

Lane stayed in the hospital for six hundred and twenty-two days with no other treatment than mild laxative medicines, a simple diet and frequent immersions in the hot waters of the King's Bath. By the end of his sojourn, the contraction in his legs was entirely removed, his muscles had regained their proper proportions and he could walk unaided though his arms were still weak and wasted.

(*left*) Portrait of Dr Rice Charleton (1710-1789) by Gainsborough, in the Holburne of Menstrie Museum, Bath.
Photo courtesy of the Courtauld Institute, London.

(*below*) Frontispiece to *The Register of Bath* by Dr Thomas Guidott. 1694.
Courtesy of Avon County Libraries.

Dr Charleton was fascinated by the dramatic success of Bath water treatment in so many of these sort of cases. The reputation of the waters in the treatment of palsy was well established long before the hospital's foundation. Dr Thomas Guidott, in practice at Bath during the latter part of the seventeenth century, published a register of over two hundred cases successfully treated by taking the waters and palsy accounts for about a quarter of all cases recorded; indeed the proportion is probably greater as some cases are simply described as 'lame.' The eminent Oxford physician, Thomas Willis considered the Bath waters were the treatment of choice for palsy.[6] So did Dr Robert Peirce, who was in practice at Bath for over half a century and described many cases of wrist drop following colic. At the close of the seventeenth century, he wrote "I find no one distemper more frequent among my adversaria, nor in none more eminent recoveries than this."[7] He delighted in naming eminent patients he had attended: the Marchioness of Normanby, the Earl of Thanett and Sir William Davis, Lord Chief Justice of Ireland, were all sufferers of wrist drop in their time.

MISERABLE COMPANION OF YOUTH

If the number of paralysed patients was large in the seventeenth century, it reached epidemic proportions in the next. The Mineral Water Hospital was full of young men dragging themselves around the wards, their arms hanging limply at their sides. Dr Charleton was particularly struck by the youthfulness of the patients affected, remarking that the palsy, formerly the attendant of worn-out nature, had now become the "miserable companion of youth."[8] Most of his cases were aged between 20 and 40. Over a thousand paralytics were admitted to the wards between 1751 and 1764, which means that almost half the patients in the hospital were suffering from this sort of disorder.

THE
REGISTER
O F
BATH,
O R,
Two *Hundred* Obſervations.
CONTAINING
An Account of C U R E S performed, and *Benefit* received, by the *Uſe* of Famous the HOT WATERS of *B A T H*, in the County of *Somerſet*, as they, for the *moſt* part, came under the *Obſervation*, and *Knowledge*
O F
T H O M A S G U I D O T T,
Phyſician there.
Being great part of his *Experience* of the EFFECTS of the *Baths* of Bath, for XXVII Years laſt paſt.

L O N D O N, Printed by *F. Leach*, for the Author, and are to be ſold by *Randal Taylor*,near *Stationers Hall*,1694

Not all had wrist drop. Some were admitted with hemiplegia, the name given to paralysis of one half of the body with or without disturbance of speech. Analysis of the *Case Book* records reveals a relatively older group of patients with this type of paralysis with a preponderance of male cases in the fifth and sixth decades. In this respect, the pattern resembles present day experience though a lot of patients are young by modern standards: we do not expect to find many strokes in thirty and forty-year-olds nowadays. Many of these strokes occurred after fevers, particularly puerpural fever due to infection of the womb after childbirth. Such fever is usually caused by streptococcal infection and, with the high probability of damaged heart valves from previous rheumatic fever, lying-in women were particularly susceptible to strokes from emboli flowing from the heart to the brain, either blocking the arteries there or producing brain abscesses. Sometimes children were admitted with strokes after contracting smallpox or meningitis, both of which may have caused cerebral haemorrhages.

Paralysed limbs also resulted from accidents. As one would expect, the great majority of these patients were male. Falls from horses and ladders were common; in this respect, things have changed the least although today's traumas generally result from riding accidents on motorbikes rather than horses. The hospital is still concerned with the rehabilitation of patients suffering from the after-effects of head injury, just as it was in the eighteenth century. At that period, many accidents occurred in the pursuit of agricultural occupations. Dislocation of the shoulder with resulting weakness or paralysis of the arm was a common injury seen at the hospital. Back strains accounted for some of the admissions, just as they do today, and sometimes they led to paralysis of the leg muscles through pressure on the spinal nerve roots.

Table analysing the treatment of paralytic cases at the Mineral Water Hospital. From Charleton's 'Three Tracts on the Bath Waters'. 1774. RNHRD.

A State of the Paralytic Patients admitted into the Bath Hospital, from May 1751, to May 1764.

Total Number admitted.——1053.

viz.

		Cured and Benefited.	No better.	Dead.	Improper.	Discharged for Misbehaviour.	Discharged at their own Request.	Eloped.	Total.
45	General Palsies	28	12	2	1		2		45
283	Hemeplegias	204	41	12	20	1	4	1	283
144	Palsies of the Lower Limbs	92	21	10	18	1	2		144
3	Dead Palsies	3							3
5	Shaking Palsies	1	3		1				5
237	Palsies from Cyder and Bilious Cholics	218	5	9	4		1		237
40	Palsies from Mineral Effluvia	38	1	1					40
17	Fevers	13	2		2				17
27	Rheumatisms	22	3	1	1				27
9	Nervous Affections	6	2		1				9
2	Suppression of the Menses	2							2
1	Miscarriage	1							1
1	Lying-in	1							1
19	External Accidents	16	2	1					19
2	Scrophula	1	1						2
24	Extreme Cold	19	2		1		1	1	24
11	Palsies without any assignable Cause	9	2						11
183	Whose Cases were not properly described.	139	16	7	12	3	5	1	183
		813	113	43	61	5	15	3	1053

Cured and Benefited - - - 813.
Not Benefited - - - 240.

FANCIFUL THEORIES

Paralysis, like rheumatism, was often attributed to damp. In one instance, a referring surgeon thought his patient's paralysed legs had resulted from wearing a damp waist-coat.[9] Indeed, for most eighteenth century patients, the cause of their affliction remained a matter for the fanciful theories of their medical advisers like that of a Dorset surgeon called Mr North who referred a paralysed carpenter to the hospital in 1752. The carpenter had been to the nearby town of Glastonbury where he had mentioned to some residents that he was suffering from corns. They persuaded him to try the effects of the newly discovered Glastonbury mineral spring by filling his boots with the water and then riding home a distance of thirty miles with it sloshing about around his ankles.[10] We do not learn whether or not the carpenter was cured of his corns but his palsy, coming on soon afterwards, was imputed to have been caused by this reckless treatment!

A NOXIOUS MINERAL

There was less theorising about one group of patients. Painters, refiners, plumbers and glass workers were frequent residents in the hospital's wards and even the earliest physicians to the hospital were aware that these particular trades exposed their artisans to the pernicious effects of lead. Even the fumes of lead paint seemed to have been hazardous. In 1753, a patient called Samuel Butts arrived at the hospital from London. Like the men from Dunster and the sailor from the West Indies, Butts suffered from violent colics which gave way to weakness of his arms and legs. The symptoms progressed until he was unable to feed or dress himself.[11] Unlike his fellows from the country, Butts did not drink cider and he did not follow any hazardous trade but his house had been freshly painted just before he was taken ill.

Dr Charleton was convinced Butts had been affected by lead in the paint fumes. "It shows," he wrote, "that a very small quantity of that noxious mineral, lead, is capable of producing the most pernicious effects. Happy it would be if some other pigment could be discovered which might supply its place, for even the very effluvia which arise from newly painted houses have sometimes proved as hurtful to the inhabitants as mixing the colours and laying them on commonly proves to the painters themselves."[12]

CORROSIVE ICHOR

Could the cider colic have also been caused by very small quantities of lead dissolved in the drink? Certainly this idea does not seem to have occurred to Dr Oliver, even though he must have seen many cases when he was practising in Plymouth during the 1724 outbreak of Devonshire colic. He was probably satisfied with the explanation of his fellow Plymouth physician, John Huxham who assumed the disease was caused by drinking improperly fermented cider. "Crude juice," wrote Huxham, "ferments vehemently in the stomach and intestines and hence distends them greatly with wind and racks and gripes them." As for the palsy, this was caused by "sharp coagulated matter" being thrown into the blood so that instead of "an exceeding soft lymph to moisten the nerves," a "corrosive ichor" created havoc on the patient's neurological system.[13]

Such an explanation seemed very plausible to the eighteenth century mind until another Devonshire physician dispelled this fanciful theory. Sir George Baker, a Devonian by birth but successful as a London practitioner, was convinced that cider colic was none other than lead poisoning and set

Cider manufacture in the West country. Lead used in the presses may have contaminated the drink.

out by chemical analysis to prove that the beverage was contaminated with small but significant amounts of the noxious element. His work was published in 1768, and came to the notice of Rice Charleton in Bath who commented:

In a very ingenious pamphlet lately published by Dr Baker, the Devonshire colic is attributed to lead, dissolved by the juice of the apples in the manufacture of cider. Lead we know is remarkably productive of this complaint. The sugar of lead, when either given internally, or externally applied, is found to bring on the disease. The same effect is produced by correcting acid wines with sugar of lead and a similar instance fell under my own knowledge of six persons who became at the same time paralytic by drinking cyder brought to them while at harvest work in a new earthenware pitcher, whose inside was glazed; which glazing is chiefly made of lead, and was undoubtedly dissolved by the cyder as appeared not only from those unhappy effects which drinking it produced, but also from its having given that astringent sweetish taste to the liquor by which solutions of this mineral are peculiarly distinguished. But whatever be the cause whence cider derives this deleterious quality, this however is certain, that all such paralytics come to our hospital from Devon, Somerset, Gloucester and Cornwall. It is very remarkable that during the 13 years to which my inquiry extends, there has been only one such patient sent us from Herefordshire and not one from Worcestershire.[14]

In fact, cider colic did occur in the latter two counties, though on a much smaller scale. It is always possible that patients from these counties did not present themselves at the hospital because of difficulty of access due to the appalling state of the roads.[15] This theory is supported by finding that less than 1% of all admissions to the hospital between 1752 and 1756 came from Herefordshire and Worcestershire compared with 47% from Somerset, Gloucester and Wiltshire.[16]

Baker's theory supposed that the cider produced from the apples in the presses of Herefordshire and Worcestershire was relatively free of lead, unlike most of that produced in the South-Western counties. Baker's findings, though based on experimental evidence, were not universally accepted and during this period, West country cider continued to be liable to contamination from dissolved lead. Devonians did not want to see their cider industry ruined and preferred to listen to other West country physicians who condemned Baker's opinions: commercial interests were sufficiently strong to obscure the truth. But ultimately the truth did prevail after James Hardy, a physician at Barnstable added further evidence that cider could easily be contaminated by lead simply by allowing it to stand in glazed earthenware jugs. The acetic acid in rough cider leached out the lead in the glaze.[17]

It may seem strange to us, in view of the huge number of paralytic cases regularly examined by the medical staff at the hospital, that the discovery of lead as the causative agent in colic-with-palsy was not made by any of the Bath hospital physicians. Admittedly, Sir George Baker was able to prove his theory by virtue of his skills in analytical chemistry but such skills were hardly lacking in some of his contemporaries in Bath. Rice Charleton spent many hours analysing the chemical content of the Bath waters[18] and his writings display a reasonable knowledge of chemical matters.

A clue as to why such discoveries were missed lies in a statement made about the hospital's role in research which appears in the early broadsides appealing for funds. *Surely, if the knowledge of the nature and efficacy of the Bath waters could be rendered more extensive and certain, it would be doing a great service to every individual person in any country or age who may hereafter have occasion for their use. Nobody can doubt but this hospital will contribute greatly towards this desirable end.*[19] Research, for most of the early history of the hospital, meant an obsessional preoccupation with the efficacy of the Bath waters and disease processes were only considered in as far as they could be fitted to explain how the waters exercised their effects on the internal workings of the body. Lead had no part in this scheme, indeed it was irrelevant to the main thesis: that the Bath waters benefit the palsy. As a result of this attitude, practical observations on the effects of the Bath waters was considered the only valid sort of research for the first century and a half of the hospital's existence.

The King's Bath, by J.C. Nattes. Courtesy of Bath Museums Service.

BATH HOSPITAL.

The following is a list of Patients, with their diseases, when admitted, who have been discharged during the last month from the Bath Hospital, and who have derived great benefit from the Bath Waters :—

Thomas Hulbert, Trowbridge, Wilts, chronic rheumatism........... *cured.*
William Collis, Timbury, Worcestershire, dropt hands from lead *cured.*
Rachael Woodwards. Trowbridge, Wilts, chronic rheumatism... *cured.*
Ann Keel, Codford St. Peter, Wilts, rigidity of limbs .... *cured.*
Thomas Pearce, Yate, Gloucester, eruption upon the body......... *cured.*
John Stroud, Preshute, Wilts, rheumatism .... *cured.*
William Weller, Butleigh, Somerset, sciatica .... *cured.*
Isaac Whitehouse, Temple, Bristol, rheumatism .... *cured.*
Charles Trove, Wellington. Somerset. dropt hands from lead ... *much better*
Thomas Bishop, St. Clement, Oxford, hemiplegia .... *much better*
John James, Kington, Surrey, palsy .... *much better*
James Bray, Kilmersdon, Somerset, rheumatism .... *much better*
James Daynton, Bradford, Wilts, eruption on the skin .... *much better*
John Bowen, Monmouth, pain and weakness after inflammation *much better*
Charles Ind, Batheaston, Somerset, paraplegia .... *much better*
Mary Wilson, Stourton, Wilts, peraplegia ... . *much better*
George Edwards, Morland Bishop. Devon, eruption on the skin *much better*
William Harroll, Maiden Bradley, Wilts, rheumatism .... *much better*
Thomas Brade, St. James, Westminster, palsy from lead........... *much better*
Thomas Ridout, Wilton Abbas, Dorset, rheumatism .... *much better*
Hannah Lewis, Frome, Somerset, palsy of the lower extremities *much better*
David Long, Mere, Wilts, eruption on the legs .... *much better*
Frederic Cannon, Islington, Mid., rheumatism .... *much better*

HENRY J. PRINCE, Resident Apothecary.
WALTER BRETT, Registrar.

Bath Hospital, July 2d, 1832.

Lists of patients discharged from the hospital were printed in the local newspapers during the 18th and 19th centuries.

CURED BY THE BATH

In fact, the Bath waters appear to have been remarkably effective in curing lead palsy. The hospital had a well defined classification by which the medical staff assessed the results of treatment when patients were discharged. According to Charleton,[20] the outcome was defined into one of five groups:

> **Cured**
> **Much better**
> **Better**
> **No better**
> **Dead.**

Not all patients could be assessed in this way because some were discharged prematurely for misbehaviour, or got fed up and took their own discharge. A small proportion of patients were classified *improper*, a term which did not relate to their behaviour but rather to the opinion that their case was not suitable for mineral water treatment. This either meant that the hospital had been given insufficient or misleading clinical detail about the patient prior to their admission, or the physicians had decided to try out the effect of the waters in the forlorn hope that they would give some benefit, the so-called "trial of the waters."

Because the outcome of all patients' admissions was published in the local newspapers, it was obviously in the hospital's interest to demonstrate a high cure rate to would-be subscribers. For this reason, a certain amount of scepticism is necessary when judging the efficacy of treatment. Furthermore, patients were often admitted for a very lengthy stay, sufficient in most instances for an improvement to be seen if the disorder commonly resolved naturally.

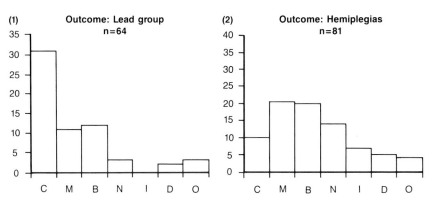

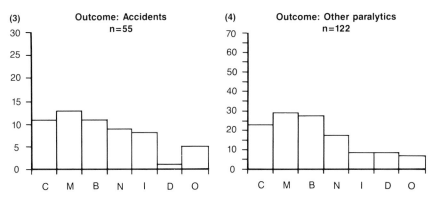

Bar charts showing the outcome of treatment in patients with
(1) palsy and colic ("lead group"),
(2) hemiplegic strokes,
(3) injury
(4) ill-defined paralyses.

The cure rate is significantly greater in the lead group.

Classification of outcome:
    C: Cured.
    M: Much Better
    B: Better
    N: No better
    I: Improper (i.e. not suitable)
    D: Died
    O: Other outcome e.g. Took own
       discharge.
(Author's analysis of 700 cases admitted 1752-56).

But even allowing for such bias, the evidence obtained from analysing the outcome of the lead-related paralytic cases admitted between 1752-58 demonstrates a remarkable success rate in the treatment of this disorder compared with other types of paralyses (*see bar-charts*). Even if the patients were kept in the hospital for a lengthy stay, the patients' referral letters often record that they had "laboured under their disorder" for a very much longer period. In some instances, patients had already been admitted to other hospitals where treatment had been unsuccessful.[21] This applies particularly to the cases with features of lead poisoning, and to patients suffering from skin disease.

Could the mineral water treatment have in some way helped rid these patients of their lead? This intriguing possibility has been recently investigated by Drs O'Hare, Heywood and Dieppe[22] who have studied the effects of prolonged immersion on reducing the lead levels of industrial workers who are exposed to the metal. Their results suggest that immersion in deep baths is of benefit and may explain why so many of the eighteenth century paralytic cases did particularly well at Bath. Together with copious and frequent draughts of mineral water, and the hospital's tough policy towards patients' sorties into the town's public houses, a sojourn of three to six months at Bath probably effected a virtual elimination of lead from most of these patients and thereby cured their symptoms.

AN ICEBERG OF PLUMBISM

Though one can only confidently attribute lead poisoning to those eighteenth century cases where there is a clear description of colic preceding palsy, or where a palsy occurred in a patient whose trade involved high risks of lead exposure, such cases are possibly only the tip of an iceberg of plumbism which affected much of the population at this time. Muscular soreness and stiffness (i.e. symptoms of rheumatism) often precede the paralytic phase, and constipation, a frequent complaint in patients admitted to the hospital at this time, was the natural consequence of the bowel spasm which chronic lead toxicity produces. Close examination of the cases in the 1752-58 *Case Book* reveals patients successfully recovered from symptoms such as convulsions, blindness, vomiting, and tremors, all of which are suggestive of poisoning by lead or other heavy metals.

Gout can also be precipitated by lead poisoning because of the toxic effect on the kidneys which leads to the retention of uric acid. Traditionally, gout is associated with port drinking and it has been suggested that fortified wines in the eighteenth century were heavily contaminated with lead. Recent chemical analyses carried out on some very old bottles of port and madeira have proved this to be so.[23] Rum from the West Indies was another potent source of lead and was undoubtedly the cause of the West Indies Colic. Though gout was extremely common in the eighteenth century, there are remarkably few cases mentioned in the hospital records at that time, though it is notable that some of the paralytic cases, like that of William Bishop with cider palsy and Allen Lane with West Indies Colic, both mentioned earlier in this chapter, draw attention to hard painful swellings on the backs of the hands which could well have been due to gout. Despite this observation, gout was primarily a disease of the affluent and well-fed who were in the daily habit of consuming large quantities of meat, the principle source of uric acid. These were not the sort of persons who would have generally required the charitable support of the hospital. The diet of the poorer classes at this time was mainly vegetarian, and this might explain why lead poisoning did not generally precipitate gout in these people. It was only in the nineteenth century, when the diet of the labouring classes became more varied, that the number of gouty patients in the hospital began to increase.

Bath doctors attending a patient with gout. Detail from a drawing by Thomas Rowlandson.

86

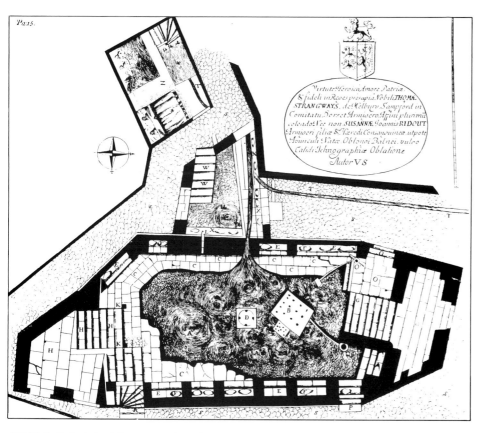

THE BLADUD LEGACY

The early records of the hospital include many admissions for leprosy. Most of these unfortunate people suffered from some quite different complaint. Leprosy, as we know it today, certainly existed in Europe during the Middle Ages but it seems to have disappeared from this country by the time of the Tudors. Despite this, the word which is derived from the Greek *lepra*, meaning scaly, continued to be used well into the nineteenth century to describe any chronic rash on the skin in which scaling or thickening was a prominent feature.

The legend of Bladud, whose leprosy was cured by bathing in the springs, provided hope to all those wanting to be made clean. People with chronic skin disease frequently came to Bath to take the waters for this purpose. Concern for "leprous" cases at Bath antedated the founding of the hospital by several centuries. In 1138, Bishop Robert of Lewes had a hand in building a small house in Bath for the leprous poor. What makes this leper hospital unusual is its siting within the city walls.[24] It was built in close proximity to the Cross and Hot Baths but its exact position is uncertain as it had been demolished by Elizabethan times. It was replaced by another "leper howse" financed by John de Feckenham which stood on the corner of Nowhere Lane,[25] so called by an apothecary in the city during the seventeenth century who had a servant girl who liked to slip out of the house to meet her boyfriend in this road. When asked where she had been, she always replied "Nowhere!"

Feckenham's leper hospital was given a boost in 1712 when Miss Strode of Downside endowed it with £5 a year.[26] Each Lady-day, between eleven and twelve o'clock in the Abbey, the money was paid over to the representatives of the leper hospital until, in 1786, the building was destroyed. Whether it was pulled down or simply fell down is uncertain but Miss Strode's endowment lay fallow for the next thirty-nine years until

(above) 17th century plan of the Hot and Lepers' Baths, with Feckenham's leper house nearby. Courtesy of Avon County Libraries.

(below) Detail of the leper house.

Graduated pewter cups for dispensing mineral water. 18th century. RNHRD.

some observant Governor of the Mineral Water Hospital remarked that as the hospital admitted cases of leprosy, it could rightly claim the endowment.[27] A decree was successfully obtained from Chancery allowing the hospital to receive the annual sum, back-dated to 1786, though the Governors were no longer required to collect it from the Abbey chancel.

Patients with skin diseases represent between 10% and 15% of admissions to the Mineral Water Hospital during the eighteenth and early nineteenth century. Between 1752 and 1764, 241 "lepers" were admitted of whom 122 were "perfectly cleansed" and 85 "much benefitted." Only sixteen received no benefit, and four of these died in hospital.[28] The remainder were discharged because they misbehaved or were unable to take the waters. One of the most florid cases that Dr Oliver and his colleagues had ever seen was a young woman from Bicester called Mary Tompkins. Born in the same year the hospital opened she developed a rash on the skin when she was five years old. At first it was mild and was diagnosed by the local apothecary (William Hicks) as being due to a *surfeit*. It was a common belief at this time that drinking large quantities (ie a surfeit) of cold liquid, particularly if the body was heated, was the cause of such rashes.[29] As Mary grew older, her rash got worse so that by the age of twelve, she was confirmed as having leprosy. Every part of her body, including her face and head, was affected. When she was 15, she was sent to St. Bartholomew's Hospital in London where a variety of medicines was tried, including the dreaded mercury. All treatment failed miserably and she was discharged as incurable. Back in Bicester, Mary's disfigurement was so appalling that nobody was prepared to have her in their house.

In 1763, Mary was sent to Bath and was admitted to the hospital on New Year's Eve under Dr Oliver's care. He wrote:

"I never saw so bad a leprous case. The girl's skin was almost universally covered with large, thick, hard, dry scabs, of a dark brown colour. These brown scabs were specked with white shining silver scales which gave her countenance a very shocking appearance. The clefts between the scabs were wide and deep so that her skin resembled the bark of a tree."[30]

Apart from the state of her skin, she was in good health and Oliver ordered her to be bled and purged and then to embark upon the usual Bath water regimen of drinking and twice weekly bathing. Bathing was discontinued after a month and she was prescribed an ointment made from a mixture of tar (*Ung. e Pice*) and oil obtained from the hooves of oxen. Neat's foot oil, as the latter preparation is known, was used quite widely in the hospital in the 18th century, not only for dermatological cases but as an application to crackling joints on the supposition that it could traverse the skin and thereby lubricate the offending organ. The ointment was applied twice daily for three weeks, and then bathing resumed. It must have been a very sticky business. In 1851, the Minutes[31] record that twelve new flock mattresses were needed to replace those soiled by ointment.

Mary Tompkins drank a pint of mineral water each day, together with a medicine containing mercury, antimony and sarsaparilla. By alternating periods of water treatment with application of ointment, her condition steadily improved and she was able to leave hospital on 8th August 1763, "perfectly cleansed."[32] Patients like this were sometimes resident in the hospital for more than a year. The diagnoses in modern terms can be no more than pure conjecture: psoriasis, eczema, tuberculosis of the skin, fungal infections, impetigo, syphilis, arsenic poisoning, all these have probably been treated at some time in the hospital. The eighteenth century descriptions are for the most part lacking in the necessary detail to allow accurate identification, though sometimes one can be fairly confident of the diagnosis. Henry Robjohn, a poor eight year old lad admitted in 1745 whose grazed elbows became scabby and crusted and failed to heal, was almost certainly suffering from impetigo.[33] Dr Oliver's explanation was simply that the graze caused an impairment of circulation through the skin and "corrosive particles" which were normally dispersed and harmlessly diluted by the fluid parts of the body, accumulated at the site of injury and began "eating away the adjacent parts, exciting intolerable itchings and covering the skin with foul scabs."[34] In fact this idea is not so far removed from modern theories of inflammation; white cells do eat away adjacent parts, particles of fibrin accumulate into foul scabs and there are chemicals in the body which excite intolerable itchings. What the physicians of Oliver's era had no concept of was the possibility of minute living organisms invading the wounded skin, a discovery not made for at least another century.

After the installation of baths at the hospital in 1830, many patients with skin disease were immersed in a foul-smelling concoction of potassium sulphide and mineral water, the so-called sulphur bath. Vapour baths, better known nowadays as Turkish baths, were installed in 1863 by the Bath engineering firm of Stothert and Pitt and used to treat skin cases.[35] By now the term "leprosy" no longer appears in the admission records. But, as with the arthritic cases in the hospital, the medical staff made virtually no attempt to distinguish the various cutaneous disorders which were referred to them. Dr James Tunstall, writing in 1850, was convinced that "such distinctions, however useful to the student, are of no practical avail to the practitioner of medicine."[36] He held that the different types of cutaneous eruptions were merely examples of the same disease modified by the patient's habit, temperament and constitution. For example, an error of diet might in one patient lead to impetigo while in another, the same dietary indiscretion could manifest as eczema. All such skin disorders

(*above*) Neat's foot oil, now used for softening leather.

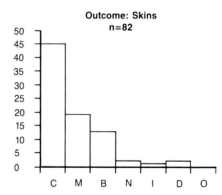

Outcome of skin cases in 18th century, showing high cure rate.

Classification of outcome:
C: Cured.
M: Much Better
B: Better
N: No better
I: Improper (i.e. not suitable)
D: Died
O: Other outcome e.g. Took own discharge.
(Author's analysis of 700 cases admitted 1752-56).

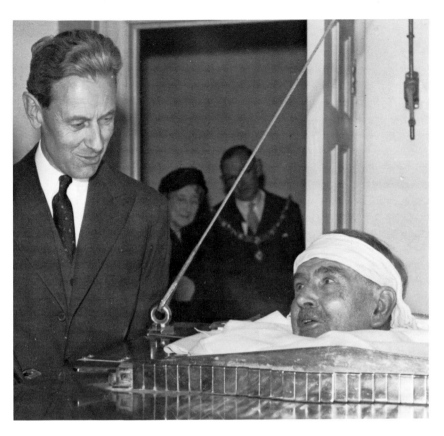

Patient in a vapour bath under the watchful eye of his physician. Courtesy Bath Museums Service.

were considered to be caused by want of cleanliness, errors of diet, cold air, hereditary disposition and various trades.[37]

The old idea that imprudent drinking of cold water frequently caused eruptions on the skin seems to have persisted well into the nineteenth century. In children, great store was put by the state of the teeth: the decay would surely find its way into the system and emerge through the skin as "unhealthy exhalations." These unfortunate youngsters had to undergo scarification of the gums in addition to their immersions in the Bath waters. This meant that one of the surgeons periodically sliced up their gums with a lancet. If the scalp was affected, the patient's hair was shaved twice a week and their head washed twice daily with petroleum soap applied with a shaving brush.[38] The soap was made in the hospital laboratory by blending it with Barbados tar.

One cannot but admire the persistence of both doctors and patients in those days. "It is wonderful," wrote Dr Tunstall in 1850, "how long an advantageous course of the waters may be borne without inconvenience. I have known them in severe and long-standing cases continued for half, and even three-quarters of a year with improvement resulting in cure, the affected parts gradually resuming a healthy state."[39]

Skin disease, along with other non-rheumatological conditions, was excluded from treatment when the hospital adopted its present name in 1935. Ironically, several rheumatic disorders are associated with dermatological manifestations and psoriasis, the "leprous disorder" of Georgian times, is sometimes associated with a severe arthritis of the rheumatoid sort. As a result, the hospital has rekindled its former interest in skin disease and, though the waters play no part in modern dermatological therapy, tar ointments are still popular in the treatment of eczema and psoriasis though they are no longer compounded with Neat's foot oil.

90

RHEUMATISM – THE COLD-MOIST CONUNDRUM

The walls are damp, the ditches smell.
Clos'd is the pink eyed pimpernel.
Hark how the chairs and tables crack;
Old Betty's joints are on the rack.

from *Signs of Rain*, by Dr Edward Jenner.

In 1754, Walter Flea, an excise officer living at Calne in Wiltshire paid
a visit to a local soap maker. The business was carried out in a particularly
damp and cold cellar and Mr Flea was obliged to stand there for some
time, watching the man at work. It was an inspection the excise man was
later to regret. During the next three years, his health took a downward
turn. Severe pains and swelling began to afflict his limbs, flying from one
joint to another. His legs became grossly swollen with fluid. Sometimes
the pains abated, leaving him in a weakened state, only to return a few
weeks later with equal vehemence. Whenever the pains were bad, he
became feverish. By 1757, he had become a cripple, both feet distorted
by severe contractures.

There was one feature of this man's disease on which all his medical advisers
agreed: the illness had been caused by the damp chilling atmosphere in
the soap maker's basement. Cold and damp were considered to be the
principal causes of rheumatism, both acute and chronic. Doctors referring
patients for treatment in Georgian times frequently allude to damp and
cold precipitating the illness: cases like that of William Eason, a sawyer
from Dorset whose rheumatism was supposed to have developed after
"taking a violent cold by sawing in rough, cold, turbulent weather,"[40] or
John Bowen from Monmouthshire whose weak back was "occasioned by
sitting on the ground when hot."[41]

Dr William Falconer suggested that agricultural workers, miners,
washerwomen and anyone employed in moist surroundings ran a high risk
of contracting rheumatism because of their exposure to cold and damp.[42]
He was so convinced of this dictum that he suggested the majority of
rheumatic cases admitted to the hospital could have avoided their illness
if only they had been more sensible in their habits.

A necessitous person may indeed suffer an attack of rheumatism from want of sufficient
clothing, scarcity of fuel, by being obliged to labour in cold wet seasons or in moist ground,
or in other employments exposed to the vicissitudes of heat and cold. But neither poverty,
nor any duty a man owes to his employers, obliges him when heated by exercise to pull
off what clothes he has and expose himself, when at rest, to a current of air, to plunge
into cold water, to drink enormous draughts of cold liquors, or to lie down and even sleep
on moist ground, and often in the autumnal season; all of which, and many similar incidences
of rashness, are so common that I am convinced more than two thirds of the rheumatic
and hip cases (admitted) might be traced to such causes.[43]

ACUTE RHEUMATISM

The idea that damp was the cause of rheumatism was still being debated
in 1928 when a large assembly of physicians attended the hospital for an
international conference on rheumatic diseases. By this time, the nosology
of rheumatic disease had become more logically based as much on its
pathology as on its symptoms though, even today, the pathology of many

By the Rev.ᵈ Henry Crow, Bath.

Portrait of Dr William Falconer.
Courtesy of Avon County Libraries.

rheumatologial conditions remains enigmatic and provokes considerable controversy amongst doctors.

Of all the rheumatic diseases, none has been associated more with damp than rheumatic fever, (also known as acute rheumatism). Once exceedingly common, its incidence began to decline in Britain after the first world war and is now so rare in this country that most doctors entering practice since 1970 have never seen a case unless they have worked in the Third World. The earliest case description from Bath dates from 1665 when Dr Robert Peirce related how a young female patient of his had developed rheumatism as a result of lying on damp ground after an attack of scarlet fever. [44]

Now that rheumatic fever has virtually vanished from English society, nobody gives much credence to damp any more. People still pull off their clothes and expose themselves to currents of air in a manner considered so reckless by Dr Falconer two centuries ago but they do not necessarily develop disease. Perhaps exposure to the inclemencies of the British climate posed more threat in the days when a large section of the population was malnourished and living in squalor. If nothing else was achieved by this theory, it was largely responsible for the improvement in the standard of housing during the nineteenth century, and Dr Falconer, in preaching prevention, must take some of the credit for this.

Peirce's observation that his patient developed rheumatism after scarlet fever highlighted a relationship which was not fully appreciated for another two centuries when the world became aware of bacteriology. Physicians began to consider that rheumatic fever might be an infectious disease. At first it was thought that almost any micro-organism might provoke the disease if it attacked a suitable person, but from 1900 onwards, more and more researchers believed the streptococcus to be the germ responsible. Ultimately, the exact nature of its pathology was worked out and revealed by three doctors from the Rockerfeller Institute who addressed the first international conference on rheumatology to be held in Bath in 1928. They presented a theory that the disease was due to an immune reaction associated with infection by streptococci, the germs which cause tonsillitis and scarlet fever.[45] Since that time, the study of immune reactions and the part they play in other rheumatic diseases has become one of the most important avenues of research in rheumatology.

THE HIP-GOUT

Pain in the hip and leg was another common "rheumatic" disorder treated at the hospital in the early days. "If you enquire of these patients where their pain is situated," wrote Dr Charleton in 1774, "some will point to the groin, some to the great trochanter of the thigh bone and others to the junction of the os innominatum with the os sacrum (sacro-iliac joint). Temporary pains are also often spoke of in the knee, the shin and ankle of the diseased limb. Many of these patients can bear to have the head of the thigh bone moved around in its socket without the least uneasiness. If the buttocks be examined, that of the diseased side will be found lower than that of the well side. The disorder is sometimes brought on by colds which have been caught by sitting on damp ground. Sometimes it is the consequence of external injuries – falls, leaping down from high places, etc. And very often no assignable reason can be given for it."[46]

Between 1761 and 1773, there were 296 patients admitted to the hospital with this sort of history.[47] They were diagnosed as suffering from sciatica or hip-gout, and were more generally classified as *hip cases*. Many were cured but some developed swellings in their thighs, became feverish and then died. Unless the swellings spontaneously burst as an abscess, one of the surgeons would have to apply his lancet to encourage the flow of *laudable pus*. Either way, abscesses nearly always heralded the patient's demise; "the flux of the matter is usually more than his strength can support and he sinks under the discharge."[48]

Pains in the hip and leg still cause diagnostic confusion though mercifully the "flux of matter," a consequence of bone infection or osteomyelitis, is seldom seen today. The condition was frequently encountered by physicians in Bath, even in the days before the hospital was established. "It is not so easily palliated or cured," wrote Dr Peirce in the seventeenth century, "because affluent sharp humours lie deeper upon the bone and thick and large muscles intervene, and therefore no outward application can so easily reach it as in a less fleshy part. The matter, being long imprisoned there, corrupts more, grows more acrimonious and becomes at length corrosive.... which in the process of time penetrates the bone itself."[49] Such cases were often the result of hip joint dislocation. One of Peirce's patients, Sir Thomas Malevorer, had fallen from his horse while hunting and injured his hip. It was some months before he was referred to Bath, and by the time he arrived in 1687, he was very weak and ill. He had to be carried everywhere and when lifted, "was ready to faint away." Two or three attempts were made to put him in the King's Bath, but his condition rapidly deteriorated and he died a fortnight after his arrival.

POST-MORTEM

On the night of the death, Peirce called together two other doctors and the patient's brother and proceeded to perform a post-mortem. It says much for the brother's stomach that he witnessed the opening of "such a suppurative abscess as well nigh filled the cavity of the left side (of the abdomen) near as high as the spleen." Peirce described it as being "the colour of an unboyled lobster, and when opened there spouted out at first some quarts (two or three as we judged) of a wheaty foetid matter which was followed by a cheesy curd..... and what remained of the thigh bone, or at least the upper part of it, was all carious and eaten into holes."[50]

There are no records of the number of post-mortem examinations done at the hospital in the eighteenth century though, despite the absence of records, such examinations were certainly performed at the time. They probably took place in a room in the basement though the absence of any plan for this level means that the site of the original mortuary is unknown. It was usual for the post-mortems to be carried out by one of the surgeons, with the medical staff in attendance.[51] There is an entry in the *Case Book* for 1752/58 which suggests an autopsy was carried out on a patient called John Stillman, a Trowbridge man, who had been referred to the hospital for treatment of severe headache and vomiting.[52] He died two months after his admission and his death is recorded with a postcript, written in a tiny hand, that approximately 10 fluid ounces of liquor was found in his brain. The first inquest seems to have taken place in 1847[53] after a patient died suddenly. A verdict of death from apoplexy was returned.

After the eighteenth century, the number of cases of osteomyelitis admitted to the hospital declined. This probably reflects a more realistic admission policy rather than a decline in incidence. Such cases were deemed *improper* because their feverish state was a contra-indication to Bath water treatment.

Post-mortem set. 19th century.
RNHRD.

SPANISH FLY

Oliver and Charleton were happy to treat sciatica as long as their patients were young and healthy. The affected buttock was usually *cupped* prior to a course of bathing. Cupping entailed applying the mouth of a glass hemisphere to the skin overlying the painful area after the air inside the glass had been heated by a piece of burning tow. As the air cooled the skin would be sucked into the cupping glass by the partial vacuum created. Irritation of the skin in this way may possibly have helped by reducing pain sensation. In the same way, lime poultices were sometimes used to irritate the skin[54] or Spanish flies used to raise blisters.

Counter-irritation, as this type of therapy became known, remained the favourite method for treating sciatica well into the present century. Only the irritants have changed. Spanish fly, or *cantharides* as it is more correctly termed, was once ordered by the hospital pharmacy in large quantities but was ultimately banned after it achieved notoriety because of its dangerous misuse as an aphrodisiac. Towards the end of the nineteenth century acupuncture was the principal method in use. Three, four, five or even more needles, about two and a half inches long, were plunged into the patient's thigh along the course of the sciatic nerve. Hugh Lane, who treated patients at the hospital with this method, wrote:

Patients, after two or three experiences of acupuncture needles, have begged for a repetition of their use with the result that they have at length derived that immunity from pain which they day after day craved for.[55]

Fifty years on, needles had given way to *cautery* and Dr George Kersley found that a line of small burns on the skin over the sciatic nerve produced effective relief. In the last few years, acupuncture has become popular again and some physiotherapists at the hospital are using the technique.

Two forms of counter-irritation. (*above*) Tincture of Cantharides Courtesy of Hale's Chemists Ltd, Bath.
(*Below*) Cupping glasses. RNHRD.

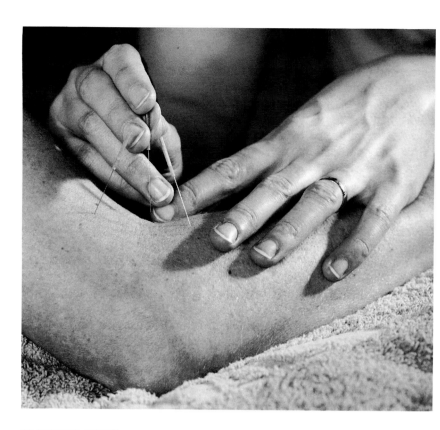

Physiotherapist at RNHRD performing acupuncture on a patient. Feb.1988.

SLIPPED DISC

Some cases of sciatica were the result of compression of nerve roots in the back. In the eighteenth century, tuberculosis often affected the vertebrae causing collapse of the spine, so-called Pott's caries. There were many such cases admitted, though the cure rate was certainly not spectacular. Often the physicians simply played for time. Matthew Ball, a twenty-eight year old Gloucestershire man was "seized with a defluxion on the lungs which continued two or three years with great weakness." He went on to develop a considerable distortion of his spine and he lost so much weight that "a consumption was thought inevitable." Five months before his admission, he began to experience numbness and weakness in his hips, thighs and legs. He was in the hospital for 404 days before being discharged in 1755, *much better*.[56] He was lucky. Others died, or were discharged improper because they developed a prolonged high temperature known as a hectic fever, often a symptom of TB or osteomyelitis. With the decline of spinal osteomyelitis, the commonest cause of nerve root compression is now the *slipped disc*. In 1934 two American surgeons, William J.Mixter and Joseph Barr, discovered that intervertebral discs could rupture and cause sciatica by pressing on the spinal nerve roots. They demonstrated how it was possible to relieve the compression by an operation known as laminectomy. Within months of their discovery, two patients with sciatica at the Mineral Water Hospital were the first to receive this revolutionary surgical treatment in Great Britain, performed by Bath surgeon Charles Kindersley.[57]

BLOOD AND STEEL

The operation was carried out at the Bath and Wessex Orthopaedic Hospital. Apart from a temporary operating room fitted out during the last war, the Mineral Water Hospital had no proper operating theatre until 1965; indeed operative surgery was a notably absent feature of the hospital's early days. In the first century and a half, only one major operation is recorded and this was such a significant event that the Governors had to

give their permission.[58] In November 1807, the house apothecary reported that Philip Harding, a patient in the hospital, was "in such a state as to require an amputation of the leg above the knee." There may have been more operations carried out, but no other is mentioned in the Minute Books. According to the rules agreed by the 1739 Act of Parliament, "When any surgeon has any considerable operation to perform he shall acquaint the physicians and surgeons of the House when it is to be performed that they may be present if they please."[59] Minor surgery seems to have been carried out as much by the resident apothecaries as the surgeons themselves. Certainly bleeding and cupping, traditionally the province of surgeons in hospital, was carried out by the eighteenth century apothecaries.

Caricature of a Bath surgeon using a large clyster syringe. From a series of drawings by Darly. 18th century. Courtesy of Bath Museums Service.

The surgical procedures carried out in the hospital at this time were of a minor nature. They included:

Bleeding	**Excision of tophi**
Cupping	**Catheterisation** (particularly in back injury)
Blistering	
Issues	**Clysters (Medicated enemas)**
Plastering	**Cauterisation**

Such procedures were probably carried out in a room set aside for the purpose. John Wood's proposed plan shows a *surgeons' room* on the ground floor, as well as the apothecary's and physicians' rooms. In 1750, the hospital Minutes mention that a dozen cupping glasses and a lamp were required in the *surgery*.[60] In 1829, the surgeons' room and adjacent matron's room were knocked into one to form a new Committee Room.[61] The matron's apartments were moved to the west wing and, on a plan of the hospital drawn in 1857, all trace of a surgeons' room has vanished. This probably indicates that there had been so few *considerable operations* performed that the surgery was no longer thought necessary. Furthermore, a proper operating theatre, complete with tiered auditorium,[62] became available to Bath surgeons in 1826 at the newly erected United Hospital in Beau Street and any patients requiring major operations could theoretically be admitted there. After 1844, surgeons and physicians were able to hold honorary appointments at both hospitals[63] which facilitated transfer of surgical patients between the two institutions. Even today, major orthopaedic procedures are transferred to the Bath and Wessex Orthopaedic Hospital at Combe Park.

CONTRACTURES

The greatest challenge for early surgeons was the treatment of patients with contracted limbs. When a limb becomes immovable from injury, paralysis, or from joint disease, the affected muscles slowly contract to pull the joints into a permanently flexed position. The early hospital records make frequent reference to patients with contractures and their treatment in the baths. Straightening was accomplished by immersing the patients and stretching their contorted limbs in the hot water. Progress was painstakingly slow and, even with regular treatment, it often took a year to effect any significant change. Mechanical contrivances were also used: in 1795, the Governors purchased a Lobb's machine, a sort of traction apparatus for stretching contracted limbs.[64]

Charles Kindersley, first *orthopaedic* surgeon to the hospital.

Simple stretching was both slow and uncomfortable. The discomfort was even greater when the problem was due to arthritic joints, but the advent of anaesthesia in the mid-nineteenth century opened the door to a much quicker and effective means of releasing contracted limbs though the first mention of anaesthesia in the hospital records does not appear until 1885.[65] Four years later, Thomas Pagan Lowe, a surgeon at the hospital, published his experiences in treating arthritis by forcible movements.[66] Publications by the honorary surgeons of this time demonstrate their interest in orthopaedics but they were essentially generalists. Charles Kindersley, appointed in 1932, was the first surgeon to be officially designated *orthopaedic*.[67] Kindersley pioneered the use of plaster of paris splints to immobilise acutely inflamed joints and to treat contractures. But Kindersley, despite his specialist interest, was still a general surgeon. Only since the last war have the consultant surgeons at the hospital confined themselves entirely to orthopaedic practice. During this time, surgery has come to play an increasingly important part in the treatment of arthritis and the replacement of diseased joints by artificial ones has revolutionised the outlook for crippled patients who would otherwise be consigned to wheelchairs.

NEW JOINTS FOR OLD

The technique has now reached such a stage of perfection that over ninety percent of patients whose hip joints are replaced can expect to be relieved of their pain and stiffness. But in years to come total hip and other joint replacements will probably prove as ephemeral as plaster-of-paris splinting. The hope amongst rheumatologists now is that the understanding of the disease processes responsible for arthritis will increase to the point where it will soon be possible to prevent and control rheumatic diseases, so obviating the need for the large volume of repair work with which the present day surgeons are burdened. The Bath Mineral Water Hospital has played an increasing role in unravelling the mysteries of those disease processes, a role which began three quarters of a century ago.

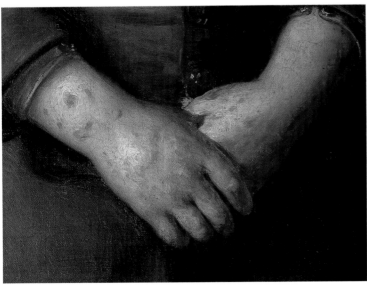

(above) Scene in the Pump Room, 1784. The man in the centre appears to have a paralytic condition affecting his legs and is being supported from behind by another visitor. There are several cripples amongst the assembled company. Detail from a painting by Humphrey Repton in the Victoria Art Gallery, Bath. Courtesy of Bath Museums Service.

(left) Detail of the hands of a child patient, possibly suffering from eczema but labelled a leprosy, from a painting by William Hoare.

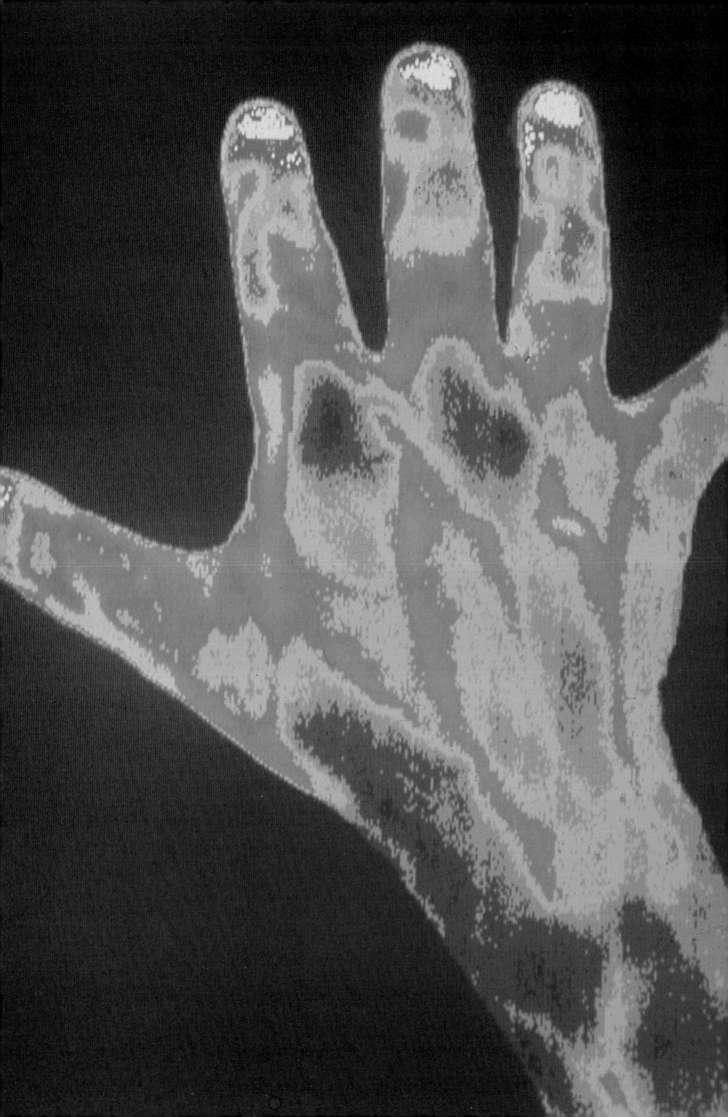

CHAPTER SIX
The Development of Rheumatological Research at Bath

In 1798, a close friend of Dr William Falconer called John Haygarth took up residence in Bath. Haygarth had been physician to the Chester Infirmary and had kept meticulous records of over 10,000 consultations he had made during 34 years in practice. During his years of retirement at Bath, he took the opportunity to analyse his records and in 1813, he published some of his results.[1] Among the many patients who Haygarth had observed, 34 appeared to have a joint disease quite distinct from the chronic arthritis which crept in behind an attack of acute rheumatism. Nearly all these patients were middle-aged women and he called their arthritis "nodosity of joints" on account of its characteristic appearance. Around the same time, other publications began to appear in England and France describing a hitherto unrecognised type of arthritis. Despite Bath's magnetic attraction for arthritic patients, no descriptions of this newly recognised disease were published by any of the hospital's physicians until 1888.[2] This is all the more remarkable considering the large number of so-called rheumatic cases admitted to the hospital over this period.

One possibility strongly debated amongst rheumatologists, is that this particular form of arthritis was rare in the eighteenth century and was only recognised later because its incidence suddenly rose in the nineteenth century. This theory is born out by analysing the hospitals case referrals for 1752-56. Out of a series of 785 cases admitted, joint symptoms are only specifically mentioned in 56 of the referral letters, and of these only 25 refer to swelling in more than one joint. Very few descriptions in the series match the clinical picture of what we now call rheumatoid arthritis, though there are some which are suggestive of the diagnosis. Forty year old Martha Smith from Chedworth in Gloucestershire, who was admitted in July 1755, was described by her own doctor thus:

Always of tender habit of body, she has had several children, one about three months ago. She hath been much afflicted with rheumatic pains these eighteen months past. Her hands, feet and legs swelled and the tendons of her hands and feet are contracted and the joints have become large. In the last few months she has become quite lame and helpless in her hands and feet.[3]

Another case, a young woman from Devon, was described as labouring under great weakness and relaxation of her wrists and ankles and also weakness in her dorsal spine. Her doctor mentioned nodes in the joints of her fingers and swellings and pains in her knees and diagnosed her condition as "scorbutic rheumatism."[4] But were these cases of rheumatoid arthritis?

William Falconer had made some attempt to describe a series of 895 cases of rheumatic disease admitted between 1785 and 1793.[5] He regarded acute and chronic rheumatism as different stages of the same disease,

(above) Dr John Haygarth who is buried at Swainswick, near Bath. Courtesy of Avon County Libraries.

(opposite) Thermogram of hand, from the hospital's thermographic department, known internationally for its development of new techniques in heat measurement of diseased joints and tissues.

distinguished from gout in as much as the joint pain was bearable and the joints themselves were never red. Falconer regarded rheumatism primarily as a muscular disorder though he accepted that the joints were commonly affected, even to the point of becoming ankylosed (fixed). Very few cases of gout are recorded in Falconer's series though he does mention a small number of patients suffering from "gout conjoined with rheumatism." As explained earlier, true gout was unlikely to occur in hospital patients of this time simply because their poverty precluded the sort of rich diet necessary for the disease to manifest itself.

Unfortunately there is no way of deciding what Falconer meant by "gout conjoined with rheumatism," though the term rheumatic gout was later used by some doctors to descibe rheumatoid arthritis; indeed the nomenclature of the various forms of arthritis remained in a state of total confusion for most of the nineteenth century. It was not until 1876 that Sir Alfred Garrod (1819-1907), professor of medicine at University College Hospital, London, first used the term Rheumatoid Arthritis to describe the distinctive form of joint disease that we recognise by this term today. But was this the same disease as that identified by the French physician Landré Beauvais in 1800, and subsequently by William Heberden, John Haygarth and several others over the next half century? Nobody really knows. Haygarth may have been describing a variation of osteoarthritis rather than rheumatoid disease. Even when we have reasonably detailed descriptions of patients' cases, as we do with the case of Martha Smith mentioned above, retrospective diagnosis is pure guess-work. Before the mid-nineteenth century, medical terminology was beset by ambiguity and confusion. And even after Garrod coined the term Rheumatoid Arthritis, the confusion remained: John Kent Spender,[6] who was the first Bath doctor to publish an accurate description of the disease in 1888,[7] at first referred to it as *osteo-arthritis*, a term now reserved for an entirely different kind of joint disease.

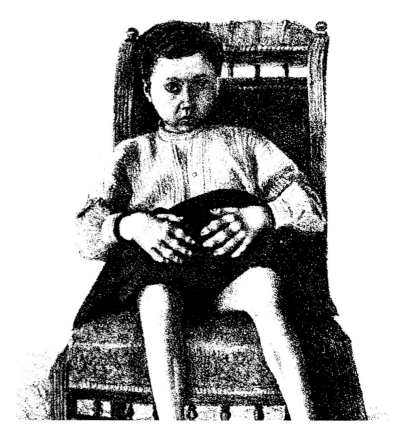

Boy with rheumatoid arthritis, drawn from a patient in the hospital in 1890.

Detail of hands.

Spender's description of rheumatoid arthritis is easily recognised as the disease which doctors still deal with at the hospital in modern times, though it seems to have been a more aggressive illness in Spender's time with a profound anaemia and often with curious pigmented spots appearing on the skin. These brown patches were subsequently known as Spender's Spots. They are rarely seen now.

It is perhaps strange, in view of the opportunities for research offered by the large concentration of rheumatic cases under one roof, that the hospital contributed so little to the advancing knowledge of chronic rheumatic disease in the first two thirds of the nineteenth century. Spender himself acknowledged these opportunities when, on his retirement, he wrote: "Nowhere else in the kingdom could I have prosecuted those researches which helped to prove the clinical identity of rheumatoid arthritis."[8]

But within a decade of Spender's retirement, a spate of observations on patients at the hospital with rheumatoid arthritis appeared in print. In 1890, Hugh Lane and Charles Griffiths, reviewing hospital cases, published the first clear differentiation of rheumatoid arthritis, chronic rheumatic arthritis and osteo-arthritis. Hugh, whose brother Sir William Arbuthnot Lane achieved eminence as an orthopaedic surgeon by using plates and screws to treat fractures, was appointed honorary surgeon to the hospital in 1891.[9]

The calibre of the resident medical officer, or resident apothecary as he was formerly known, may have been the decisive factor in determining what, if any, research was done during the early history of the hospital. Evidence from the minute book suggests that much of the data collected for William Falconer's publication in 1795 was the result of meticulous recording by William Balne Farnell who was the long-suffering and dedicated house apothecary at that time. A half-century later, James Tunstall analysed records he kept while he was resident apothecary so that, at the end of his term of office, he was able to publish a book about the sort of diseases which were most benefitted by spa treatment.[10] By the final decade of the nineteenth century, the quality of applicants for the resident medical officer's post had improved to such an extent that the Governors were able to appoint candidates in possession of higher medical degrees.[11] Rheumatological research was now in full flow and the resident medical officers contributed a large part to it. One of these was a young doctor called Arthur Wohlmann who graduated with honours from Guy's Hospital in 1891 and obtained his MD degree in the following year.

INADEQUATE APPARATUS

Perhaps the most promising development in the work of the hospital since the last war has been the expansion of laboratory investigation into the nature and treatment of rheumatoid disease. The hospital's research laboratories are now housed in a building opposite, known as the Bath Arthritis Research Centre but in 1893, when Arthur Wohlmann arrived at the hospital to take up his appointment as resident medical officer, the concept of a research laboratory was about as alien to the hospital's board of governors as the election of women onto the Committee. Dr Wohlmann was anxious to develop his interest in the fashionable scientific pursuit of bacteriology. Year by year since the mid-nineteeth century, diseases hitherto attributed to obscure physiological imbalances, genetic defects or adverse climates were proving to be caused by micro-organisms. In 1882, the famous German bacteriologist, Robert Koch, had demonstrated bacilli in tuberculous joints and a year later others found gonococci in cases of

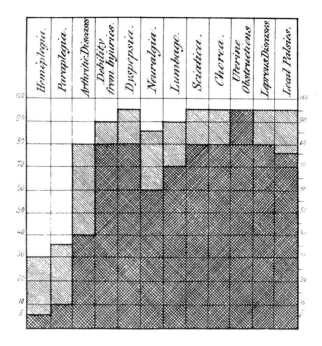

STATISTICAL TABLE

Shewing the proportion of cases per cent. cured and relieved by the Bath Waters. The cross lines represent the numbers cured, and the faint lines those who derive great benefit.

(right) The efficacy of the Bath waters in treating various diseases. From a survey carried out by Dr J. Tunstall, resident apothecary, 1843-1850.

(below) Dr Gilbert Bannatyne, physician to the hospital 1894-1912. Bannatyne was the first doctor to publish an x-ray photograph of rheumatoid arthritis in 1896 in his book on the disease. Courtesy of Bath Clinical Society.

gonorrhoeal arthritis. Might not rheumatoid arthritis, the disease which Spender claimed was "merely one sign of a profound nerve disorder," also be caused by bacteria? Dr Wohlman, together with a newly appointed honorary physician called Gilbert Bannatyne were convinced that it was.

For some time, Dr Wohlmann and I, looking at the clinical nature of the disease and at the course of the symptoms, had practically made up our minds that the disease was microbic in character. The absence of post-mortem material complicated the case, but we decided to obtain what specimens we could from the living subjects. In this way, we were led to aspirate affected joints and examine the fluids so obtained microscopically and by cultivation. On staining we were readily successful in determining a micro-organism was present, but at the same time were troubled with the difficulty of staining it properly and getting it free of precipitate. Our first culture attempts utterly failed, but by degrees we got fair results.

Having arrived at this stage and feeling the utter inadequacy of our apparatus, I felt compelled to call to our assistance more skilled aid. [12]

They enlisted the help of Dr Blaxall, a bacteriologist at the Westminster hospital, who agreed to examine more samples of synovial fluid collected from the joints of patients at Bath. With some difficulty, Blaxall confirmed the presence of small bacteria in the specimens sent to him. [13] But even though Bannatyne and his colleagues believed they had discovered the causative agents of rheumatoid arthritis, others remained sceptical. In all probability, they were nothing more than contaminants.

What is most remarkable about this project is that it ever happened at all. Facilities for this kind of research were woefully lacking in the hospital. The only scientific equipment which the hospital possessed at this time was a microscope and apparatus for analysing urine. Pathological research was regarded as having no place in the hospital's constitution and the only permissible studies were on the efficacy of the Bath mineral water. Medical staff who wished to observe other aspects of the cases under their care were expected to satisfy their intellectual curiosity in their own homes at their own expense. Pathological research was certainly not something to be financed out of the charitable funds of the hospital.

It took an outsider to change this attitude. In 1905, a Cambridge University pathologist with the somewhat curious name of Dr Thomas Strangeways Pigg Strangeways, had set up a small clinical research hospital in Cambridge to study patients with rheumatoid arthritis. One of Dr Strangeways' proteges was a young medical graduate called James Lindsay who in 1906 was elected resident medical officer to the Bath Mineral Water Hospital. Dr Strangeways was anxious to investigate a possible link between rheumatoid arthritis and the presence of infection elsewhere in the body. He encouraged Dr Lindsay to make such a study of patients at Bath. One hundred and seventy two hospital cases were analysed and Lindsay's findings were published by Dr Strangeways in 1907. At first sight it looked as though vaginal infections and gum disease had some link with rheumatoid disease because Lindsay found well over a third of his female cases were suffering from these complaints.[14]

In October 1908, Dr Strangeways wrote to the Governors of the Mineral Water Hospital seeking their permission to send a research pathologist to carry out further bacteriological studies on patients. The pathologist would require a laboratory but if the hospital could provide a room with gas and water on tap, Cambridge University would fit it up with the necessary apparatus.[15] The Committee, happy that the project would not involve the hospital in any expense, agreed to provide a room next to the mortuary.[16] The research pathologist, Dr Emily Morris, moved in just before Christmas and became the first woman doctor to work in the hospital. She stayed four and a half months, collecting numerous vaginal swabs from patients with rheumatoid disease. She probably had a hard time for she concluded in her report[17] that "the investigation was unsatisfactory because the vagina only was examined, the circumstances under which it was carried out did not permit an examination of the cervix." It must have been virtually impossible to perform satisfactory vaginal examinations in the gloom of the gas-lit night wards.

These early investigations tended to support the notion that rheumatoid arthritis was linked to foci of infection elsewhere in the patient's body and led doctors to adopt an obsessional preoccupation with tooth extraction and the surgical removal of other offending organs, such as tonsils and gall bladders, where occult infections might be smouldering. The theory of an infectious aetiology was also responsible for maintaining the time-honoured ritual for flushing out the bowel, performed in the nicest possible way at Bath with mineral water enemata, so that the bacterial flora suspected of inducing the patient's arthritis could be safely swilled away. A dental chair and a Plombière Douche became prominent amongst the hospital's therapeutic armamentaria, and the Governors felt it expedient in 1906 to appoint an honorary dental surgeon to the hospital. Just how many teeth were drawn in the hope of curing patients' joint disease must, like the teeth themselves, remain buried in obscurity.

After Dr Strangeways and his colleagues had completed their programme of research, they offered the apparatus in the laboratory to the hospital for £25. The Committee refused to buy it and the medical staff had to raise the money amongst themselves. The hospital's microscope was so antiquated that Dr Bannatyne loaned his own instrument. And so the Governors rather reluctantly took up the cause of laboratory medicine and invited Dr Lindsay to become the hospital's first honorary pathologist.[18] But despite the medical staff's enthusiasm, the Committee were resolute

Dr James Lindsay, first pathologist and honorary physician to the hospital, 1912-1930. RNHRD.

105

that no money could be granted from hospital funds towards the new laboratory.[19]

By 1913, the Committee's attitude to pathology had undergone a dramatic turn about. When Dr Bannatyne retired and removed his microscope from the laboratory, the Committee agreed unhesitatingly to buy a replacement.[20] The hospital management seem to have woken up to the realisation that they were in the twentieth century. Pressure was put on the three honorary physicians, now rather long in the tooth, to resign and make way for new blood. They were replaced by Frederick Thomson, Richard Llewellyn, Rupert Waterhouse and Gilbert King Martyn. James Lindsay was also made an honorary physician, thereby relinquishing his post as pathologist. Where he had been content to work in a tiny box-room laboratory, his replacement required a laboratory with more room. Two new pathologists were appointed: John Munro, a doctor of science, and a medical graduate George Almond who was later killed in action on the Western Front in the closing months of the first world war. Together, the new medical team stood poised to forge the hospital into a nationally and internationally recognised centre for rheumatology.

The large number of cases of gout, rheumatism and allied conditions which pass yearly through the wards offer a wide field for collective clinical observation and research, and carefully compiled statistics with regard to etiology, course and effect of treatment in a large number of these cases should prove distinct value towards elucidating the many obscure points which still exist in connection with these diseases.[21]

Portrait of Dr Rupert Waterhouse, physician to the hospital, 1912-1932. Courtesy of Bath Clinical Society.

The original research laboratory. The building had previously been used as a nurses' home and was on the site of an inn known as the Sedan Chair.

The new laboratory was fitted out in a house in the hospital's garden, previously used as a nurses home (and the site of an inn known as the Sedan Chair). Annexed to the laboratory was a medical museum for pathological specimens relating to bone and joints, and a small medical library. The latter was started by Sir William Osler who was invited to Bath to open the new facilities on June 4th 1914 and donated ten pounds, a not inconsiderable sum in those days, for the purchase of books. By the end of the year, the library contained over 500 volumes.[22] But within a few months of the new laboratory's opening, the wards of the hospital were full of wounded soldiers returning in droves from the front lines; the "requirements" of a country at war precluded any further ideas of expanding research until the decade ended.

By 1920, with the last of the soldiers discharged, the hospital had returned to its more usual role as a treatment centre for rheumatic diseases. The medical staff resumed their aspirations to create a rheumatological centre of excellence with national and international reputation.

The first post-graduate course in rheumatology to be held at the hospital (1920) attracted a large number of physicians from all over Britain and provided much needed publicity about the work of the hospital amongst the medical profession. The mood amongst the medical staff was one of optimism and a desire for expansion. The closure of the Blue Coat School meant a sizeable premises adjacent to the hospital became vacant and the medical staff encouraged the Committee to make an offer for its purchase to provide accommodation for research work and surgical facilities. A research fund was started and the Medical Research Council approached to help finance the project.

In June 1921, the hospital bought the old school building for £1200 but there was insufficient money in the Research Fund to do anything, so the building was temporarily let to a firm of estate agents in the hope that the finances would soon improve. The Committee was hoping to raise money by admitting patients of 'moderate means' and charging them fees, but this was such a dire departure from the original intentions of the hospital's founders that the charity commissioners continually stalled on their approval of the scheme. The MRC were also stalling and after three years of procrastination on all sides, the hospital management were obliged to return the Blue Coat School to the market where it was sold to the city council. (Ironically, the building is being considered to accommodate extra research laboratories at the present time).

Despite the disappointment over the Blue Coat School, quite a lot of research did go on at the hospital during these years. In 1913, the hospital's pathologist, J.M. Munro, was paid £400 a year to pursue "a certain series of pathological, bacterological and biochemical investigations" and a local printer and publisher, Cedric Chivers, offered to pay the salary of a biochemical assistant. Some of the money was used to finance a study by two Oxford biochemists (Peskett and Raiment) into the biochemical effects of drinking Bath mineral water. Four male beds were lent to admit non-rheumatic patients on which to carry out the investigations.

Munro's research focused on the effects of hydrotherapy on normal individuals, and biochemical and metabolic investigation of various types of arthritis. He also studied the way in which antibodies react with bacteria involving a substance called complement.

Munro and his colleagues hoped to fund their research with a grant from the MRC but this august metropolitan body was unmoved by the enthusiasm of provincial researchers. For one thing, the laboratory facilities were Dickensian. The laboratory building was adjacent to the local newspaper's print shop and vibration from the presses was so bad that it was impossible for the pathologists to accurately weigh anything on their balances. Until 1927, there was neither electric power nor electric light in the building. Progress in rheumatological research could hardly be expected in such an environment, but the medical staff were still quite pleased with their achievements. In 1921, Dr F.G.Thompson wrote:

During the last 8 years investigations have been carried out in the Pathological Department of the hospital in an attempt to elucidate some of the problems connected with the pathology of arthritis. These investigations afford strong evidence of the presence of infective processes in a large proportion of patients, though in many cases the precise location and determination of the infective agent may be quite impossible, and remain a matter of inference. The chronic infective processes associated with arthritis are found with extreme frequency among the community in general, and only a certain proportion of those affected develop joint change. In other words, *certain persons appear to be more susceptible to arthritis than others under the same conditions. The personal factors which predispose the individual to the onset of arthritis are at present an unknown quantity, and biochemical investigations into this aspect of the question are urgently needed.* Research on these lines would of a certainty be a long and difficult business and could only be satisfactorily carried out by whole time research workers of the highest technical ability. [23]

Dr Thompson's words were prophetic. It was indeed to be a long and difficult business but, over sixty years on, the technology of biochemical investigation has advanced sufficiently to prove the link between the patient's genetic constitution and their susceptibility to arthritis. Today's research scientists can work out the molecular structure of patient's genes in order to discover which particular bits are associated with rheumatic diseases.

INSTITUTION FOR THE STUDY OF DISEASE

Throughout the thirties, appeals for money to fund research and rebuild the hospital went hand in hand. Though most members of the hospital management committee now appreciated the need to improve the facilities for research, not all were convinced. Dr Preston King, one of the old guard of physicians who stepped down from office after the Great War, complained that the hospital was being diverted from its proper use as a mineral water treatment centre and was fast becoming "an institution for the study of disease." Pathological research and biochemical work carried out in the laboratory was, in Preston King's view, both costly and unnecessary.[24] The younger physicians, like Vincent Coates, an internationally respected rheumatologist who was tragically killed in a train accident in 1934, inevitably took the opposite view and were concerned that the hospital was already losing ground in its efforts to keep up to date.

(below) Dr Vincent Coates, physician to the hospital 1921-1934.

(left) Old Blue Coat School. (now replaced by a Victorian building.)

(above) A view of post-war laboratory research. RNHRD.

(below) Bas Relief plaque of Sidney Robinson, a major benefactor of hospital research in the twentieth century.

In 1934, a large donation was offered by one of the Governors, Sidney Robinson, to fund the full-time research worker for whom the medical staff had been canvassing for so long. Robinson's daughter, Violet Prince, suffered from rheumatoid arthritis and both she and her father were major benefactors of the hospital in the years between the two wars. The Medical Research Council were also adopting a more positive approach to providing research funds, having been encouraged by news of the Governors' proposals to rebuild the hospital on a new site. With sufficient funds now at their disposal, they appointed a Jewish refugee, Dr Walter Levinthal, as a full-time research pathologist. Dr Levinthal had been assistant professor of pathology in Berlin before fleeing Nazi Germany. During his sojourn at the hospital, he became interested in the possibility that rheumatoid arthritis was caused by an abnormal response of the body's immune system. A series of observations on blood and joint fluid led him to conclude that persons subject to rheumatic diseases had fewer antibodies in their blood but their tissues were much more immunologically sensitive.[25] This rather simplistic theory marks the commencement of the hospital's continuing interest in the immunological basis of rheumatic disease, a line of research which is still being investigated in its laboratories fifty years later.

MOST PROGRESSIVE IN THE WORLD

Part of Levinthal's work involved animal experimentation. Despite assurances that no vivisection was going on, voluminous correspondence from concerned readers began to appear in the local press.[26] Amid protests, the work continued, carried out in a refitted laboratory in the Sedan Chair building, and by 1938 at the International Rheumatology Congress taking place in the city, the hospital was acknowledged as the most progressive rheumatology unit in the world despite its building being declared by Lord Horder as "only fit for rats to live in."[27] With a substantial sum collected for a new 250-bedded hospital near the river, the Queen was invited to lay the foundation stone on 11th September 1939. Eight days before the ceremony was due to take place, Britain found herself at war and the building scheme had to be postponed. Money for medical research dried up and Dr Levinthal was laid off in 1941. The ultimate blow literally came when the laboratory was wrecked by a bomb blast which destroyed much of the hospital's west wing during one of the German *Baedecker* raids on Bath. With half the medical staff called up for military duties, research came to all but a standstill.

RESEARCH DIRECTOR

It was to be largely the enthusiasm and dedication of one man that resurrected it after the war was over. George Durant Kersley was born at Bath in 1906, the same year that James Lindsay, then a young resident medical officer at the hospital, was busy conducting his research on arthritis. Unbeknown to either of them at the time, they would eventually practice medicine together. Years later, when Kersley was himself a young doctor at St Bartholomew's Hospital, he received an invitation from Dr Lindsay to join his practice at Bath. Dr Kersley had already become particularly interested in rheumatology and Lindsay's offer presented a chance not only to work in his native town but also become honorary physician to the foremost rheumatology centre in the country, a post to which he was elected in 1935 and held with love and devotion for a further 38 years.

After the war, the damaged Sedan Chair building was refurbished and named the Sidney Robinson Laboratory after its main benefactor. Dr Kersley was particularly keen to revitalise rheumatological research at the hospital and, in 1947, he facilitated the creation of a research fellowship under the auspices of Bristol University and funded by the remainder of the Robinson money. The first fellow was a Mauritian doctor called Max Desmarais whom Dr Kersley discovered in a middle-eastern convalescent depot during the war and who arrived at the hospital in 1945 to become its first medical registrar. In 1948, fifty of the hospital beds were appropriated for clinical research to form a new Rheumatism Research Unit.

Useful research papers began to flow from the unit and over the years, there has been a prodigious output of publications from the various doctors, including many from abroad, who have worked there. Working conditions were still very primitive in the first few years and Dr Kersley recalls how he sometimes had to carry on his medical research at home in his own kitchen. During the early post-war years, the hospital lead the field in rheumatological research. Pioneer work on the microscopic appearance of tissues affected by rheumatoid disease was carried out by the hospital's pathologist, Hubert Gibson. Research in those days was not for the faint hearted. George Kersley had to inject some of his own muscles with irritants and then cut bits of them out so that Dr Gibson could examine them beneath his microscope to compare the appearance of diseased and healthy tissue.

Since that time, the laboratory accommodation has steadily improved. After 1965, when the war damage was finally repaired, the extra storey added to the West Wing provided much-needed new accommodation for research. The considerable cost of equipping the new Princess Marina Research Laboratory was assisted in part by a grant from the M.R.C. but largely from the public appeal in the early sixties which raised £20,000 in two years. In subsequent years, the main financial support has come from the Arthritis and Rheumatism Council. The laboratory includes a thermography unit, directed by Francis Ring, which has gained international recognition for its work on the temperature measurement of diseased tissues. Pioneering work on arthroscopy, the technique of looking inside the knee joint, was also done in this laboratory.

In 1975, the hospital's regular pathological service was transferred to a central laboratory at Combe Park which served all the hospitals in the Bath district. The former laboratory at the Mineral Water Hospital was given over to immunological research. With the opening of the Bath Arthritis Research Centre opposite the hospital in 1981, more laboratory space became available and most of the microscopic work is now performed in this building. The investigations carried out into the pathology of bone and joint disease, together with clinical enquiries, immunological, genetic and epidemiological studies, and research into the technology of relieving physical handicap, make the hospital a leading centre for research into the nature and relief of crippling disease.[28]

Dr George Kersley, physician to the hospital for 33 years and Mayor of Bath in 1979.
Photo: Edward St Maur.

A selection of publications by
doctors connected with the hospital.

113

CHAPTER SEVEN
Cured by the Bath

"The Bath Waters are so powerful in their action that a course of treatment by them must be entered upon with caution and not without a certain amount of responsibility."[1] Such was the fascination of these waters that they caused numerous men and women to contribute hundreds of pounds towards Britain's first national hospital, instituted for the reception of impoverished invalids with infirmities reputedly cured by a regular dip in the salutary springs. The waters were so much the raison d'etre of the institution that it became known as the Royal Mineral Water Hospital. Nowadays, the thermal waters no longer flow into the hospital's baths and the institution makes no mention of them in its title. The power of the Bath waters seems to have run out.

The use of water as a treatment for disease dates back to antiquity, to the days of the Assyrians, Babylonians and ancient Egyptians. It was the Romans who popularised hot mineral springs and established the first spas in many provinces of their empire. Some of these places still flourish as spas. Aix-les-Bains, Weisbaden and Baden-Baden are examples. Bath was also a Roman spa but the mineral springs are no longer used to treat disease.

MORE THAN TAP WATER

Some people lament the demise of the mineral water treatment and firmly believe it offers something special, almost magical, and thereby more efficacious than ordinary water from taps. The waters emerge from each of three springs near the centre of the city at temperatures between 42°C and 47°C. Geologically they are even more special having originated in part from rain which fell on the land around Bath many thousands of years ago. This extraordinary time lapse allows them to pick up a varied assortment of minerals, gases and radioactivity as they percolate through the rock. But what of their medicinal qualities? Do they really have curative properties?

(*opposite*) The kitchen in the King's Bath, c 1738, showing the crutches abandoned by cured cripples. From an engraving by Fayram.
Courtesy of Avon County Libraries.

The Great Roman Bath shortly after its excavation. Note the absence of the modern colonade.
Courtesy Bath Medical History Group.

115

The physicians of the seventeenth and eighteenth centuries were so convinced of the existence of an innate curative principle in the waters that they spent long hours trying to discover the nature of the elusive quintessence. "For what can be more necessary, and therefore useful than to know the principles of any waters we recommend to our patients," wrote Dr Thomas Guidott in 1676.[2] In practice, the most important principles were the heat and dryness. It might seem contradictory to describe water as 'dry', but the term is used in the sense that wine is called dry and refers to its mineral qualities. This fits in well with the traditional idea of disease etiology – the imbalance of humours. Phlegm being cold and wet required a hot drying remedy to neutralise it and the Bath waters possesed both qualities.

By the mid-eighteenth century, excess of phlegm was thought to be far too simple an explanation of disease. Humours there might be, but they were thought of as being acrid and corrosive rather than hot and moist. Logic could easily be twisted, and the waters were now considered relevant for diluting and washing out malicious humours and noxious effluvia which built up in various parts of a person's body causing disease in them. This theory introduced the possibility that ordinary water might work as well as the mineralised variety, an assertion which has continued to provoke controversy into the present day. As Smollett wrote over two centuries ago:

Without the interposition of any unintelligible influence, I can easily conceive how extraordinary cures may be performed by the mechanical effects of simple water upon the human body; and I fully believe that in the use of bathing and pumping, efficacy is often ascribed to the mineral particles which belongs to the (water) itself, exclusive of any foreign substance.[3]

Smollett's opinions were not popular with physicians at the Bath Mineral Water Hospital, all of whom were ardent advocates of the mineral water. Even in recent years some hospital physicians had lingering doubts:

The value of external application of natural (mineral) waters rather than tap water is still under debate, and little controlled scientific work has so far been carried out in this field.[4]

But the consensus opinion within hospital circles now favours Smollett. The effects of drinking tap and mineral water were compared in 1925 by Drs Peskett and Raiment who failed to show any essential difference in their action,[5] though their experiments were criticised at the time because the mineral water was given with meals and not, as had always been the custom, on an empty stomach. More recently, Drs Paul O'Hare and Audrey Heywood compared the effects of immersion in tap water and Bath mineral water. Ironically these observations were conducted twelve miles away in Bristol as no suitable baths could be made available for use in Bath. The studies revealed that although some quite profound changes in the body's physiology resulted from prolonged immersion, these changes were identical whichever sort of water was used.[6]

The counter argument in Smollett's lifetime asserted that the Bath waters only worked if taken fresh from the spring. Removing them to Bristol, or anywhere else for that matter would cause the *aerial impregnations* to be dissipated as the water cooled down. According to Dr Oliver, even corks could not confine this volatile part.[7]

The idea that the waters lost a volatile curative principle on cooling was a fundamental premise put forward by physicians from the time of the earliest

Crystalline deposit obtained from evaporation of the Bath waters. From Charleton's "Three Tracts on the Bath Waters". 1774.

publications. This runs parallel with the notion that there was some vital difference between the geothermal heat of the Bath waters and the heat of ordinary tap water raised to the same temperature by artificial means. Dr Robert Peirce (1622-1710), an author often quoted by later writers, described his observations on their slow rate of cooling. He suggested that this was due to fermentation of particles which "until they are wholly evaporated continue the water more or less warm." Cynics might say that a belief in a labile and elusive component which readily disappears on cooling was propounded of necessity by the local medical establishment as a means of getting their fee-paying patients to Bath for their treatment rather than receiving it in bottles at home.

In fact the water does lose some of its components as it surfaces. The first of these to be recognised was the dissolved gases, identified in the late eighteenth century by Dr William Falconer, honorary physician at the hospital (1784-1819). Falconer believed that the *fixed air* (carbon dioxide), which he discovered in samples he tested, gave them an antiseptic quality which might explain their efficacy. In 1800, Sir George Smith-Gibbes, another of the hospital's physicians, published his own analysis.[8] According to Gibbes, the Bath waters contained 80% azotic gas (nitrogen), 15% carbonic acid gas (carbon dioxide) and 5% oxygen. This must have been a bit disappointing to everyone because even the most credulous of persons were not likely to be convinced that components of dissolved air were the cause of the waters' wonderful effects.

RADIOACTIVE CURES

Another evanescent component came to light a century later. In April 1901, the Lancet reported that R. Strutt and Sir James Dewar had discovered "the costliest substance known" lurking in the Bath Waters. It was estimated that it had cost them a million times more to collect this latest discovery, helium, than the equivalent volume of coal gas.[9] There was even more excitement to follow. Two years later, Strutt informed the city's Baths Committee that he had discovered small quantities of radium in mineral deposits collected from the conduits feeding the baths and in 1912, Sir William Ramsay announced the presence of a radioactive gas called niton (known now as *radon*) which was released in relatively large quantities at the spring heads. Here was the evidence that everyone had suspected for so long: the etherial quintessence radiating healing properties which rapidly escaped into the air. Radiation certainly had dramatic biological effects which is more than could be said for the chemical components of the water.

General interest in the biological effects of radium followed its discovery by Pierre and Marie Curie and the foundation of the Laboratory for Radium in Paris at the turn of the present century. Reports began to appear in the medical press of successful radiation treatment for high blood pressure, diabetes, gout, and lack of sexual vitality. In the 1920's, an anonymous member of the Bath branch of the BMA wrote:

Although it is unlikely that the immersion method will ever be superseded at Bath, it will probably be supplemented in the near future by others designed to utilise the 5000 litres of highly radioactive gas which are here daily available. Sir William Ramsay considers that, when a patient is taking a bath, in addition to the niton that may be absorbed by the skin, some undoubtedly enters the lungs. He has recommended a form of electrical bath which would consideralbly augment the cutaneous absorption of niton by means of ionisation.[10]

(*above*) Sir George Smith Gibbes (1771-1851).
Courtesy of the Royal College of Physicians, London.

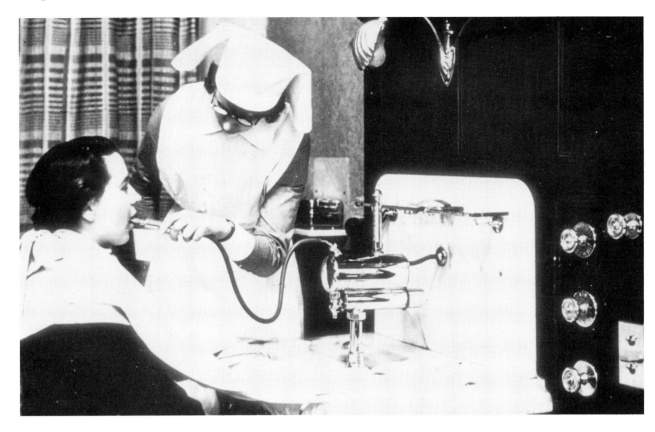

(above) The Radium Inhalatorium at the New Queen's Baths. Early 20th century.
Bath Museums Service.

(below) Bathing chair being carried by chairmen. Detail from a painting of the Circus by J.R.Cozens.
Courtesy of Avon County Libraries.

After the second world war, enthusiasm for advertising the springs' radioactivity dampened as people began to recognise that ionising radiation did more harm than good. Radioactivity became a dirty word. It was quietly dropped from the Spa Brochures whilst the city's Radium Inhalatorium was redeveloped as a tourist gift shop. (In fact the level of radioactivity in the waters is only marginally higher than that in ordinary ground water and poses no danger to bathers).

Other constituents of the waters have received attention from time to time but have later lost favour. In the 1920's, mineral waters were given a rating known as their "zymosthenic index," the value of which depended on their ability to enhance fermentation by the body's digestive juices. This effect is due to the presence of trace elements in the waters, and similar catalytic actions were thought to be facilitating cures within patients. Others thought that the mysteries of balneology could be explained by "the interrelationship between radioactive substance, ions and colloids."[11]

Ions have come back into vogue in recent years. An excess of negative ions in the atmosphere is associated with an increased sense of well-being. Ionisers in factories are supposed to increase the productivity of those who toil in them and mountain air owes its bracing qualities to the abundance of negatively charged particles at high altitudes. Conversely, stuffy rooms and thunder storms are denizens of positive ionisation, sapping vital energy and producing a generally unhealthy environment. Is the air immediately around the Bath mineral springs charged with negative ions, perhaps another reason for taking the cure at source?

TAKING THE WATERS.

During the two and a half centuries of the hospital's existence, patients have "taken the cure" in every form imaginable. They have been immersed in it, had it sprayed and douched in every possible bodily orifice, suffered it hot and cold or mixed with pine and sulphur, tasted it neat or mixed with cardomoms, sat steaming in it in a sweating box, had it mixed with mud and been subjected to electric shocks through it.

In the early days the treatments were relatively simple. Mineral water was not piped to the hospital until 1830 when two baths were constructed for men and women respectively. Before this, patients made use of the corporation baths. Men and women were never allowed to bathe together, the former visiting the baths on Tuesdays, Thursdays and Saturdays and the women on the other weekdays. Those who could walk were expected to hobble to the baths as best they could but the hospital possessed several wheelchairs and three closed bathing chairs which Smollett suggests[12] were constructed from a design by Archibald Cleland, the surgeon dismissed in 1743 for misconduct. The original chairs were made in 1749 by Mr Jelly, the hospital carpenter[13] and one of these still survives.

Bathing commenced at 10 a.m. in the Hot Bath, though hospital patients used the larger King's Bath from 1750 onwards. They were accompanied by two *bath guides* employed by the hospital whose job was to help patients in and out of the water and who, in some measure, may be regarded as embryonic physiotherapists. One of their duties was to check the temperature of the water and regulate it to between 98° and 100° F, the level recommended by the hospital medical staff.[14] Even today, the water in the hospital hydrotherapy pool is maintained in this temperature range.

The hospital provided special garments for patients to wear whilst bathing. The men wore canvas shirts and the women canvas shifts.[15] In July 1743, the Committee heard that several male patients were seen "without their linnen and swimming naked in the bath."[16] Even worse, the guides were reported to be drinking spiritous liquors with the patients while bathing.[17]

(above) 18th century bathing chair in possession of hospital. RNHRD.

(below) Bathers in the King's Bath. From an engraving by George Cruikshank in the Victoria Gallery, Bath.
Courtesy of Bath Museums Service.

The Hot Bath, c.1738.
Courtesy of Avon County Libraries

The Hot Bath as used by the hospital patients no longer exists as it was demolished before 1776 when John Wood the Younger designed the Old Royal Baths to replace it. Wood's building was closed in 1978 and still lies derelict despite several abortive plans to re-develop it. The original Hot Bath, pictured on the early maps of the city lay to the west of the later building and was sited directly over the hot spring. It was roughly rectangular in shape and had a *cross* in its centre. Central structures were a feature of all four principal baths. The one in the centre of the King's Bath was known as the *kitchen* because bathers sitting in the niches sweltered from the great heat of the water there. Thomas Baldwin redesigned this bath in the late eighteenth century and the magnificent centre structure, already in danger of collapse through subsidence, was demolished and replaced by a more modest pile. At present, there is no central structure, nor indeed any floor, in what remains of this bath. It was removed in 1979 to gain access to the Roman reservoir beneath.

Hot bathing was not recommended for everyone. One school of thought in the eighteenth century favoured invigorating dips in cold water. On the rare occasions when the hospital physicians prescribed such chilling therapy, the unfortunate patient had to go to the nearby village of Widcombe, just south of the city, where a gentleman called Thomas Greenaway had built a bath-house supplied by a cold spring of mineral water.[18] Sadly this Cold Bath house was demolished in the 1970's to make way for a new road.

PUMPING WITHIN AND WITHOUT

Besides general immersion, particular parts of the body were treated by directing jets of water at them. In Elizabethan times, this form of treatment must have been a rather hit or miss procedure because patient's simply had buckets of water thrown at them. Samuel Pepys described in his diary how he was *bucketted* and was obliged to wear a crownless large-brimmed hat to protect his head. By the middle of the seventeenth century, the corporation installed hand pumps in and on the side of the baths. Physicians had to specify the number of pump strokes their patient was to receive, sometimes as many as several thousand. The poor fellow operating the pump must often have been in need of treatment himself after such exertion.

By forcing the mineral water against the affected part, physicians imagined it would pass through the pores of the skin to act on the underlying tissues. General immersion in hot water was thought injurious if a patient's organs were too "hot." Kidneys seem to have often been a cause of concern in this repect. Our own age seems only to recognise hot headedness.

Localised douching was called *dry pumping*. The patient usually perched on a stool while the affected organ was sprayed. This method continued into modern times and, coupled with massage, was used to treat painful muscular disorders. The French preferred to massage their patients on a rubber covered slab while hot mineral water rained down from a series of showers, the so-called *Vichy massage*. By 1890, when a suite of massage baths was added to the hospital, such refinements were available for hospital patients. One invention called a needle bath consisted of a circular array of pipes perforated on their inner aspect so that the patient could be soused with fine jets of water. The lower the temperature of water, the more *tonic* the treatment. Despite these innovations, jets of water from hose pipes were still frequently used as an adjunct to bathing, though a steam engine rendered the job of the *pumper* redundant.

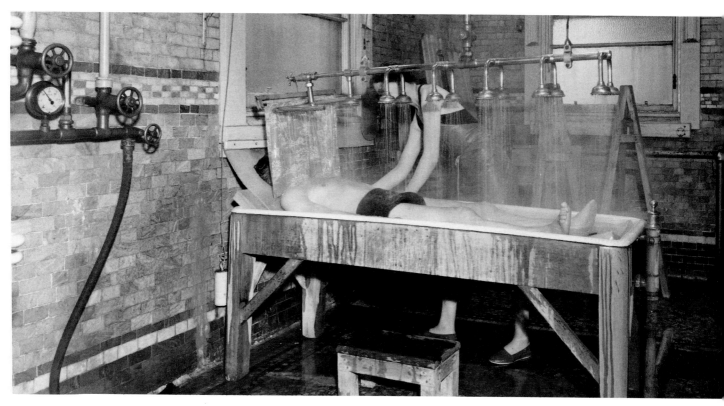

(top) Vichy massage.

(left) Needle Bath.

(below) Aix Douche.

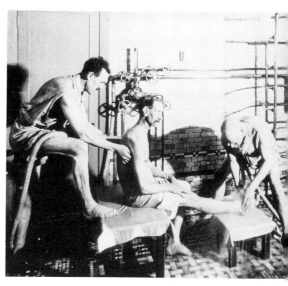

These three types of hydrotherapy
were available in Bath until 1976.

Douching was not confined to external parts of the body. Injections of mineral water into the vagina were recommended for uterine diseases as early as the seventeenth century. Dr Robert Peirce described the case of a Bristol woman who was sent to Bath in 1661 for treatment of a profuse vaginal discharge. He relates:

> I made her drink these waters and sometimes moderately to bathe; and, in the bath, to inject the water with an instrument I got purposely for her and taught her the use of and which... I have since caused to be used by many.[19]

Archibald Cleland's dismissal from the hospital in 1743 seems to have resulted from his habit of personally administering this form of therapy and it is noteworthy that relatively few cases of uterine disorder were admitted after his departure. The medical staff preferred to remain on safer ground examining paralytic limbs and leprous rashes. In the following century, internal irrigation was resumed, this time via the patients' bowels which had to endure the ebb and flow of warm mineral waters. Known discretely as the *Plombière Douche*, this method of administering the Bath waters was still available to patients as recently as the 1970's. Irrigating the bowels in this way was thought to benefit rheumatic disease by removing the source of toxic absorption causing the condition.

Mud packs, impregnated with mineral water, were also used until comparatively recent times. Mud, or rather scum and dirt obtained from the sides of the baths, was advocated as early as the seventeenth century. Guidott described a miner who, in 1640, was treated for a palsy by applications of a poultice made from scum.[20] Peirce relates its use in treating skin disease.[21] In more recent times, a sticky mix of fuller's earth and hot mineral water applied to an arthritic joint provided an effective means of pain relief. Hot packs are still used but they are no longer made from local materials.

Patient treated with a mud-pack made from fuller's earth and Bath mineral water. Mid 20th century. RNHRD.

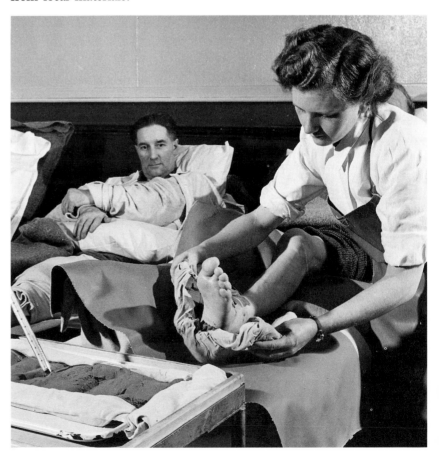

SWEATING IT OUT

Vapour baths were another early innovation. In 1562, William Turner suggested the waters be administered in this form by constructing a little house raised on a scaffold over the hottest part of the spring "in such manner that the hot vapours might strike hot upon certain places of a man's body. This manner of receiving the hot vapours is much better for some kinds of dropsies and gouts than the water itself."[22] In 1899, Dr Gilbert Bannatyne wrote "In the acute attack of gout in the extremeties, little can be done beyond treatment by the Berthollet vapour bath."[23] In three and a half centuries, little had changed. The *Berthollet* was a somewhat diminutive version of Turner's "little house"; a dust-bin shaped tank filled with steam which had projections for the hands and feet – a sort of vapourised version of the village stocks.

Other gadgets were available to promote sweating at this time. With the advent of mains electricity in the hospital at the turn of the present century, patients could be baked as well as boiled. The *Greville Electric Hot Air Bath* was a popular model. Fitted around the shoulders, patients assumed the semblance of electrically operated armadillos. It was theoretically possible to treat the whole body, though Dr Preston King recommended that it was probably better to treat only one or two joints at a time "as exposure of the entire body to heat is naturally somewhat trying." Temperatures frequently reached 300°F.[24]

The obsession with heating patients in boxes seems to have started quite early in the history of the hospital. In 1759, Jerry Peirce presented the hospital with a *sweating box*.[25] Though there is no description of the apparatus, it is described in one of the hospital's case books as a *sweating chair*. Its employment as a method of treatment was not taken on lightly. In April 1760, a certain Michael Aberdeen, whose lumbago and shoulder pains failed to improve after the usual course of bathing, "was ordered to try what effect the sweating chair might have on him" and accordingly was put into it one evening in the presence of a physician and two surgeons. He was incarcerated for one hour during which time it was reported that he "sweat pretty much, particularly in his face, in the pit of his stomach and down his back.... he bore the operation very well and was no ways fainty."[26] Despite some temporary improvement, the patient was ultimately discharged *no better.*

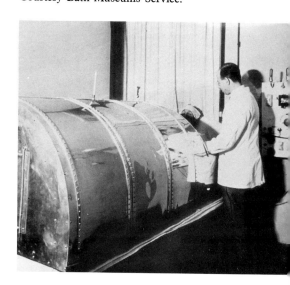

A Difcourfe of Naturall

BATHES,

And Minerall

VVATERS,

Wherein firft the originall of Fountaines
in generall, is declared:

Then the nature and differences of Minerals, with examples of particular Bathes from moft of them.

Next the generation of Minerals in the earth, from whence
both the actuall heat of Bathes, and their vertues
are proved to proceed.

Alfo by what meanes Minerall Waters are to bee examined and difcouered.

And laftly, of the nature and ufes of Bathes, but efpecially of our Bathes at BATHE in Sommerfet-fhire.

The third Edition, much enlarged.

By ED. JORDEN; Dr. in Phyfick.

LONDON,
Printed by THO. HARPER. MDCXXXIII.
And are to be fold by *Michael Sparke* in Green Arbour.

(above) Frontispiece to Edward
Jorden's treatise on the waters. 17th
century.
Courtesy of Avon County Libraries.

(below) Sir Thomas Browne.
Courtesy of National Portrait
Gallery, London.

(below right) 18th century drinkers
in the pump room. From Thomas
Rowlandson's "Comforts of Bath."
Courtesy Bath Museums Service.

A DELUGE OF WATERS

Beside the slime, the vapours and the bath, the mineral waters were also quaffed by invalids until comparatively recent times. The vogue for drinking the waters seems to have fluctuated over the centuries. In the earliest work recommending the inward use of the water entitled *The Bathes of Bathes Ayde*, (1572), its author John Jones advised taking as much as the stomach would bear at all hours of the day. In the following century, professional opinion varied from one physician to another. Dr Edward Jorden thought the springs so polluted as to render the water impotable. Sir Thomas Browne and Sir Alexander Fraser, who attended Catherine, wife of Charles II, on her visit to Bath in 1663 were both enthusiastic advocates of drinking. Between these extremes lay Dr Thomas Guidott (1638-1705), an outspoken physician who took refuge in Bath to escape the ravages of the Great Plague in London. In Guidott's opinion, the body's fibres and juices were so diluted and softened by the deluge of waters taken inwardly that any good effects produced by their external application to the affected parts were no longer in evidence. Realising the confusion caused by the divergent opinions of his learned colleagues, Guidott published a pamphlet guiding the reader on whether the waters should be drunk hot or cold, whether bathing and drinking could be done on the same day, what times of the year were the most proper to drink and whether leap years and dog-days had any malign influence.

By the time of the hospital's foundation, professional opinion had settled in favour of recommending drinking as a supplement to bathing. A pump room had been built on the north side of the King's Bath and it was possible to obtain reasonably pure water through conduits running from the spring head. Each day, the hospital's chairmen went to the pump to fetch a supply of the water which they carried back in leather bottles called *jacks*,[27] but most of the patients drank the water fresh from the pump when they visited the bath.

124

In 1830, a conduit was laid under the streets conveying mineral water from the King's spring to the hospital. The steam engine, installed by Mr Stothert, pumped the water up to a tank in the roof where, over the years, enhancements of its flavour were unwittingly produced by the addition of avian excrement and drowned rodents. Notwithstanding the pollution, many people found the taste of the waters unpalatable and the prospect of drinking between three and six pints a day (the amounts usually prescribed in the eighteenth century) was daunting. One solution was to mix it with tinctures of aromatic herbs like cinnamon and cardomoms, or boil it with asses milk and administer the whey after separating the curds, thus "reconciling the stomachs and palates of many who would not else be able to bear it."[28]

It is unlikely the earliest hospital patients were offered such mixtures as Dr Oliver was most averse to corrupting the mineral water in this way:

I cannot forbear mentioning a very offensive custom of putting milk, and a variety of medicines, into the waters at the pump, which then become mere vehicles, their specific properties being destroyed by the mixture.[29]

The prescription of mineral water in considerable quantity during the customary six months admission period would have provided patients with a significant mineral intake. Just what effect this had on them is open to conjecture, but the calcium content may have facilitated the elimination of the excessive lead levels from which many of the patients suffered in the eighteenth century.

In the nineteenth century, the amounts prescibed were less generous. Dr R.W. Falconer, physician to the hospital (1856-1881), thought their administration could be attended with side-effects of headache, thirst, dry tongue, epigastric discomfort, diminished appetite, nausea and vomiting. Like everyone else, he maintained that their benefit was maximal only when they were drunk fresh from the spring. In that way, they could "accelerate the pulse, increase temperature of the body, and excite the secretions; and these effects which are generally manifest soon after drinking them, are more permanent than might at first be anticipated."[30] It is no small wonder that the Governors insisted on keeping the men and women apart!

DIRT AND NASTINESS

Hygiene was not a prime consideration in the eighteenth century. John Wood commented that the walls of the baths were "encrusted with dirt and nastiness" and the slips at the corners where the bathers descended into the water were like "cells for the dead." Some thought the dirt and the slime were therapeutic. In the seventeenth century, it was considered a rich source of sulphur and was recommended as an efficacious application for scaly eruptions of the scalp. Sulphur was long held to be one of the prime constituents of the Bath waters, a misconception perpetuated by physicians at the hospital through most of the eighteenth century. Dr Rice Charleton was so anxious to establish sulphur as a constituent that he redefined the word to embrace oily substances in general. "If any oily substance can be found in these springs, it has all just right to be called the sulphureous principle howmuchsoever it may differ from common brimstone."[31]

The water was changed once a day to protect bathers from *Bath Mantle*, a condition characterised by a rash of pimples on those affected. This may

Silhouette drawing of
Dr R.W. Falconer.
Courtesy of Avon County Libraries.

The King's Bath drained for
cleaning. An engraving by
J. Fayram. c.1738.
Courtesy of Avon County Libraries.

have been what is now termed swimming pool rash, caused by the
bacterium *pseudomonas*. Smollett was particularly concerned about the
risk of infection.

Two days ago I went into the King's Bath by the advice of our friend Charleton in order
to clear the strainer of the skin for the benefit of free perspiration; and the first object
that saluted my eye was a child, full of scrofulous ulcers, carried in the arms of one of
the guides under the very noses of the bathers. I was so shocked at the sight that I retired
with immmediate disgust and indignation. Suppose the matter of those ulcers, floating
in the water, comes into contact with my skin when the pores are all open, I would ask
you what must be the consequence? Good heavens! the very thought makes my blood run
cold! We know not what sores may be running into the waters while we are bathing and
what sort of matter we may thus imbibe; the King's Evil, the scurvy, the cancer and the
pox; and no doubt the heat will render the virus the more volatile and penetrating. [32]

Risk of contamination seems to have also worried the surgeon, Archibald
Cleland. In 1739 he wrote to the Mayor suggesting that serious accidents
might arise when people with "foul and catching diseases" mixed with
others in the water. Cleland's opinions were largely ignored and the hospital
authorities do not seem to have been unduly worried until 1852 when a
patient complained that she, along with the majority of patients in her
ward, had suffered from the *itch*. The infestation was attributed in part
to the admission of a filthy patient onto the ward but also to "indiscriminant
use of bathing dresses and the *foul state of the baths from leprous
patients*." [33]

Spa water bathing is certainly not without hazard: as well as contagious
diseases like dysentery and poliomyelitis spreading from one person to
another, the water has frequently been contaminated by the excrement

of animals and birds. In 1956, the Medical Officer of Health for the city recommended that patients at the hospital should not be given the mineral water to drink as it had been found to be contaminated with an avian strain of bacteria, though this information was never made public for fear of adverse repercussions on spa treatment which was then still a going concern. It was not until 1978, when a young girl who had been bathing in one of the spa swimming baths died of a rare form of meningitis, that the public were informed that bathing was attended by serious risk. In the water lurked an amoeba called *Naegleria Fowleri* which had a nasty habit of penetrating the lining of the bathers' brains if they happened to sniff spa water up their noses. With such a horror story making headline news, the spa, already a faltering institution, had no chance of survival. But even though mineral water no longer flows into the hospitals's baths, hydrotherapy has retained its importance as a method of treatment.

Bathing in the Kings Bath, c.1800. Note the man on the right using a "wet" pump. Detail from a painting by John Nixon.
Courtesy Bath Museums Service.

PHYSICAL THERAPIES

Hydrotherapy reached its zenith in the early twentieth century, a time when physicians could choose from a bigger selection of gadgetry than at any other time before or since. Needle baths, douches, hydro-mechanical and hydro-pneumatic contrivances, reclining baths, upright baths, vapour baths and electric baths. As methods of administering the waters became more complex, the methods themselves began to adopt more importance than the media.

Modern investigation tends to show that the beneficial result of the external application of natural waters depends as much on the means their application affords for the conveyance of heat, pressure, percussion, and other purely physical effects, as on any specific healing properties of the waters themselves. [34]

SUBTLE MEDIA

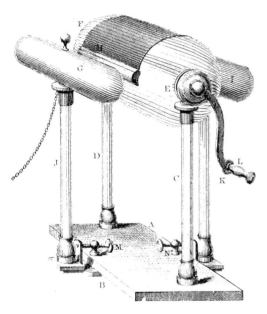

The type of machine used for electrotherapy in the 18th century.

Though hydrotherapy has been the physical treatment par excellence at the hospital, indeed the very raison d'etre of the institution, it has not been the only non-pharmacological therapy to be used there. Whilst the first patients were being admitted, a Lay Clerk of Worcester Cathedral called Richard Lovett was busy *electrifying* his fellow citizens. Lovett had no medical qualification but he realised the potential of using electricity therapeutically and his publication, *Subtil Medium*, which appeared in 1756, influenced others to adopt the novelty. Similar publications had already appeared on the continent. One Christian Kratzenstein had, in 1745, advocated electricity in the treatment of paralytics.[35] It may have been one of these publications which influenced Dr Edward Harington to try the effects on some of the paralysed patients in the Mineral Water Hospital before his death in 1757, though he apparently had little success.[36] Dr Charleton, writing in 1774, was also unconvinced of its worth[37] but in 1788 a London optical glass maker called Nairn presented the hospital with "an electrical machine and apparatus thereto belonging,"[38] though there is no information about its use. Indeed, one wonders if it was used at all because a year earlier, the hospital physicians had stated that many of their patients who received benefit from the Bath waters "have, before their admission, had various experiments of electricity made upon them to no purpose."[39]

The machines in use at this time were generators of static electricity, produced by friction between a revolving glass globe or cylinder and a small cushion of leather, a rod of amber, sulphur or sealing wax. The electric charge was collected in a Leyden jar. The *apparatus thereto belonging* was a glass-legged platform on which the patient had to stand so that his body was insulated from the ground. Treatment was effected by electrifying the patient and drawing sparks from the affected part, or administering shocks.

Static electricity continued to be used into the present century and the stream of sparks bombarding the skin provided pain-relief by so-called counter irritation. In 1905, the hospital hired a Whimshurst machine[40] and Dr Kersley recalls[41] how, in the 1930's, patients were placed near such a machine from which they were subjected to a sort of miniature thunderstorm in order to get their muscles twitching vigorously. This was thought to break down adhesions which were considered to be the cause of *fibrositis*. Fortunately for today's patients, both fibrositis and Whimshurst's machines are out of fashion.

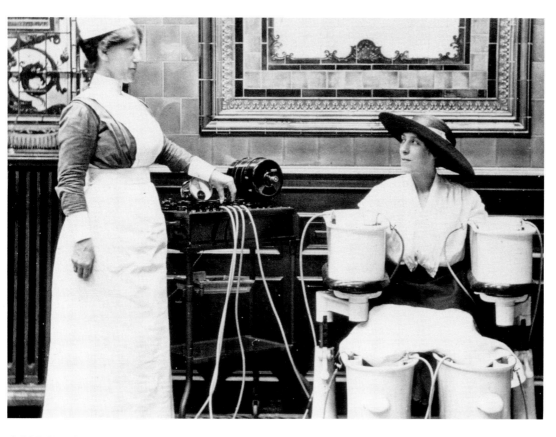

GALVANISED

Other innovations in the realm of electro-therapeutics came with the invention of the battery in 1799. The application of current from a battery was known as *galvanism*. It was first adopted by fringe practitioners who brought it into disrepute trying to resuscitate hanged criminals and drowned men.[42] The hospital purchased its first galvanic machine in 1821 for £5[43] which was replaced in 1850 by a more powerful model.[44] The vogue for the *electric bath* seems to have first become popular at this time, and a local druggist, Mr J.P. Tylee, published his *Practical Observations on Galvanism, Electricity, and Electromagnetism as employed in the cure of disease with remarks on the advantages of their application through the medium of baths.*[45]

Though the hospital possessed various electrical gadgets throughout the nineteenth century, the coming of *mains* electricity at the end of the century opened up much greater scope for electro-therapy, so much so that in 1913 the medical staff asked the Governors to officially recognise an *Electrical Department*. In some ways, this new department can claim to be the forerunner of the present day physiotherapy department. But modern physiotherapy does not just concern itself with electrical machines; today's physiotherapists can claim to have evolved as much from masseurs as they have from electrotherapists.

SCRUBBERS AND RUBBERS

In 1820, the senior physician Dr Edward Barlow, lamented how the hospital nurses were so inept at shampooing.[46] He was not concerned about the appearance of his patients hair: the term *shampooing* was then used to describe frictional massage on any part of the body and was a task which nurses were expected to perform in the early days. They used firm bristled instruments called flesh brushes, though there are no details of how often

(above) Patient calmly awaiting treatment in a four-cell Schnee bath. Courtesy Bath Museums Service.

(below) Advertisement for electrotherapy by J.P. Tylee. Courtesy of Avon County Libraries.

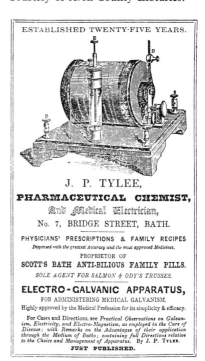

129

this happened, or who instructed the nurses in this delicate art. By 1852, it had become a sufficiently specialised occupation to warrant the hospital engaging a *rubber*, Mary Isles, who remained in office 27 years before being dismissed for "providing liquor to patients."[47]

With the completion of the massage baths in 1889, an advert was placed in the *British Medical Journal* for a masseur and masseuse.[48] Perhaps the Governors hoped to attract a higher calibre of person by using French terms, though the lady who had replaced Mary Isles was retained on the staff as the "general rubber and shampooer." Dr Murrell,[49] an eminent authority on the use of such terms, likened the difference between massage and shampooing to "playing a difficult piece of music as opposed to striking the keys of a pianoforte at random." Not all the hospital's masseurs could be classed as such virtuosos. Mr Donovan, masseur to the hospital in 1902, had to be relieved of his duties after breaking a patient's elbow and generally administering his massages in a most unsatisfactory manner.[50] But despite such catastrophies, massage became increasingly important as an adjunct to hydrotherapy. One Bath physician thought massage so important that it was "nothing short of bigotry to refuse to employ so potent an agent for the relief of human suffering."[51]

Before 1904, the masseurs only spent six hours a week visiting the hospital to treat patients, but the governors, by making another member of staff[52] redundant, were able to increase the weekly hours to 15. This was still considered insufficient and the masseuse was asked to give instruction to some of the nurses.[53] Training was probably given quite informally until 1912 when Miss Margaret Clements, a local masseuse recommended to the hospital by the *Incorporated Society of Trained Masseuses*, (the forerunner of the *Chartered Society of Physiotherapy*), was engaged to teach nurses the theory and practice of massage, together with a course of lectures on anatomy and physiology. There were two lectures a week for six months and the first pupils sat the Society's examinations in May 1913.[54] Miss Clements was paid 13 guineas a year for her services.[55]

Princess Marina, visiting Bath in 1938, meets a patient having treatment in a small whirlpool bath. RNHRD.

130

PHYSIOTHERAPY

The four years of the Great War really established physiotherapy at the hospital, though the term was not generally used until 1921.[56] With so many war casualties on the wards, the number of trained masseurs was increased to five. Preference was given to blind therapists, many of whom had lost their sight on the front line. Guided by touch, they were often particularly skilled at massage.

The war also stimulated increased expenditure on gadgets. In 1917, a Shanks whirlpool bath was added to the hospital's paraphernalia,[57] providing patients with what is now popularly called a Jacuzzi. This proved particularly effective in treating the chronically infected wounds sustained on the battlefields of Flanders. Other pieces of apparatus, which in these days are more familiar to frequenters of health clubs than to hospital departments, were purchased in rapid succession: radiant heat lamps, solaria, and *Zander machines*. The latter, named after the inventor of mechanotherapy, J.G. Zander, allowed patients to exercise weak limbs by treadling or cranking weighted levers and wheels.

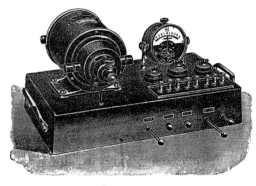

Much of the equipment from this time is now obsolete. The *Leduc's Pulsating Current Generator*, the *Plurostat* and the *Smart and Bristowe Faradic Coil* are only remembered by the more senior of the hospital's physiotherapists. When it comes to paraphernalia, physical medicine is about as fickle as a Paris fashion house. Electric baths and galvanotherapy have been quietly forgotten. Short wave diathermy was prone to cause great havoc to pictures on people's television sets unless they were worked inside a wire cage. Ultrasound and *Megapulse* are currently in vogue. As a general trend, the equipment gets smaller, though its design is no less impressive. There are far fewer sparks flying about these days and the treatments are more comfortable. Modern apparatus is less likely to strike terror into the hearts of patients than the humming, buzzing and flashing contraptions of the past, but ironically, fear may have played a part in the success of past treatments, at least in rheumatoid arthritis. Stress causes an increase in the hormone *ACTH* which in turn stimulates the adrenal glands to produce more corticosteroids. Before the 1950's, when an injectible extract of the hormone became available for therapeutic use, physicians at the hospital tried to increase the natural output of *ACTH* by giving 130 volt shocks to patient's heads after administering an anaesthetic and a muscle relaxant drug.[58]

From above: Leduc's Pulsating Current Generator, Plurostat, Smart and Bristowe Coil.

REHABILITATION

The Mineral Water Hospital's long association with physical treatments made it the obvious place in which to develop a school of physiotherapy. After the Great War, the hospital's *School of Massage and Electrotherapy*, under the guidance of Miss Clements, became well known.[59] It issued its own embroidered badge[60] and in 1921, admitted male students as well as women.[61] Miss Clements resigned as superintendent in 1926 and the school seems to have subsequently gone into decline. In 1933, John Hatton, one of the most enthusiastic Spa directors the city council has ever employed, proposed that a hydrotherapy training school should be set up as a joint venture between the council's spa department and the hospital[62] but plans to rebuild the hospital on a new site, and then the second world war, served to delay matters. The war, like its predecessor in 1914-18, emptied the hospital of its usual clientelle and filled the wards with servicemen requiring rehabilitation from their injuries.

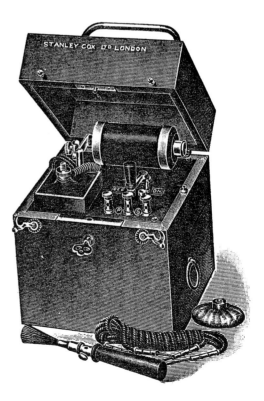

(above) The original hydrotherapy
pool at the Mineral Water Hospital.

(right) Hydrotherapy in 1988.

Such was their need that, in 1943, a *Rehabilitation Department* was created under the management of Dr Aldred Brown offering hydrotherapy, massage, electrotherapy, physical training and curative workshops.[63] The hospital's first occupational therapist, Miss Hick, was appointed at this time to give instruction in the curative workshops and physical training was provided by Miss Toley. In the following year, the Rehabilitation Department was completed by the addition of a Welfare Officer, Miss Catherine Cox, who provided a service akin to the present-day medical social workers. The hospital still plays a major role in rehabilitation and in 1977, Dr Tony Clarke was appointed as a consultant physician to develop the various services available to help the physically handicapped.

SCHOOL OF PHYSIOTHERAPY

During the last war, rehabilitation focussed the need for a first class approach to physiotherapy and thoughts naturally turned once more to its tuition. It happened that the assistant matron of another Bath hospital, St. Martin's, had before the war been the superintendent of the Cardiff School of Physiotherapy and Hydrotherapy. Miss Rudland Hills gave up her post at St Martin's hospital in 1941, and after working for a short time in Bristol with the orthopaedic division of the Emergency Medical Service, was posted to Canada to give instruction in physiotherapy and plaster work. On her return to Bath, she was the obvious choice for the proposed hydrotherapy school and was invited to become its principal. On her arrival at the hospital, she was somewhat perturbed to find that the treatment baths were also being used for ablution purposes and the governors had to hurriedly purchase some second hand bath-tubs to remedy this undesirable feature lest the hydrotherapy school failed to get its accredition.[64]

Dr G.R.P. Aldred-Brown, physician to the hospital 1930-45.

The first six-month course was advertised to commence in October 1946, but the school did not officially open until the following January.[65] The courses were only available for qualified physiotherapists and the hospital and, in particular, Dr George Kersley were keen to develop a full physiotherapy school which would involve all the major hospitals in Bath. With half the Mineral Water Hospital still in ruins from war damage, there was no room to accommodate pupils and so Weston Manor, recently vacated by the Americans who had built a war hospital around it, was chosen as the site of the new Bath School of Physiotherapy which opened in 1947, also under the superintendence of Miss Rudland Hills.

The school is still flourishing in Weston Manor, though its annual intake of 25 pupils are now accommodated in lodgings or flats around the city. Tuition in hydrotherapy is centred primarily on the Mineral Water Hospital and still remains a post-registration course, despite hopes of including it in the basic curriculum. The hospital was re-accredited as a national centre for hydrotherapy tuition in 1987.

(*above*) New Queens Bath. Early
19th century.

(*below*) Detail from an engraving of
the King's Bath. 17th century.

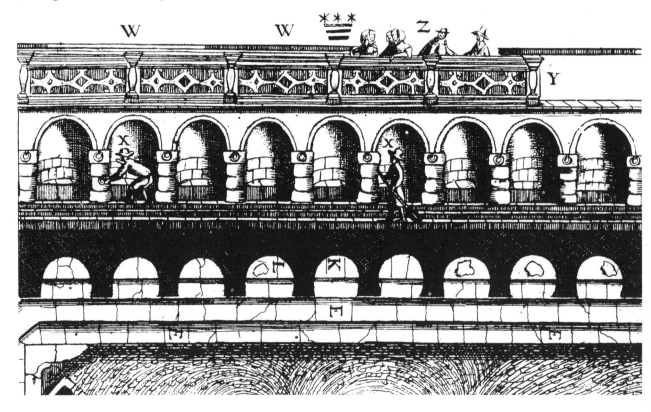

Watercolour of the King's Bath by
John Nixon. Victoria Gallery, Bath.
Courtesy of Bath Museums Service.

Visitors in the Pump Room, from
Thomas Rowlandson's "Comforts of
Bath".
Courtesy of Bath Museums Service.

135

CHAPTER EIGHT

Pennyroyal to Penicillamine
– changes in pharmaceutical practice

Opodeldoc is not a name familiar to modern pharmacy. It was one of the more exotic sounding preparations used to rub into painful joints of Georgian patients treated at the hospital. The resident apothecary had the task of making the ointment from a receipe which might nowadays be mistaken for the ingredients of a curry sauce. A Pharmacopoeia of 1722 recommends using a mixture of angelica, origanum and basil, cummin seed, the berries of juniper and bay and lavender flowers together with some rather less appetising ingredients. They all had to be heated together for many hours before adding them to soap and camphor, the basis of the ointment.[1]

Amongst those cured by this wonderous preparation was a Miss Scriggins of Bristol whose hip-joint was rendered pain-free after several anointments. Unfortunately, "the pains then flew about her and attacked several other joints" but rather than stay her time in the Mineral Water Hospital, she discharged herself to Glastonbury on hearing that the waters of that town were more efficacious than those at Bath. It seems that the rumour was ill-founded because, a year later, she was back in the hospital again and Dr Oliver was recommending that she be purged and bled prior to a course of bathing.[2]

CATHARTHSIS

Purgatives were the most commonplace of all drug treatments in the eighteenth century, and the Mineral Water Hospital was no exception. Even when "the viscera were sound and performed their duty regularly,"[3] the physicians still deemed it necessary to accelerate matters by administering one of the many aperients available. The case-notes were full of references to block-busting medicaments like *Elect. Caryocostinum*, *Jalap*, *Calomel* and the *Lenitive Electuary*, a sweet medicine containing senna.

With the exception of senna, still dispensed as a laxative, it is doubtful if a single medicinal preparation stocked by the hospital's first apothecary, John Morris, could be found amongst present-day prescriptions. A few of the drugs given to patients in those early days can still be found in the hospital but they no longer appear on the dispensary shelves. Marjoram, sage, rosemary, angelica, horseradish, common amongst herbal treatments two and a half centuries ago, are now the concern of the kitchen staff. Indeed the hospital no longer has its own dispensary. Economies have dictated that there should be only one pharmacy, based at the Royal United Hospital, to provide the needs of all the hospitals in the city. Like many facets of the hospital's work, pharmacology has undergone a revolutionary change during the last quarter millenium.

Key to opposite plate

a. Sweet cicely
b. Cinchona bark
c. Pill roller.
d. Opium poppy heads
e. Mortar inscribed Bath Hospital 1742.
f. House apothecary's Vade Mecum. 1811.
g. An apothecary's bill. 18th cent.
h. Chinese Rhubarb
i. Glass Carboy,18/19th cent.
j. Elder Flowers
k. Basil
l. Senna pods
m. Colchicum corms
n. Garlic
o. Rosemary
p. Ipecacuanha
q. Modern anti-rheumatic drugs
r. Colchicum seeds

Materia medica by courtesy of Bath University. Carboy by courtesy of Hales Chemist Ltd. Apothecary's drawers from a private collection.

VIPERS

Drugs have always played an important role in the treatment of disease. For hundreds of years, medicines were derived from a large selection of plants each of which was considered to have specific properties for use in particular conditions. The rationale for their use was often totally unscientific. Lungwort, with leaves vaguely shaped like human lungs, was thought to be suitable for pulmonary ailments. Similar unwisdom led to jaundice being treated with yellow flowers like saffron and buttercups. Other plants like hyssop, which was advocated for cleansing leprosy, had a tradition going back to Biblical times. Animal material was also used for compounding drugs: *millipedes* (woodlice) and *vipers* are amongst some of the materia medica appearing in the hospital's order book for 1749, though it does not make it clear whether the vipers were dead or alive. Even at this time inorganic substances were incorporated in the pharmacopoeia. Steel filings, dissolved in sulphuric acid, were used as a strengthening medicine and may well have worked as such because iron sulphate is an excellent treatment for anaemia. Mercuric salts, often used in ointments, effectively destroyed micro-organisms. Unfortunately, they were equally efficacious in destoying humans. It is a popular fallacy to suppose that old-fashioned drugs, even those of herbal origin, had fewer side effects than modern medicines. Nothing could be further from the truth.

Dispensing today is much easier than it was in Georgian times. Then, the apothecary had to make up all his medicines from raw materials and the hospital had a laboratory where distillation and the basic chemical work was carried out. An assistant was employed at a salary of 4 guineas (£4.20) a year to help with this work. The first "Elaboratory Man", Robert Borrey, worked for nearly forty years in this capacity and despite his modest salary, he bequethed £300 to the hospital after his death in 1787.[4] In 1839, the elaboratory man was redesignated *dispenser* and from that time on, the resident apothecaries progressively reduced their involvement with drug preparation in favour of medical practice. In 1870, the redesignation of *Resident Apothecary* to *Resident Medical Officer* marks the final schism and the emergence of the pharmacist in his own right.

COBWEBS AND CROCODILES

The first dispensary was situated on the ground floor of the original building and was known as the *Shop*, even though nothing was sold there. Unfortunately we have no description of what it was like but we can only hope that it was a little better than the one described in a satirical poem entitled the *Diseases Of Bath* (1737) as —

> A nauseous littered magazine
> Of all that is unwholesome and unclean.
> From the low roof on hempen lines are hung
> Dried insects, bladders and stale simples strung.
> Here cobwebs dangle from a crocodile;
> There, spiders spin from the prescription file;
> Above, on dusty shelves in lessening rows
> Stand empty galley-pots for idle shows.
> Beneath, in ranks, gilt lettered drawers are seen
> Titled from damaged drugs contained within.
> In this glass case a skeleton is stowed
> And in that box lies a dissected toad.

Mortar inscribed Bath Hospital, 18th century. RNHRD.

The medical staff had a monthly duty to inspect the apothecary's shop and report on the quality of drugs therein. After some years, this seems to have lapsed.

No doubt some of the materia medica ordered by the early apothecaries originated locally, like the stale beer which was used to make poultices and posset drinks.[5] Most of the materials were sent down from a firm of wholesale druggists in London called Joseph Hall & Co. of Bishopsgate St. Others came from more natural sources. In 1753, the hospital paid for the carriage of several gallons of sea water at a cost of a shilling a gallon. This was the year in which a Quaker called Benjamin Beale presented to the public on Margate sands a hut on wheels which could be towed out to sea by a horse while the bather inside took the opportunity to undress "under decent cover." The medical gentlemen of the Bath Hospital must have taken note of the emergent vogue for sea-bathing. Quite what they did with so much sea water when it arrived at the hospital remains a mystery.

FOUR FULL PUKES

One of the most frequent arguments about the treatment patients have received in the hospital has been over the heavy reliance on drug therapy. In the early days, the critics were of the opinion that drugs in some way nullified the beneficial effects of the Bath waters; nowadays it is to deplore the pharmaceutical approach for having shouldered out the waters altogether. Even Dr Oliver was criticised for his great reliance on drugs. One of his patients, corresponding with a friend, said that she wished he would not try too many medicines "which is thought to be his failing."[6] Oliver was particularly keen on emetics in addition to purging and bleeding. In his book on the treatment of gout, he seems to recognise the importance of alcohol intake in the etiology of the disease he was treating. He mentions the use of *ipecacuanha* in wine as a sort of aversion therapy for patients who were fond of the bottle: "When the emetic begins to operate it is to be worked off with two parts of Camomile-flower tea to one of Old Mountain or Red Port wine. If the patient is used to drinking too much wine, I choose he should promote the vomitings with that sort that he likes best, because it gives him an aversion to it for some days afterwards, and he is more easily induced to submit to the restraint his physician ought to lay upon him in the article of drinking. Three or four full pukes are sufficient."[7] With such drastic treatment, it is not surprising that some of his patients protested, particularly the private ones to whom these remarks are most applicable.

It was not only patients who criticised the use of drugs. Dr William Baylies (1724-1787), piqued at being refused the opportunity to become an honorary physician to the hospital, published a critical account of patient management in which, besides accusing Dr Oliver of nepotism, he claimed that combinations of medicines and Bath waters were frequently used on patients, prejudicing their recovery, and endangering those of a fragile disposition.[8] The hospital physicians seem to have taken a more pragmatic approach, declaring that "the waters are by no means a panacea and often require assistance from medicine whilst they are drunk; neither will they defend those who use them externally or internally from the various disorders incident to them at their own houses."[9]

There were, however, economic considerations which could not be ignored. The drug bill in the eighteenth century threw a significant burden on the hospital's finances and "physicians and surgeons belonging to the hospital

Ipecacuanha wine.

had to be at all times attentive to the interests of the house by ordering as little medicine as possible."[10]

Some idea of the cost of individual materia medica can be obtained by inspecting the hospital's *incidentals book*. Most of the preparations listed are herbs which may have been grown locally and inexpensively. Though more than sixty preparations appear in this book, it is evident from the published hospital prescriptions[11] that a far bigger selection of materia medica was in use. Many of the drugs used in these prescriptions were compounded from plants only found in foreign countries and were presumably amongst the packs of drugs sent down from the hospital's London supplier.[12]

Page from the hospital's *'Incidentals Book'*. 18th century. showing items ordered for the apothecary's shop. RNHRD.

Incidents To the Apothecary	£.	s.	d.
July 31 To Rose Buds	0	1	8
To 5 Bus: of Rose leaves a 4 p B:	1	0	0
To Pepper-Mint	0	12	0
To Baum 9d. a 1	0	7	6
To car: of Sea Water & porteridge	0	15	3
To twine for the Shop	0	1	5
Aug:12 To 120 of Mint	0	10	0
To penny-royal	0	3	0
paid	3	10	10
Sep:26 To Vipers	0	11	6
To Mulberries	0	1	9
paid	0	13	3
29 To Stale Beer for poultice	0	1	0
Octo: 9 To 3 Leeches	0	0	9
10 To sweeping one Chimney	0	0	4
13 To Mosh	0	5	0
To Quinces	0	2	0
17 To stale beer for poultice	0	1	0
To Ditto for posset drink	0	1	4
paid	0	11	5

RHUBARB ON TRIAL

By the end of the eighteenth century, the increasing threat of war with Napoleon led to escalation in the price of imported drug materials. The hospital Committee, ever mindful of saving money, must have been gratified to learn of a study conducted by the medical staff to compare the effects of Chinese rhubarb with a locally grown variety. Rhubarb, even today, has a reputation for awakening the sluggish bowel, though those who hope for results after enjoying a rhubarb tart will be disappointed as it is not the edible garden variety which produces the salutary effect but the root of a pale broad-leaved cousin known as *rheum palmatum*. It was to this plant that Drs Falconer and Parry, aided by the Bath Agricultural Society, turned their attention in the closing years of the eighteenth century.[13] The hospital's apothecary, Mr Farnell, who is described in the Society's paper as "a very sensible, accurate and well informed person," was entrusted with the preparation of medicines made respectively from imported Chinese rhubarb and a locally grown variety. The effects of the two preparations were compared on some of the hospital patients and proved equally efficacious, thereby heralding two concepts which remain of paramount importance in hospital practice today; the comparative clinical drug trial and the policy of economic prescribing.

The results of the rhubarb trial published by the Bath and West Agricultural Society.

CONQUEST OF THE GOUT

Despite two and a half centuries of research, specific drugs to cure rheumatic diseases have been slow to emerge. Each year some progress is made towards this goal and there are now several drugs which effectively control the progress of disease and prevent the irreversible damage which has been the fate of so many patients in the past.

The treatment of gout has been attended by the most successful progress in the field of drug research, much of which was carried out in the hospital. As a result, victims can now effectively prevent attacks by taking a drug called *allopurinol* which prevents the formation of uric acid in their bodies. Treatment of acute attacks is also much more effective; we have moved on a long way from Dr Oliver's "three to four full pukes."

DEADLY SEEDS

Portrait of Edward Barlow. From his book on the Bath waters.
Courtesy of Avon County Libraries.

The first drug which had any appreciable effect on gout, *colchicum*, was introduced into the hospital practice by Dr Edward Barlow (1785-1848) in the 1820's. The drug is derived from the wild flower, meadow saffron, a plant used in medicine in ancient times by Arabian physicians as a remedy for gout and rheumatism. Because of its reputation as a deadly poison (the seeds were powdered down and added to the victim's alcoholic drink), it was not favoured by English physicians who omitted it from the London Pharmacopoeia until 1788, though king James I is said to have been prescribed the herb by his physician who mixed small portions of the root with the powder of unburied skulls.[14] In tiny doses, the herb causes diarrhoea and mild sedation but anything more has the effect of gradually paralysing the central nervous system so that the victim slowly asphyxiates or has a heart attack because the root also contains a cardiac poison, veratrine. In the second half of the eighteenth century, it became increasingly popular as a remedy for gout after a Swabian physician, Dr Anton Stoerk (1731-1803) described a safer way of extracting the drug from the plant.

Barlow treated his gouty patients in the hospital with an alcoholic solution of colchicum seeds. He described the action:

Colchicum purges, abates pain, and lowers the pulse. Its sedative powers, though sensibly connected with its evacuant action, are not however wholly dependant on them. The motions are copious, frequent and watery. I have known even twenty motions occasioned by a dose of colchicum – the patient not complaining of the least debility. These circumstances will guide our employment as a remedy for gout[15]

By means of the treatment now prescribed, a paroxysm of gout is capable of being effectually relieved, the constitution re-established, the powers of the affected limb preserved and the gouty disposition diminished.

Certainly the drug produced great benefit to 47-year-old John Kenny, admitted to the hospital in April 1821. The patient had suffered from intermittent attacks of gout for fifteen years and at the time of his admission, "his locomotive powers were so much diminished that he had not been able to walk for 14 months."[16] He was treated with colchicum and bathing, and was discharged in the August "greatly improved and able to walk short distances. He was so sensible of the benefit which he had derived from colchicum under the paroxysm that he solicited copies of his prescriptions in order to resort to them under any future attack."[17]

Colchicum, and later its alkaloid, *colchicine*, continued to be used in treating the acute attacks of gout. Colchicine still has a place in its management though safer drugs are now available.

THE BARK COMES OF AGE

Because gout is caused by an excessive amount of uric acid accumulating in joints and other tissues, any treatment which prevents this build up will serve as an effective prophyllaxis against the disease. Long before uric acid was discovered, physicians talked about *gouty matter*. Dr Oliver, in his book on the subject[18] considered that unless the patient was properly prepared with emetics and purgatives, there was a danger that bathing would dissolve the gouty matter so quickly that it would saturate the blood and cause fever and further attacks of gout.

The earliest drug to produce any appreciable reduction in uric acid levels of gouty patients was first used for this purpose in 1908. Called *Cinchophen*, it was a chemical derivative of cinchoninic acid, a substance extracted from the bark of the cinchona tree. Cinchona bark, variously known as *Peruvian Bark* and *Jesuits' Powder*, was widely used in the time of Dr Oliver as a treatment for fever. Cinchona bark is a potent source of the anti-malarial drug, *quinine*. The supposedly specific action of the bark in a disorder known as the *ague* has lead to the idea that this ancient ailment was malaria. More likely, ague was a term used to describe any feverish illness of an intermitting nature, and the bark worked because it contained drugs, including quinine, which reduced the the patient's fever. Substances which act in this way are known as antipyretics. Many modern anti-rheumatic drugs have this property.

(above) Meadow saffron, the source of colchicine.
Courtesy of J. Kirkup.

(below) Quinine, an extract of cinchona bark.

Because of the increasing cost of imported drugs, physicians were keen to find home-grown alternatives to cinchona bark. Daniel Lysons, physician to the hospital between 1781 and 1800, experimented with elm bark as a treatment for skin disease.[19] In 1798, William White who was apothecary to the Bath City Infirmary and Dispensary, demonstrated how the bark of the English broad-leaved willow was just as effective in the treatment of fever as the more expensive cinchona.[20] Willow was originally advocated in the belief that diseases common in damp environments would probably be cured by plants growing in a similar situation, a piece of pseudo logic known as the doctrine of signatures. However, in the case of willow, its efficacy was later proved to be founded on more scientific principles for it contains salicylic acid, a compound from which several modern anti-rheumatic drugs have been derived including the best known drug of all, aspirin.

Despite its widespread use by the 1930's, aspirin does not seem to have been used very much by the physicians at the Mineral Water Hospital at this time. Coates and Delicati's book, *Rheumatoid Arthritis*, makes very little mention of drugs at all.[21] Even with gout, the treatment was largely dietary, with abundant swilling of Bath waters, low protein and high carbohydrate intake.[22] One of the reasons for the reluctance to use drugs at this time was their considerable toxicity. Cinchophen may have effectively cured patients with gout but it probably killed quite a number.[23]

The saga of cinchona bark and its derivatives did not finish there. People had noticed that sufferers of rheumatoid arthritis sometimes improved when they travelled abroad and took anti-malaria tablets. In 1952, Drs Mandel and Kersley tried the effect of two anti-malaria drugs, plaquenil and camoquin, on a series of patients with the disease. Although the patients

Hospital of the Nation

(*right*) Steroids, though dangerous in large doses by mouth, can be used safely and effectively by injection into arthritic joints. RNHRD.

(*below*) Willow trees. The bark is a source of salicylic acid.

(*below right*) A large assortment of anti-rheumatic drugs is now available.

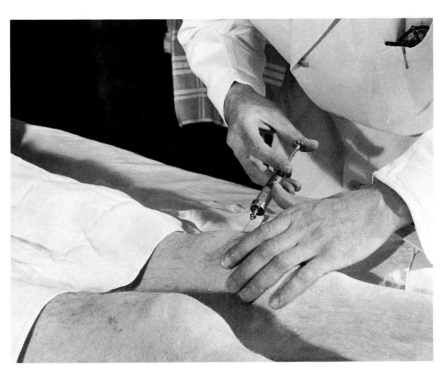

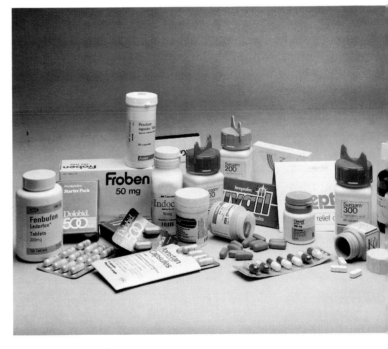

enjoyed a suppression of their disease, the high doses necessary to produce an improvement were accompanied by serious side effects.

Many other drugs have been tried out on hospital patients in the last 40 years, including early trials with steroids and gold compounds. Great care is taken to monitor the bad effects as well as the good. Though there is now a large number of anti-rheumatic drugs from which to choose, none of them are entirely free from adverse effects, particularly irritation of the stomach from the so-called non-steroidal anti-inflammatory drugs. By looking directly into the patients' stomachs with an instrument called a gastroscope, physicians at the hospital have recently become aware of the extent of this problem. Hopefully, the next generation of drugs will prove safer and more efficacious. In the meantime, drugs are just one of the many facets of treatment which the hospital is able to offer.

Portrait of John Morris, the first apothecary to the Mineral Water Hospital. RNHRD.

RESIDENT MEDICAL STAFF

Although the house apothecary was the antecedent of the resident medical officer of later years, he combined the role of doctor, pharmacist and general manager. The first apothecary, John Morris, was appointed by the Governors in 1741. He received a salary of £60 per year, together with board and lodging. This was a very generous sum for a hospital apothecary in those days. By comparison, the salary of the resident apothecary to the Bristol Infirmary was only half this amount. Morris seems to have been embarrassed by his level of remuneration and volunteered to drop his salary to £40 in 1744 when the hospital faced economic stringencies. After Morris' retirement in 1757, the Governors fixed his successor's salary at the more realistic level of £30, though it rapidly climbed again during the next half century.

PRAYERS AND PROVISIONS

As well as the usual professional duties of drug preparation and dispensing, the apothecary was expected to visit the wards twice daily and "administer aid to patients according to the direction of the physicians and surgeons."[24] He was also responsible for recording the progress of patients in the case books. These were bound in leather and were the form in which clinical records were kept until 1891 when they were replaced by the more modern practice of recording each patient's notes individually in folders kept on the wards. (Unfortunately, having survived two centuries and an enemy bomb, the medical board thought it expedient in 1943 to destroy all except one of these early case books, along with many other early clinical records).[25] The apothecary, together with the matron, also looked after the general running of the hospital and in this respect the apothecary took over the role of the *master* associated with mediaeval hospitals and hospices. The hospital rules laid down that the apothecary could never absent himself from the building while the matron was out, and vice versa, ensuring there was always someone with ultimate responsibility on the premises.

Although the ordering of provisions was initially entrusted to a *house steward*, the Governors decided to do away with this appointment in 1774 after learning a certain Noah Elliot, who was then steward, had managed to embezzle vast quantities of meat and coal during the preceeding year.[26] The steward's responsibilities were devolved between the house apothecary and matron who were given slight rises in salary to compensate for their extra work.

The apothecary also had to read prayers on the days the chaplain was absent, read the hospital rules to the patients once a week in each ward, write up the diet tables defined by the physicians and periodically attend the male patients at the baths.[27]

SECURITY

The main attraction of the job must have been the security offered. Though an apothecary could earn considerably more in private practice, there was so much competition in the city that it could take an outsider years to build up a worthwhile business. There are no records of how the early resident apothecaries were selected, though advertisements were placed in the local papers when vacancies arose. In the nineteenth century, with the advent of the Lancet in 1823, advertisements were also placed in medical journals. During the eighteenth century, the Governors appointed relatively older men and those elected appear to have regarded the post as a permanent position. William B. Farnell, elected 1784, was still staggering around the wards forty four years later at the venerable age of 79, though he had become so infirm that the Governors were obliged to employ an assistant for him.[28] This led to a difference of opinion between members of the Committee on whether to continue the ailing apothecary's pay and his board and lodging, an issue which precipitated Thomas Falconer, one of the Governors, to tender his resignation and write an anonymous letter of indignation at the way the more cheese-paring Committee members were behaving towards the long serving apothecary.[29] In the end, compassionate feelings prevailed and Farnell was allowed to end his days in the hospital where he died in 1829.

Though married quarters as such were not provided, regulations did not preclude a married man holding the post and certainly John Morris had a wife, for her portrait still hangs in the hospital. The Morris family portraits adorn most of the top landing and were the work of a cousin who was a lesser known limner in the city.[30] Apart from the portraits, little else is known about John Morris. At least two men (John Floyer Hughes in 1745 and J. Chaffy in 1746)[31] were apprenticed to him after he had taken office, though the Committee generally disapproved of resident apothecaries taking apprentices.

It is not clear how much free time the early apothecaries were allowed. In 1850, the Committee admonished the resident apothecary for being out late at night (ie. after 10 pm) and for attending public lectures and meetings in the town.[32] The next apothecary complained that he rarely finished his work before 7.30 pm and asked that he be allowed to stay out until eleven.

STEPPING STONE

The house apothecaries of the nineteenth century held their appointments in a much more transitory way than their predecessors and regarded the job as a means of gaining experience before setting up in practice on their own. A typical example is provided by Edwin Skeate who was appointed resident apothecary in 1835 at the age of 24 after qualifying with MRCS and LRCP from St. Bartholomew's Hospital, London. Skeate left after eight years residence and continued as a general practitioner in the city until his death in 1907. His successor, James Tunstall, was resident apothecary for a similar period. Unsuccessful at his application to become school doctor at Marlborough College,[33] Tunstall continued as a Bath general practitioner and in 1867 was elected honorary physician to the hospital. While he was resident apothecary, he found time to study for his Edinburgh MD degree and to write a guide-book of walks around Bath which can still be followed today,[34] though the advent of motor vehicles has rendered road rambling a hazardous pastime.

MESSIAH

Only one of the house apothecaries entirely forsook his career in medicine. Born in 1811 at 5, Widcombe Crescent, Bath, Henry James Prince was the last of a family of five children. His father died shortly after his birth and his mother, to make ends meet, took in lodgers. When Henry was fourteen, he was forced into a medical career, much against his own inclinations, and was reluctantly apprenticed to an apothecary at Wells. He finished his medical studies at Guy's Hospital and returned to Bath where he was elected resident apothecary to the hospital in 1832. Prince was frequently ill with a "stomach complaint" and ultimately resigned on account of his poor health.

Prince now changed direction and set out to become a minister of the church. After a brief residency at St David's College, Lampeter to prepare for his priestly duties, he became curate to the small parish of Charlynch in Somerset. Here he made a great impression on his parishioners by convincing them he was the Messiah. Children were struck dumb, women were entranced and men were driven to fight each other in the streets with empty cider flagons. Windows were smashed and heads were cracked. The sounds of all this fury, the clamour of embattled churchgoers under the spell of a lunatic curate, was all too much for the Bishop of the diocese who saw no alternative but to terminate Prince's curacy. A year later, the Bishop of Ely was driven to equal distraction when Prince set the East Anglian parish of Stoke ablaze in a similar state of frenzy.

Prince was now about to reach the zenith of his career, not in the Church of England where one Messiah was regarded as enough, but in the company of two other clergymen and a bevy of suggestible virgins. Prince had a way with women, particularly rich women, and he was soon in a position to purchase two hundred acres of land in the Quantock village of Spaxton where he built an establishment known as the *Agapemone*, or Abode of Love. Here, shielded from public gaze in a large house behind high walls, the one time resident apothecary of the Bath Mineral Water Hospital assumed the title of the Holy Ghost personified and outraged Victorian morality by ceremoniously deflowering one of his flock before the chapel altar.[35]

MEDICAL OFFICERS

After 1870, the house apothecary was officially known as Resident Medical Officer. The appointments were seldom held for more than two years but the job provided one of the best experiences of rheumatological and physical medicine in the country and several well-known specialists in the early part of the present century, R. Llewellyn Jones Llewellyn, Rupert

Waterhouse and James Lindsay, started out as RMOs at the hospital. The first woman resident, Dr Laura Bates, was appointed during the Second World War. Apart from two short intervals,[36] there had always been a medical practitioner living in the hospital until comparatively recently. There are now three house officers employed by the hospital. Though they can rent hospital accommodation, few avail themselves of this opportunity. Provided they live within reasonable distance of the hospital, they can be on call at night from their own homes. The hospital also employs two doctors at registrar grade, as well as providing opportunities for other doctors engaged in research, a proportion of whom come from abroad. There are many distinguished rheumatologists in practice today, both in Britain and abroad, who hold affectionate memories of Bath from their former associations with the hospital.

TEACHING AND TRAINING

In the last fifty years, the hospital has become internationally important as a training centre for doctors wishing to pursue a career in rheumatology, as well as providing opportunities for undergraduate medical students to examine patients with rheumatic diseases and receive teaching from experts. In the immediate post-war years, Bristol and Birmingham Universities both sent medical students to the hospital as part of their courses, and medical students are still welcomed at the hospital today.

The hospital's main role in medical education revolves around the training of graduate doctors wishing to further their abilities in diagnosing and treating rheumatic diseases. In 1932, the hospital was the first anywhere in the country to offer a postgraduate rheumatology course designed primarily for general practitioners. Half a century later, general practitioners can still attend courses to learn or improve their skills in practical techniques like joint injections. There are also many courses arranged for specialists and rheumatologists from all over the world who come to visit the hospital at various times.

Its huge potential as a teaching and research centre has long made the hospital an obvious place in which to incorporate a university chair of rheumatology. Dr Kersley made tremendous efforts in the 1950's to secure a grant from the Nuffield Foundation and thereby win academic recognition for the hospital but the scheme floundered because the professor of medicine at Bristol was antagonistic to specialist hospitals and was not willing to support a new chair in his university. Instead, the first chair of rheumatology in Britain was set up at Birmingham.

Ironically, no less than three professors of rheumatology in British universities have emerged from the Mineral Water Hospital, despite the absence of a local chair. But happily the situation has at last changed. In 1987, the University of Bath expressed an interest in creating a new chair of medicine, financed by a grant from Glaxo pharmaceuticals and in the following year, Dr Peter Maddison, a physician at the hospital, was elected Professor of Bone and Joint Medicine, finally securing the academic recognition the Mineral Water Hospital has so long deserved.

The London Evening-Post.

From SATURDAY July 8, to TUESDAY July 11, 1738.

Since our laſt arriv'd the Mail from France.

Peterſbourg, June 10.

Courier is juſt arrived from Veldt-Marſhal Lacy, with Letters dated the 28th of May from the River call'd Moloſhnoy Vode, giving an Account, that a Party of his Don Coſſacks and Calmucks had defeated about 1000 Crim Tartars, and taken two of their Colours, which the Courier has brought to the Czarina. The Priſoners that are taken have aſſured the Veldt-Marſhal, that the Tartar Cham, who is near the Perecop, has not with him above 10,000 Men, which he drew together with Difficulty; for the Inhabitants of the Crimea would willingly ſubmit themſelves to her Czariſh Majeſty, becauſe in Caſe the Ruſſian Troops deſtroy the Country again this Year, they muſt periſh for want of Bread, having no Corn but what is brought them from abroad.

Letter from Paris, July 7.

' The Count de Lautrec arriv'd here from Geneva ' the 4th Inſtant, and the next Day waited on the ' King at Verſailles, gave his Majeſty an Account of ' the Succeſs of his Negotiations, and met with a ' moſt gracious Reception. The Republick of Geneva being deſirous of giving publick Marks of their ' Eſteem for the Count de Lautrec, have cauſed a Medal to be ſtruck with that Nobleman's Buſto on one ' Side, and on the Reverſe three Vertues with this ' Motto, *Fortitudo, Prudentia, Equitas, conſpicua in* ' *uno.*

' ' The Count de la Mark, whom his Moſt Chriſtian ' Majeſty has appointed his Embaſſador to the Court ' of Madrid, is to receive his Inſtructions in that ' Quality in a few Days: His Excellency is principally charg'd to remove the Obſtacles which prevent his ' Catholick Majeſty's Acceſſion in form to the definitive Treaty concluded between the Emperor and the ' King. The Commander de Solar, Embaſſador from ' the King of Sardinia, has deliver'd a Memorial to ' our Miniſters containing the Motives which determined his Sardinian Majeſty to take Poſſeſſion of ' ſome Fiefs in the Milaneze.'

COUNTRY NEWS.

Bath, July 8. Laſt Thurſday being the Day appointed for laying the Foundation-Stone of the intended General Hoſpital of this City, above twenty of the Truſtees and Contributors met at the Rummer Tavern, and proceeded from thence to the Place appointed for erecting that Hoſpital, where the firſt Stone was laid, on which was the following Inſcription:

This Stone was the firſt which was laid in the Foundation of the General Hoſpital at Bath, July 6. *A.D.* 1738. *God proſper the Charitable Undertaking.*

When the Ceremony was over, the Gentlemen return'd to the Rummer, where his Majeſty's Health, that of the Prince and Princeſs of Wales, General Wade, and other abſent Benefactors, were drank, and all the Demonſtrations of Joy poſſible ſhewn on this Occaſion, every one appearing pleas'd with a Deſign ſo excellently well calculated for the Good of Mankind in general, and the Welfare and the Happineſs of the Poor, Wretched, and Miſerable in particular.

An handſome Preſent was made to the Workmen, and the Bells rung on this happy Occaſion.

A Liſt of Contributions for making Mrs. Stephens's *Medicines publick, paid into the Hands of Mr.* Drummond, *Banker, at* Charing-Croſs, *in the Month of* June.

	l.	s.	d.
COL. John Selwyn	5	05	0
Mr. John Cay	2	02	0
Dutcheſs of Portland	21	00	0
Earl of Clarendon	25	00	0
Mrs. Archer	26	05	0
Duke of Leeds	21	00	0
C. D.	10	10	0
Lord Lymington	5	05	0
Mrs. Jane Lowther	2	02	0
Lord Gallway	30	00	0
Ditto for ſeveral	19	19	0
Rev. Dr. Birch	5	05	0
Unknown	0	05	0
Meſſ. Snow and Poltock	10	10	0
Sir William Wynne	1	01	0
J. Windham Aſhe, Eſq;	1	01	0
Mrs. Aſhe	1	01	0
J. Windham, Eſq;	1	01	0
Mrs. Windham	1	01	0
Robert Andrews, Eſq;	1	01	0
Mr. Graves	1	01	0
Edward Hooper, Eſq;	2	02	0
Mr. Manning	2	02	0
Rev. Dr. Leigh	1	01	0
Rev. Mr. Scriven	0	10	6
Mr. J. Crow, Staymaker	1	07	0
James Harris, Eſq;	4	04	0
George Proctor, Eſq;	10	10	0
John Norris, Eſq;	5	05	0
Mr. Heckford	1	01	0
Major General Churchill	10	10	0
Mr. J. Trott	2	02	0
Col. Read	1	01	0
	233	10	6
Paid in before	888	05	0
Total	1121	15	6

It is thought proper to give Notice, that Mr. Drummond has purchas'd 1000 l. South-Sea Annuities with 1120 l. of this Money, and veſted it in the Names of the firſt three Truſtées.

There are ſeveral Perſons in different Parts of this Kingdom who have begun to collect ſmall Sums, in order to compleat this Contribution: And it would be a great Act of Benevolence to Mankind, if the Clergy, the Phyſicians, or any other charitable Gentlemen, would undertake ſuch Collections in 'a general Way, both in Town and Country.

LONDON.

A few Days ſince died at Oxford, of a Conſumption, Sir Robert-Banks Jenkinſon, of Walcot in the County of Oxford, Bart. He worthily repreſented the ſaid County in ſeveral Parliaments, and was a Gentleman of great Integrity and Honour: He marry'd a Daughter of the late Sir Robert Daſhwood, of Northbrook in the ſaid County, Bart. and is ſucceeded in Dignity and Eſtate by his eldeſt Son, now Sir Robert Jenkinſon, Bart. a Minor at Wincheſter School.

Yeſterday General Wade ſet out for Scotland, to take upon him the Command of the Forces in that Part of Great Britain.

The Dutcheſs Dowager of Marlborough deſigns to paſs the Seaſon at her Seat at Wimbledon in Surrey.

On Saturday Night laſt Henry St. John, Lord Viſcount Bolingbroke arrived hear from Calais.

Mr. Thomas Jones is appointed by his Majeſty, Comptroller of the Treaſurer of the Chambers-Office,

under the Right Hon. Lord Hobart, in the Room of Edward Seymour Eſq; who died laſt Week at Bath.

Mr. Charles Carne, Maſter Glazier to all his Majeſty's Palaces, is appointed Glazier to his Majeſty's Min. Royal in the Tower of London, in the Room of Mr. Young, who has left off Buſineſs.

Laſt Saturday the Lady Frances Williams, Daughter of the late Earl Coningſby, and Wife to Charles Hanbury Williams, Eſq; Knight of the Shire for the County of Monmouth, was ſafely deliver'd of a Daughter at his Houſe in Albemarle-Street.

A great quantity of Timber has been contracted for in Hampſhire, Wiltſhire, and Berkſhire, to be employed in the new Bridge at Weſtminſter.

The Haberdaſhers Company have newly rebuilt their Barge at the Expence of 700 l.

The Act of Parliament occaſion'd by the Murder of Capt. Porteous, was read laſt Sunday ſe'nnight in the four Reading Churches of Edinburgh for the 12th and laſt Time.

On Friday died at her Houſe in Wheatſheaf-Alley, Thames-Street, Mrs. Walley, of the Wounds ſhe receiv'd the 10th of June laſt from her Huſband, by ſtabbing and cutting her Throat, of which wounds ſhe linger'd till Friday laſt, in a deplorable Condition. The Coroner's Inqueſt brought in their Verdict Wilful Murder againſt her Huſband, now in Newgate for the ſaid horrid Crime.

On Saturday Morning died Mrs. Lewen, at her Father's, the China-man in Cheapſide; ſhe went to bed ſeemingly in good Health, but with a ſtrong Prepoſſeſſion that ſhe ſhould die in a few Hours, which ſhe declared to her Maid, who lay by her; about One ſhe was hear'd to groan ſeveral times, and being ſhook, by the Maid was with Difficulty brought to any Signs of Life. The Family being alarmed, a Doctor, a Surgeon, and Apothecary were ſent for, but in a ſhort time ſhe expired.

Yeſterday died at his Lodgings in Norfolk-ſtreet whither he came from Somerſetſhire laſt Week, Samuel Pitt of Cricket in that County, Eſq; a young Gentleman of about 2000 l. per Annum, and 100,000 l. perſonal Eſtate.

Laſt Night was buried, from his late Dwelling-Houſe in Queen's-Square, the Corpſe of Thomas Bowdler, Eſq; who died in the 77th Year of his Age. As he had always liv'd, ſo he continued to the very laſt, a faithful and zealous Member of the Church of England. This worthy Perſon was bleſs'd with a ſtrong and clear Judgment, accompany'd with ſingular Penetration and Vivacity, whereby he was qualify'd to read Men as well as Books, both which he had done to ſo great Advantage as to render his Converſation on all Occaſions not leſs entertaining than inſtructive to all thoſe who were ſo happy as to ſhare in it: His Heart too was ſo well practis'd in all Acts of Generoſity and Charity, that no one whatever knew better, when and how to do them in the moſt acceptable manner. In a Word, having diſcharg'd all the Offices, and Relations of ſocial Life with equal Capacity, Diligence and Integrity, it may without Flattery be ſaid of him, that he juſtly merited the Character of the beſt Subject, the tendereſt Parent and the moſt diſintereſted Friend.

Sunday Night laſt one Mr. Bridges, who lately lived at Dunſtable, going to Highgate by the Back-lane at Iſlington, between 11 and 12 o'Clock, was attack'd by two or three Footpads, who demanded his Money; and at the ſame Time one of them ſtruck him on the Head, but recovering himſelf, and having an Oak Stick, he knock'd one down, the other immediately fir'd a Piſtol and ſhot him in the Breaſt, then robb'd him of a Silver Watch and about 7 or 8 Shillings, and after giving him ſeveral Wounds on his Head, left him; he with much Difficulty return'd to a Houſe at Iſlington, where he was taken in and all proper Means uſed, but he died yeſterday about ſix in the Evening.

The London Evening Post for July 11. 1738, describing the laying of the foundation stone for the Mineral Water Hospital. RNHRD.

149

The Bath Esculapius,

Pub. by Darly 39 Strand July 4.
1777

CHAPTER NINE
Balneologists and Rheumatologists – the Evolution of the Spa Doctor

When Sir Richard Steele visited Bath in the early part of the eighteenth century, he commented: "The doctors here are very numerous but very good natured. To these charitable gentlemen, I own that I was cured of more diseases in one week than I have had in the rest of my life."[1] For the medical profession of those times, Bath was an Eldorado filled with valetudinarians and health seekers and every aspiring doctor's ambition was to gain a foothold in this lucrative medical market-place. Some became hugely successful, while others failed miserably. The surgeon-turned-novelist, Tobias Smollett, was one of the failures. Perhaps this is why he was so disparaging towards his competitors when, in 1750, he wrote "Amongst the secret agents of scandal, none were so busy as the physicians, a class of animals who live in this place like so many ravens hovering about a carcass."

COMFORTABLE CONSIDERATIONS

Throughout the Augustine era, the number of medical practitioners in the city steadily increased. Whereas in 1737, there were 19 apothecaries residing at Bath,[2] twenty years later the number had increased to "above thirty who constantly live there, many of whom make fortunes without dealing in the waters. These may be thought comfortable considerations for the sick who need not fear the want of any other physical aid in case the waters should fail at Bath or their sources be exhausted."[3]

The medical profession at this time was split into three distinct branches. The physicians, who regarded themselves as the intelligentsia of the profession, distinguished themselves by having a university degree and were allowed to call themselves *Doctor*. The other two branches, surgeons and apothecaries, learnt their craft by apprenticeship and had to use the title *Mr*. In country districts, with perhaps only one medical practitioner to serve the needs of a large rural area, the distinction between surgeon

(opposite) One of a series of caricatures by Darly lampooning Bath doctors. Late 18th century. Courtesy Bath Museums Service.

(left) A consultation of Bath physicians. Cavities in the heads of the canes held close beneath their noses contained aromatic herbs to defend against unhealthy odours. From 18th century edition of The New Bath Guide.

151

Oliver Biscuit Tin.
Courtesy of Dr M. Rowe.

and apothecary became blurred. A more rigid distinction was maintained in the case of hospital staff. At Bath, the surgeons had to confine their treatments to external therapies, like plastering, lancing and blood-letting. They also advised on the correction of deformities. The resident apothecary was allowed to carry out external treatment like bleeding and cupping, but only under the direction of the surgeons. Only the physicians were able to prescribe medicines for internal use.

SPECIALISTS

Though the medical profession is still split into three main branches – physicians, surgeons and general practitioners – there has been a considerable divergence from their eighteenth century counterparts. Nowadays, all branches come along the same basic educational pathway, culminating in a university degree in medicine and surgery. Thence the paths start to diverge and each pursues a period of postgraduate training culminating in the doctor's chosen vocation. In recent times there has been a relentless trend towards specialisation. Only general practitioners remain unsullied by specialist tendencies, though even they sometimes regard themselves as "specialists" in primary care. Gone are the days when one man could encompass the entire medical cognizance.

To some extent, the medical staff of the Bath Mineral Water Hospital have always been specialists: the very nature of the charity made them so. In the eighteenth century they regarded themselves as experts in the use of the waters. The spectrum of disease amenable to this sort of treatment was limited and so, within their hospital practice, they concerned themselves predominantly with chronic physical disability. Outside the hospital, the eighteenth century physicians practised entirely as generalists. It is only in relatively recent times that the physicians have confined their whole clinical interest to rheumatology and rehabilitation.

FIRST PHYSICIANS

Three honorary physicians were appointed to the Mineral Water Hospital when it first opened. The most famous, William Oliver, has become a household name, not because of any significant contribution to the advancement of medical science, but on the account of having invented a biscuit, much appreciated by lovers of cheese and wine. The two others, Alex Rayner and Edward Harington have all but been forgotten.

All three men were in their early forties when they were appointed, there being a mere three years difference in their ages. All had submitted theses to their universities to obtain MD degrees, Oliver to Cambridge and the others to Oxford. More important, all were established Bath practitioners and had made social connections with persons involved in raising funds during the years leading up to the hospital's foundation, though none more so than William Oliver. If any one man held the reins of management during the early years of the hospital's existence, it was this quiet spoken Cornishman whose muse might have led him to forsake his patients for poetry had he not enjoyed such success as a physician. His unfailing devotion to the hospital's affairs was remarkable. Rarely did Oliver fail to chair the weekly committee meetings during his twenty four years association with the hospital.

William Oliver was thirty three when he came to Bath in 1728 with his Cornish cousin, the Reverend Walter Borlase. Oliver was already established as a physician in Plymouth and had done great service to its citizens in

1724 by introducing the relatively new practice of smallpox inoculation there.[4] This technique, which involved pricking material from the pocks of a smallpox sufferer into the skin of a person requiring immunisation, was widely used in the eighteenth century until Edward Jenner pioneered the safer technique of cowpox inoculation, or vaccination, at the end of the century. The idea of inoculating to produce smallpox immunity seems to have originated in Turkey and was first described in this country by Emanuel Timoni who communicated his observations to the Royal Society in 1713 but nobody took much notice of him.

Eight years later Lady Mary Wortley Montague, who had also been travelling in Turkey, popularised the technique in London. By this time, the young Oliver had graduated in medicine from Cambridge and was attending a course of lectures in Leyden University given by Dr Herman Boerhaave, the greatest medical teacher of his time anywhere in Europe. Boerhaave broke with the traditional medical teaching of the sort experienced at Oxford and Cambridge. These two universities, the only centres of medical education in England at this time, taught medicine purely as a theoretical subject. During his six years at Cambridge, Oliver would have studied little other than the classical texts and attended lectures purely with theoretical concepts of disease and its treatment. It was hardly surprising that physicians had a reputation for diagnosing, prognosticating and prescribing without as much as a glance at their patients. Indeed, they often relied only on a description of the case conveyed to them second hand by the patient's surgeon or apothecary. But those physicians who were fortunate enough to have been pupils of Boerhaave were imbued with the idea of bed-side diagnosis, for the great man taught his students by demonstrating patients to them. This concept was a complete innovation in the history of medical education.

On his return from Leyden, Oliver resumed his practice in Plymouth.[5] This busy Devonshire port in the South West was a far cry from the echelons of London's Royal Society but Oliver, like so many inquisitive minds and gentlemen philosophers scattered around the provinces, maintained contact with the Society's affairs and a friendship with some of its members.

In 1723, he communicated a case description to the Royal Society of a patient from Fowey who had a malformation of his genitalia.[6] By curious coincidence, the case was described by another Plymouth physician, John Huxham, and appears in the same edition of the *Philosophical Transactions*. Even more remarkable is the fact that the two doctors' descriptions are substantially different. Subsequently, the surgeon who actually attended the patient wrote to the journal, accusing Oliver of gross carelessness and inaccuracy in his case description. Such a rejoinder must have been an embarrassment to Oliver and it is curious he did not try to vindicate himself with a published reply. Indeed the whole episode is puzzling. Huxham, despite being regarded highly as an author, had a notorious reputation in Plymouth where it was rumoured he was a liar and a cheat.[7] It is therefore not inconceivable that Huxham, wanting to get rid of his rival physician, hatched up an embarrassment which ended in the two contradictory case reports being published. Whatever the explanation, Huxham's rival soon moved off to a more successful career at Bath.

BUYING DEGREES

Establishing a practice in Georgian Bath could be a daunting business for a freshly arrived physician, and even those who managed it might later

Portrait of William Oliver by Thomas Hudson.
Private Collection.
Photo courtesy of Avon County Libraries.

fall on hard times. The Reverend Richard Warner, who delighted in satirising Bath society when he was not preaching to his congregation in the Abbey, epitomised the plight of the failed physician in his character Dr Borecat. The satyrist's character, believed to be based on a real Bath doctor called Burkitt, bemoans his predicament :

A thousand times have I cursed that foolish ambition which induced me to leave my pretty business in the country, go to the expense of £15 for an Aberdeen Diploma and settle at Bath as a physician. You will hardly believe I should be so mad as to quit a practice that cleared me about £200 per annum (all lying within the circumference of sixty miles) and come here upon speculation... When I have reflected upon this dangerous situation and compared with my present one – chance half-guinea fees and half my time no fees at all – the sneers of my more fortunate bretheren and jealousy of those who are upon the same lay as myself ; ... I have more than once resolved to put my parchment in the fire, quit my present character and abode and go back to my old sign of the pestle and mortar in the village of Rattleguts. [8]

Buying medical degrees may seem a somewhat dubious business, though Oxford and Cambridge graduates can still suffix an MA degree to their name by simply paying an appropriate fee. Towards the end of the eighteenth century, several of the newly founded Scottish universities were happy to confer MD degrees on established surgeons and apothecaries, provided they were sponsored by another medical graduate and were able to pay the fee. Though this was open to abuse, and provided graduates of the two ancient English Universities with ammunition for cynicism, it should be remembered that surgeon-apothecaries were often more experienced and able as doctors than theoretically trained physicians. One of the most celebrated doctors of the time, Edward Jenner, purchased his MD in this way.

WEALTH AND REPUTATION

The Bath Mineral Water Hospital appears to have been a bastion of Oxbridge graduates until the latter part of the eighteenth century. This led to a lot of bad feeling from the graduates of other universities who were anxious to be elected honorary physicians to the hospital, an appointment which added to their reputations and enhanced their private practice. Many of the hospital's physicians were wealthy men. Oliver owned several properties in and around Bath, including a house in Queen Square and a farm at Bathford, three miles from the centre. Rice Charleton (elected physician in 1757) and Abel Moysey (elected in 1747) both commissioned Gainsborough to paint their portraits. Moysey was Gainsborough's personal physician until he upset the artist by telling him his daughter had hereditary mental disease, a diagnosis which was subsequently proved to be correct. [9] According to the scaremongering Reverend Warner, Dr Moysey's methods of earning a living were not always beyond reproach. Warner intimated that the doctor had an arrangement with a London physician to refer wealthy old ladies to him on the pretext that they needed some Spa treatment. On one occasion, a lady arrived at Bath with a letter and Moysey was summoned to her lodging. The doctor read the letter and put it in his pocket. Having taken the patient's history and examined her pulse, he pronounced his opinion, recovered his fee and left the room. As he left, he pulled a handkerchief from his pocket and failed to notice the letter slip to the floor. The old lady, being of a curious nature, read the contents:

"Dear Doctor,

I send you herewith an old fat goose whom I have long been in the habit of plucking : one wing I reserve for myself, the other is at the service of my friends"

Portrait of Dr Abel Moysey
(1715-1786) by Thomas
Gainsborough.
Courtesy of Gainsborough House.

The following morning, the doctor revisited his patient and was about to take her pulse when she "thanked him for his kind intention to strip her of her remaining feathers but observed that though she might be an old goose, she was not so far advanced in her dotage as to suffer such harpies as Sir T... and himself to prey longer on her unfortunate carcass."[10]

Satirical jibes at the medical profession were at least veiled by the use of pseudonyms (Warner disguised Dr Moysey as Dr Fleecem). The doctors themselves were less obtuse with their sneers. In 1757, William Oliver was involved in a public slanging match with an Irish physician called Charles Lucas who had taken issue with Oliver over his analysis of the Bath waters. A heated correspondence arose between the two men and the letters, liberally sprinkled with phrases like "scurrilous mouth," "rancorous heart" and "infidel in physic" were subsequently published.[11]

ELECTION

The honorary staff of the Mineral Water Hospital were elected by a ballot amongst the Committee of Governors. For most of its history, the number was restricted to three physicians and three surgeons. In the early years, vacancies were announced on broadsides posted in the Pump Room. By the end of the eighteenth century, the posts were advertised in the local press. The successful applicant was usually a medical man already established in practice in the city. Abel Moysey moved to Bath in 1743, having previously practised in Sherborne, and was elected honorary physician after the short period of four years practice in the city. He was still a relatively young man of 31, and it was more usual to elect physicians in their forties and fifties, after they had been established in a Bath practice for at least ten years. Surgeons appear to have been selected by similar critera for age and experience.

155

Social connections were important in determining the selection of the eighteenth century medical staff. Many of the Governors who lived locally were members of the city council and might therefore be expected to show a preference for medical men with a similar involvement. In this respect it is no surprise to find a significant number of the medical staff amongst the list of mayors for the city. Henry Wright, elected surgeon in 1742, was mayor on two occasions. Each of six successive surgeons elected at the end of the Georgian era were mayors. Physicians also played the civic role, though more so in the nineteenth century. (The most recent physician to have been elected mayor was George Kersley, but very few local medical practitioners concern themselves with local politics nowadays).

Portrait of Henry Wright, surgeon to the hospital 1742-94. RNHRD.

Family connections were also helpful. Philip Ditcher (elected surgeon in 1744) was a friend of James Leake, a well known bookseller in Bath who was one of the earliest Governors. Leake introduced Ditcher to his cousin, daughter of Samuel Richardson, the celebrated novelist and publisher. Ditcher subsequently married the girl after much wrangling over the dowry.[12] Another early surgeon, Joseph Phillott, (elected in 1797) was able to mobilise the influence of his three brothers. One was a Bath banker and the other two were immediate neighbours of the hospital. To its right Henry Phillott was landlord of the Bear Inn and to its left, Rev. James Phillott was the incumbant of Rectory House (later to become the site of the hospital's west wing).

In general, the local connection is far more evident with surgeons. This is probably a reflection of the way they were trained. Several had been apprentices of their senior colleagues.[13] For instance, Thomas Palmer, the son of a Wiltshire clerk was apprenticed to Jerry Peirce, the senior surgeon. Palmer was subsequently elected surgeon in 1742. In the same way, Joseph Phillott had been apprenticed to his more senior hospital colleague, Henry Wright.[14]

NEPOTISM

Many of the medical staff at this time were from medical families, and sometimes family names reappear in the list of physicians and surgeons. Edward Harington, elected physician in 1740, was the uncle of Henry Harington who became honorary physician to the hospital in 1780. The Harington family, well-known in Georgian Bath, was descended from the celebrated Sir John Harington of Kelston who distinguished himself as the inventor of the water-closet, some three centuries before its Victorian rediscovery. Kelston Hall had to be sold in 1759 when the Harington then in residence, the brother of physician Edward, fell into debt. Dr Henry Harington (1727-1816), formerly a physician at Wells in Somerset, moved to Bath in 1757. Prolific in literary and musical creativity, Harington was a man of sharp wit and famed as a raconteur.[15]

(above) Portrait of Dr Henry Harington. Engraved from a painting by Thomas Beach. Private Collection.

(left) Memorial to Dr Henry Harington in Bath Abbey.

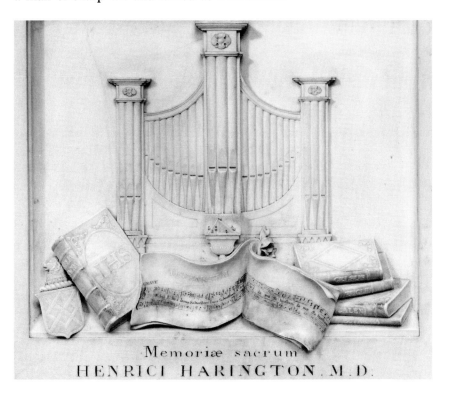

Memoriæ sacrum
HENRICI HARINGTON. M.D.

Musical score by Dr Henry
Harington.
Private Collection.

Claims that the selection of the medical staff was riven with nepotism may
have been well founded. William Baylies, an aggrieved Bath physician who
failed to get elected to an honorary post, learned that William Oliver's
son would have been elected physician in 1758 had it not been for the
objection of one of the Governors who said "Call it no longer the Bath,
but Oliver's Hospital."[16]

Similarly the names of two Falconers and two Parry's feature amongst
the list of physicians. William Falconer was born at Chester in 1744 and
commenced practice at Bath at the age of twenty-six on the advice of his
friend and fellow physician, John Fothergill. He was a man of great literary
distinction, publishing many books and papers on diverse subjects. He
was appointed physician to the Mineral Water Hospital at the age of forty
and in 1797 he attended Horatio Nelson during his stay in the city, charging
him a guinea for his services.[17] William Falconer had one son, Thomas,
who turned from medicine to the church and, though never a physician
to the hospital, was a governor for some years. Thomas's son, Randle
Wilbraham Falconer also took a medical degree and returned to practise
in Bath where he followed in his grandfather's footsteps by being elected
honorary physician to the hospital in 1856. R.W. Falconer wrote the first
history of the hospital and his image is perpetuated in a rather sombre
bust which currently surveys the out-patients waiting hall.

Caleb Hillier Parry, appointed physician to the hospital in 1799, had four
sons. The eldest, Charles, took a medical degree at Edinburgh and then
travelled to Germany with the poet Samuel Taylor Coleridge to study at
Gottingen University. He eventually returned to Bath and was elected
physician to the hospital in 1818. Charles' youngest brother, William
Edward, achieved both knighthood and fame as an arctic explorer.[18]

PERIPATETIC ACTIVITIES.

What distinguishes the early medical staff more than their medical qualifications, is the breadth of their interests and the diversity of their achievements. From Oliver onwards, the physicians display a human mosaic of tremendous educational accomplishment, in literature, in science, in commerce and in the arts. Thomas Brewster, elected physician in 1744, has an entry in the *Dictionary of National Biography*, not so much as a physician as a translator of the six *Satires of Persius*. David Hartley, who was elected in the same year as Brewster, is remembered far more as a philosopher than a physician.[19] Indeed his reputation in medicine was considerably stained by his championship of a quack remedy for treatments of urinary stones, a condition from which Hartley suffered. Brewster and Hartley were appointed as supernumerary physicians shortly after the hospital opened, together with Richard Bostock, a Recusant who had obtained his MD degree at Utrecht[20] and William Woodford, the Regius Professor of Medicine at Oxford. Woodford, one of the less distinguished professors of physic at the university, seems to have spent a considerable amount of time in Bath as his name regularly appears amongst the Committee in the Minute Book during the years leading up to his election as physician, indicating attendance at the meetings. The Governors may have elected Woodford as honorary physician through a desire to give the hospital credibility in the world of academic medicine. He was also a fellow of the Royal College of Physicians and their Censor in 1733.[21]

Portrait of Dr David Hartley, physician to the hospital 1744-48. Courtesy of the Royal College of Physicians, London.

Dr Caleb Hillier Parry, physician to the hospital 1799-1817.

An interest in the developing sciences is reflected in the considerable number of eighteenth century medical staff who were fellows of the Royal Society. William Oliver and Jerry Peirce were both FRS, as were William Falconer and Caleb Hillier Parry later in the century. At the same time, names of the hospital medical staff appear amongst the founding members of the Bath Philosophical Society, the Bath and West Agricultural Society and the Fleece Medical Society, one of the earliest provincial medical societies in the country. Caleb Parry was a member of all three societies. The Fleece Medical Society was so named because meetings were held at the Fleece Inn at Rodborough, a small village in the middle of Gloucestershire. It was at one of these gatherings in 1788 that Dr Parry told his audience that angina pectoris was caused by coronary artery disease, though it took another 125 years for the medical profession to accept his theory.[22] Caleb Hillier Parry distinguished himself both financially and professionally and is reputed to have enjoyed an annual income in excess of £7,000 at the height of his career.[23] He was the author of many perceptive publications, and was a keen naturalist, agriculturalist and balloonist as well as a musician and painter. He was the first physician to describe the association between overactivity of the thyroid gland and the staring gaze known as exophthalmos, though the paper which he read to the members of the Fleece Medical Society was not published for some time afterwards, by which time another physician called Graves had described the condition which came to bear his name.

The Fleece Medical Society had a small select membership, including the great pioneer of vaccination, Edward Jenner, who was one of Parry's closest friends. The last meeting of the society took place in 1793[24] and there were no further medical societies launched in the vicinity of Bath until the early nineteenth century. Edward Barlow (elected physician 1819) was one of the founder members of the Bath branch of the the BMA, originally known as the Provincial Medical and Surgical Society, and was eventually elected president of the Association. Local branch meetings were often held in the hospital's board room and provided the opportunity for exchange of views and discussion of difficult or interesting cases. The Bath Medical Book Society was also founded about this time by Dr Thomas Sandon Watson (elected physician 1834) and encouraged local practitioners to discuss cases and articles published in books and journals. A society still flourishing today, the Bath Clinical Society, was founded in 1908 by Rupert Waterhouse (elected physician 1912) and has provided great impetus in recent years to foster postgraduate medical education amongst local practitioners.

JOINT APPOINTMENTS

Many of the medical staff held honorary appointments at other Bath medical institutions, though not so much in the early days when the hospital was virtually the sole medical institution in the city. As the number of medical charities grew, so did the opportunity for honorary appointments. In the nineteenth century, appointment to one of the city's dispensaries or small specialist hospitals was often a stepping stone to later election to the staff of the Mineral Water Hospital. After the amalgamation of the City Infirmary and Casualty Hospital in 1826, the resulting Bath *United* Hospital became a principle rival in the attraction of honorary staff and from the end of the nineteenth century onwards, the United Hospital had usurped the Mineral Water Hospital's position at the top of the election hierarchy. Whereas Daniel Lysons (elected physician 1781) was appointed honorary physician to the City Infirmary eleven years before his election to the Mineral Water Hospital, his successors, a century later, were always elected in the reverse order. This reversal in the prestige of two institutions ultimately had unfortunate consequences for the Mineral Water Hospital which, despite its rightful claim to be a national hospital, has to fight to prevent its autonomy being buried beneath the administrative weight of the Bath Health District which is geographically and spiritually centred on the site of the United Hospital.

PAPERS AND POETRY

If all the published work written by the medical staff of the hospital since its foundation were to be bound up, there would be enough volumes to fill a sizeable library. The medical treatises and papers alone would fill many volumes, not to mention poetry by Oliver, musical scores by Harington, philosophical essays by Hartley and Falconer, observations on farming by Caleb Parry and topographical sketches by James Tunstall. Both physicians and surgeons were frequent contributors to the *Lancet* and *British Medical Journal* in the nineteenth century. William Falconer was awarded the Fothergill Gold Medal of the London Medical Society for his essay, *The Influence of Passions on Disease*, and Sir George Smith Gibbes (elected physician 1804) gave the Harveian Oration to the Royal College of Physicians in 1817. In recent times, physicians have been no less prolific in their authorship and several standard textbooks on rheumatology have emanated from the pens of the hospital's medical staff.

DILIGENCE

In January 1745, the Governors wrote to the President of the hospital, complaining that some of the surgeons were failing in their duty and desired him "to exhort such surgeons as have been remiss to attend the house more diligently."[25] The honorary physicians and surgeons were expected to attend the patients twice weekly at noon, each Monday and Saturday (changed to Monday and Friday in 1743).[26] They were conducted on a ward round by the house apothecary to see their respective patients and to recommend their discharge if appropriate. Each week, a particular physician and surgeon were nominated at the Committee meeting to be responsible for the care of all patients admitted during the next seven days. The "taking-in" physician also had to read through the current batch of letters requesting admission and advise the Committee of their suitability on medical grounds.[27]

On the first Monday of each month, all the Medical Staff who were Governors met in the apothecaries shop and examined the condition of the drugs. Once a year, they had to furnish a report to the Governors about the annual cost of drugs. This insured that the apothecary remained as cost conscious as possible.

The system of having a weekly rotation of taking-in medical staff continued until 1907, after which time the physicians were allotted approximately fifty beds each.[28] However, they were still expected to attend the hospital only two days a week though, by 1912, the Management Committee was beginning to tighten up on the medical staff's obligations. Physicians had to sign an attendance book and as their number had, by this time, increased to five, it was thought expedient to have them visiting on different days, rather than the old traditional gatherings on Mondays and Fridays.

The insidious creep of regulatory bureaucracy probably sowed the first seeds of discontent amongst the medical staff which germinated as hitherto unthinkable suggestions of remuneration. In 1917, with the hospital overflowing with soldiers, the medical staff put in their bid to claim the three pence per day capitation fee which the army was paying the hospital. Rather surprisingly, the Committee approved, though two of the physicians subsequently refused to accept payment.[29]

Further hopes of payment were launched in the 1920's when the medical staff were keen to open a wing to treat patients of "moderate means" from whom the hospital hoped to recover a fee, but the plan never materialised. But with their private "spa" practices providing a healthy income, the majority of the consultant medical staff were more than happy to gratuitously serve the patients in their hospital right up to the day, in 1948, when it ceased to be a charitable institution and was absorbed into the National Health Service.

The creation of the Health Service profoundly altered the position of the consultant medical staff. For the first time in the hospital's history, they could claim a salary for their work and were no longer entirely dependant on a flourishing private practice. The consultant physicians were now expected to devote a lot more time to the hospital, much of which was taken up doing clinic work. Indeed, there was no outpatient department in the pre-NHS days as all patients were referred for admission. There was also a much greater distinction between the role of the hospital doctor and the general practitioner, a distinction which had sometimes been blurred before the days of the NHS. With the lost opportunity for general practice and a reduced commitment to private practice, the hospital consultants identified themselves primarily as rheumatologists while the financial security offered by their NHS salaries allowed them to happily shed the "spa doctor" image. As a result, the spa, although still administered and owned by the city council, became little more than an extension of the hospital outpatient department. At first, this was seen as a great benefit. The council welcomed the financial security of a large annual grant from NHS. Confidence in the spa's future was boosted in 1966 by publication of a *Bath Development Plan* in which it was suggested that the city should retain and improve its existing function as a spa. Yet within a mere ten years, Bath ceased to be a spa at all.

On Friday, 6th December 1976, the Physical Treatment Centre in Bath Street was unusually crowded. Media persons, patients and spa preservationists hovered about the foyer like passengers awaiting the final train from a doomed station. That afternoon, the large brass cocks controlling the flow of mineral water were shut down for the last time. Their closure represented the end of an era for Bath. The Mineral Water Hospital's own supply was also compromised at this time by leaks in the Stall Street conduit and the hospital had to make use of heated tap water until 1978 when the repairs were finished. Within a matter of months, the mineral water was cut off again, this time because of the discovery of amoebic contamination. Since that time, all hydrotherapy in Bath has been carried out in heated tap water.

Inevitably, the closure precipitated a flurry of letters in the local press expressing sorrow, indignation and bewilderment. A doctor, visiting from Germany, told the city council they were misguided to throw away their greatest treasure and an 83 year old gentleman from Surrey, using the Elizabethan Charter, declared he would sue the Minister of Health and the Bath City Council, maintaining that closure of the baths would be a criminal act! Fortunately for the officers of these institutions, the Surrey gentleman was 262 years too late to file a successful litigation. But despite the exhortations of a small group of enthusiasts calling themselves the Action Committee for Bath Spa Preservation, there was a general feeling of indifference from the majority of Bath residents and the medical profession. The preservationists came mostly from the ranks of patients, not doctors. Unlike their predecessors whose prosperity was heavily dependant on the reputation of the waters, present-day local medical practitioners had little to lose by the spa's demise.

QUACKERY

There is little doubt that the decline of British spas in recent times has been largely due to a scepticism of their worth by doctors. Their image had long been tarnished by the stains of quackery and empiricism. Spas had always been a popular resort for fringe practitioners, and Bath was no exception. "Empiricks and juggling medicasters do so much abound here," wrote Dr Guidott in 1669, "that 'tis almost as hard now to meet with a regular and accomplished physician as it was in former times for Diogenes to meet an honest man." According to Dr Guidott, quacks not only boasted of curing the impossible, but charged exhorbitant fees for their first consultation. They made unnecessary repeat visits to patients as well as frequenting the baths each morning to advertise their presence. They were usually itinerant. "Tinker like, yet with more grace, they ride from town to town and from house to house to seek work."[30]

With the advent of the Bath newspapers in the eighteenth century, quacks frequently placed advertisements in the papers announcing their arrival and whereabouts. One of the most colourful characters to set up in Bath at this time was a Scot called James Graham, better known as the Emperor of Quacks. At the age of 26, he travelled abroad and practised as an itinerant ear and eye specialist. During his travels, he learnt of Benjamin Franklin's experiments with electricity. The idea of electricity excited him for he saw in it a power that might be used for his own profit when applied to the treatment of diseases in desperate patients eager for something new. He returned to England in 1774 and set up practice in Bristol where he advertised his wonderful cures. In the following year, he moved to Bath but stayed only for the summer season, reasoning that there were greater fortunes to be made in London. In 1777, he returned to Bath and it was there that his fortunes took an upward turn for one of his patients was Catherine Macaulay who afterwards married his younger brother William.[31]

While in Bath, he published a book entitled *The General State of Medical and Chirurgical Practice, Ancient and Modern, showing them to be inadequate, ineffectual, absurd and ridiculous*. In it, he advised that his remedies could only be taken with advantage under his own eye, a sure way of guaranteeing a steady income, though his personal supervision of naked mud bathing is suggestive of more voyeuristic motives. Sometimes he preferred to place his patients on magnetic chairs or into baths through which he passed electric currents, a technique which was eventually adopted by more orthodox doctors at Bath. What annoyed the established Bath practitioners most was Graham's denunciation of their treatments and implications of his superior abilities. He claimed to have cured paralytic patients who were discharged incurable from the Mineral Water Hospital.

A

NEW, PLAIN, AND RATIONAL

TREATISE

ON THE

TRUE NATURE AND USES

OF THE

BATH WATERS:

SHEWING

The Cafes and Conftitutions in which thefe Waters are really proper to be ufed, and the beft Methods of ufing them, and likewife the Cafes in which they are hurtful and very dangerous;—and demonftrating the great Errors in which Mankind have hitherto been under, in regard to bathing in, pumping with, and drinking thefe wonderful and powerful Waters;—and alfo as to their Regimen of Food, Drink, Airing, Exercifing, &c.

To which are added,

Several very remarkable CURES performed by Doctor GRAHAM, under the immediate ocular Infpection, and attefted by th Hand-writing of feveral of the principal Nobility of Europe and fome great CURES performed at Bath.

By JAMES GRAHAM, M.D.

Of EDINBURGH, but now at BATH.

BATH, PRINTED BY R. CRUTTWELL,

And fold by all the Bookfellers; and by Dr. GRAHAM's Servant, at his Apartments, No. 10, New Bridge-ftreet.

MDCCLXXXIX.

(*above*) Dr Graham's cold earth and warm mud bathing establishment. Drawing by Thomas Rowlandson. Courtesy of the Yale Centre for British Art. U.S.A.

(*below*) Frontispiece of Langworthy's book on the use of the tractors. Courtesy of Avon County Libraries.

A VIEW

OF THE

Perkinean Electricity,

OR,

AN ENQUIRY INTO THE INFLUENCE

OF

METALLIC TRACTORS,

FOUNDED ON A

NEWLY-DISCOVERED

PRINCIPLE IN NATURE,

AND EMPLOYED AS

A Remedy in many painful Inflammatory Diseases,

RHEUMATISM,	PLEURISY,
GOUT,	TUMEFACTIONS,
QUINSY,	SCALDS, BURNS,

AND

A VARIETY of other TOPICAL COMPLAINTS:

WITH A

Review of Mr. Perkins's late Pamphlet on the Subject,

TO WHICH IS ADDED,

AN APPENDIX,

CONTAINING,

A Variety of Experiments, made in LONDON, BATH, BRISTOL, &c.
with a View of ascertaining the Efficacy of this Practice.

BY CHARLES CUNNINGHAM LANGWORTHY,

SURGEON, OF BATH.

THE SECOND EDITION.

Oppose no principle, because 'tis new;
But first examine if the thing be TRUE:
Up to its source each novel science trace,
If false, reject it; but if true, *embrace*.

BATH, PRINTED FOR THE AUTHOR, BY R. CRUTTWELL;
AND SOLD BY
C. DILLY, POULTRY, AND JOHNSON, ST. PAUL'S CHURCH-YARD, LONDON;
AND BY BULGIN AND CO. BRISTOL.

1799.

PLACEBOS

Unorthodox practitioners still abound in Bath, though they are now more politely called complementary or alternative therapists. Relationships between doctors and the medical fringe is much less fraught than it used to be and rheumatologists acknowledge that many of their patients will seek the help of osteopaths, chiropractors and acupuncturists. There are almost as many alternative therapists in Bath now as there are regular doctors and they offer a wide variety of remedies, some of which are quite as bizarre as anything dreamed up two centuries ago. The outlandish nature of some therapies has made doctors reluctant to accept the value of complementary treatments unless they can stand up to comparison with placebo (i.e.dummy) therapy. One of the earliest comparative studies took place at the Mineral Water Hospital in 1799.

The experiment was conducted by Dr Haygarth and his colleague Dr Falconer to evaluate an invention by an American physician, Dr Elisha Perkins of Connecticut. Perkins had patented a device consisting of two small pointed rods made from secret alloys, one being the colour of brass and the other of silver. When applied to the skin and stroked downwards and outwards, these "metallic tractors" were supposed to bring benefit to patients suffering from gout, rheumatism, headaches, epilepsy and several other disorders. The tractors were distributed in England by Charles C. Langworthy, a Bath medical man who combined a flourishing practice in the city with the superintendancy of a mental asylum. [32]

"The tractors," wrote Haygarth, "have obtained such high reputation at Bath, even amongst persons of rank and understanding, as to require the particular attention of physicians." To this end, Haygarth made two wooden replicas the same shape as the metallic tractors and painted them in resembling colours. He collected together five patients at the Mineral Water

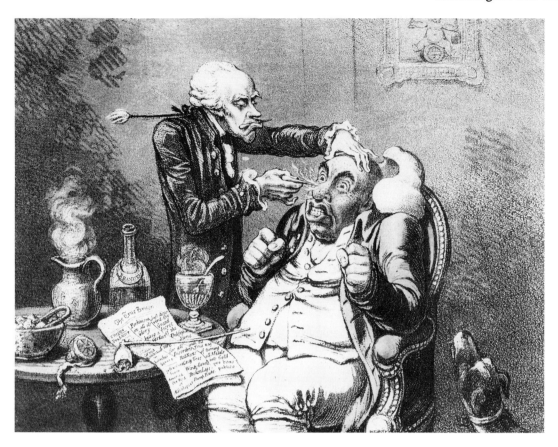

Hospital where on January 7th, 1799, the wooden tractors were employed. All five patients except one assured them their pain was relieved and three were much benefited by the first application of the remedy. One felt his knee warmer and could walk much better. Another had relief of pain for nine hours until retiring to bed. A third experienced a tingling sensation for two hours. Yet "the wooden tractors were drawn over the skin so as to touch it in the slightest manner. Such is the wonderful force of imagination." On the following day, the Perkins tractors were used with almost identical results, "distinctly proving to what a surprising degree mere fancy deceives the patient himself".[33]

Perkin's Tractors as illustrated by Gillray.
Courtesy of the Wellcome Institute for the History of Medicine.

SPOOKS

The discrediting of Perkin's tractors heralded a new critical approach to assessing the value of treatments and the part played by "mere fancy," known now as the placebo effect. It was the increasing preoccupation with this approach that ultimately led to the conclusion that any difference in the effects of spa water and tap water was also due to mere fancy. In 1933, when Dr George Kersley was working on the professorial unit at St Bartholomew's Hospital, he mentioned to the Professor of Medicine, Sir Francis Fraser, about his intention to practice at Bath. Fraser turned gravely towards him. "What's this, m'boy, do I take it that ye wish to prostitute your soul by associating along with every quack in the universe?"[34] It was a remark which rang loud in Dr Kersley's mind for the rest of his life and determined him to forge a crusade to rescue rheumatology from the clutches of the arcane arts and elevate it to a scientific discipline acceptable in the eyes of the academic medical establishment. This had two major effects for Bath and its Mineral Water Hospital. It allowed the hospital to achieve its present world-wide recognition as a centre of excellence in both the study, and teaching of rheumatology, but it also led to the demise of the spa.

Paradoxically, Dr Kersley is now one of the most vigorous campaigners to re-establish the city as a spa, lamenting that perhaps he and his colleagues in the heady days of the 1950's had "knocked the spook out of the waters" too thoroughly, forgetting the phenomenal effect of mind over matter when they insisted on complete scientific appraisal of all treatment.[35]

For a decade following the spa's closure, the preservationists have waited with bated breath whilst geological engineers have fathomed ways of obtaining uncontaminated mineral water through bore holes and would-be developers have announced their intentions of revitalising Bath's oldest asset. Various plans have been proposed for the spa buildings, but only the shopping developments seem to have born fruit. At the time of writing, the medical facilities lie in a sad state of abandonment. But whereas the city of Bath may no longer have any claim to be called the *hospital of the nation* as it did two and a half centuries ago, the Royal National Hospital for Rheumatic Diseases is still very much a national asset.

APPENDIX 1

Appendix 1a. List of physicians appointed to the hospital.

PHYSICIAN	APPOINTMENT	PHYSICIAN	APPOINTMENT
OLIVER, William	1740-1761	TUNSTALL, James	1867-1868
HARINGTON, Edward	1740-1750	HENSLEY, Henry	1868-1891
RAYNER, Alex	1740-1750	BRABAZON, A. Beaufort	1875-1896
HARTLEY, David	1744-1748	SPENDER, John Kent	1881-1894
BOSTOCK, Richard	1744-1745	CARTER, Richard	1891-1912
BREWSTER, Thomas	1744-1757	BANNATYNE, Gilbert Alex	1894-1912
WOODFORD, Prof. William	1747-1757	KING, Preston	1896-1913
MOYSEY, Abel	1747-1780	THOMSON, Fredrick George	1912-1921
SUMMERS, John	1748-1752	LLEWELLYN, R. Llewellyn Jones	1912-1921
CHARLETON, Rice	1757-1781	WATERHOUSE, Rupert	1912-1932
GUSTHART, Robert	1761-1780	LINDSAY, James	1912-1930
HARINGTON, Henry	1780-1790	KING MARTYN, Gilbert	1913-1924
LYSONS, Daniel	1781-1800	COATES, Vincent	1921-1934
STAKER, John	1781-1784	GORDON, Ronald G.	1922-1930
FALCONER, William	1784-1819	NIXON, Horace C.	1924-1927
PARRY, Caleb Hillier	1799-1817	WATSON, A. Gordon	1927-1938
HOLMAN, James	1800-1804	ALDRED-BROWN, G. R. P.	1930-1945
GIBBES, Sir George Smith	1804-1818	BENNETT, John B.	1930-1966
DAVIS, John Ford	1817-1834	McKEAG, D. Philip Wolfe	1934-1957
PARRY, Charles	1818-1822	BARNES BURT, Joseph	1938-1945
BARLOW, Edward	1819-1844	KERSLEY, George Durant	1935-1973
MUTTLEBURY, James	1822-1833	HILL, Leslie Charles	1945-1966
DANIELL, John Bampfylde	1830-1844	LOVELL HOFFMAN, Henry	1945-1950
WATSON, Thomas Sandon	1834-1867	COSH, John Arthur	1957-1979
CARDEW, John	1844-1846	DIXON, Allan St John	1966-1986
PRING, John Hurly	1844-1845	JAYSON, Malcolm	1969-1977
HODGES, Edward	1845-1857	BACON, Paul	1973-1983
TARLETON, Edwin De Laval	1846-1849	CLARKE, Anthony K.	1977
LINDOE, Robert Fredrick	1849-1857	DIEPPE, Paul A.	1978
BURNE, John	1851-1856	MADDISON, Peter	1979
FALCONER, Randle Wilbraham	1856-1881	CALIN, Andrei	1983
COATES, Charles	1857-1875		

Appendix 1b. List of surgeons appointed to the hospital.

SURGEON	APPOINTMENT	SURGEON	APPOINTMENT
PEIRCE, Jerry.	1740-1761	DITCHER, Philip	1744-1781
CLELAND, Archibald	1742-1743	PHILLOTT, Joesph	1797-1820
PALMER, Thomas	1742-1762	ATWOOD, Harry	1781-1807
WRIGHT, Henry	1742-1794	NICHOLLS, Morgan	1794-1817
DONNE, John	1742-1797	TUDOR, William	1807-1836
JONES, Giles	1744-1755	KITSON, George	1817-1842

Appendix 1b. List of surgeons appointed to the hospital (continued).

SURGEON	APPOINTMENT	SURGEON	APPOINTMENT
ELKINGTON, J.G.	1820-1821	FRASER, Forbes	1913-1924
TERRY, W.	1821-1827	FULLER, A. Leonard	1919-1930
GEORGE, Richard F.	1827-1860	MUMFORD, William George	1919-1930
LEIGHTON WOOD, George	1836-1867	TERRY, Cecil H.	1930-1945
SODEN, John	1842-1854	HAMILTON BAILEY, Henry	1930-1930
BARTRUM, John Stothert	1855-1875	MITCHELL, Douglas A.	1930-1945
STOCKWELL,		ATKINSON, E. Miles	1931-1935
Thomas Goldesborough	1860-1897	KINDERSLEY, Charles	1932-1948
SPENDER, J.K (see phys. list)	1867-1879	LEIGH, Arthur	1935-1952
CARTER, Richard (see phys. list)	1875-1891	BASTOW, John	1945-1964
GREEN, Fredrick King	1879-1906	BURTON, Arthur	1946-1975
LANE, Benjamin Hugh	1891-1895	YEOMAN, Philip	1964
HARDYMAN, George	1896-1919	KIRKUP, John R.	1969
PAGAN LOWE, Thomas	1897-1913	BLISS, Philip	1970
SCOTT, R.J.H.	1906-1918	MORRISON, Peter J. M.	1975

Appendix 1c. List of resident apothecaries and RMOs 1741-1948.

NAME	RESIDENT	NAME	RESIDENT
RESIDENT APOTHECARIES		LINDSAY, James	1906-1908
MORRIS, John	1742-1757	Elected Hon. Pathologist in 1909.	
COLE, Edward	1753-1763	Elected physician.	
SKUSE, John	1763-1784	CANE, H.J.B.	1908-1908
FARNELL, William Balne	1784-1829	MARRIOTT, Matthew	1908-1909
BUSH, George Fredrick	1829-1832	MACKAY, James F.	1910-1912
PRINCE, Henry James	1832-1835	Elected first radiologist	
SKEATE, Edwin	1835-1843	LECKIE, A.J. Bruce	1912-1913
TUNSTALL, James	1843-1850	Elected assistant pathologist.	
TERRY, Charles	1850-1859	GROVE WHITE, Mr	1914-1914
PARRY, Henry H.	1859-1863	MEERWALD, O. Spencer	1914-1918
ROBERTS, John	1863-1864	BURROW, Vincent	1918-1918
COOKE, John	1864-1867	WATSON, Capt. A.H.	1918-1919
CLOTHIER, Henry	1867-1870	BEAVER, Maj. R.A.	1919-1919
		LINDLEY, Hon. Lennox Hannay	1919-1920
RESIDENT MEDICAL OFFICERS		MARSH, James	1920-1920
COPPINGER, Albert	1870-1881	HALLOWES, Kenneth R. Collis	1920-1921
BUSBY, Alexander	1881-1884	HUTCHESON, J.I.	1921-1921
MERCES, James	1884-1885	GILCHRIST, E.G.M.	1921-1922
GRIFFITHS, Charles T.	1885-1890	MORRISON, Henry	1922-1923
KING, Preston (Dr)	1890-1893	THOMSON, W.	1923-1923
Elected physician		MORTON, Ralph.	1923-1924
WOHLMANN, Arthur Stanley	1893-1895	THOMPSON, Brian G.	1924-1925
WALSH, Leslie H.	1895-1897	BENNETT, John B.	1925-1926
BAYLISS, Richard A.	1897-1899	Elected physician	
WALKER, George C.	1899-1899	LITT, John	1926-1927
PARKER,R.D.	1899-1900	DELICATI, J. Leo	1927-1939
LLEWELLYN JONES, Richard.	1900-1900	BATES, Laura	1939-1939
Elected physician.		ROGAN, John J.	1939-1940
MALINS, J.W.	1902-1903	ROSS, Winifred	1940-1942
WATERHOUSE, Rupert	1903-1905	TASKER, Dorothy E.B.	
Elected physician.		(non-resident part-time)	1942-1948
DUNLOP, J.B.	1905-1906	BROOKS, David Hall	1947-1948

Appendix 1d. List of matrons.

NAME	RESIDENT	NAME	RESIDENT
Mrs Whitlock	1742-1760	Sarah Morgan	1826-1832
Mrs Lewis	1760-1772	Miss Higgins	1832-1836
Margaret Manns	1772-1773	Anne Stone	1836-1853
Elizabeth Whiting (Whitten)	1773-1778	Miss Brooke	1853-1884
Mrs Butler	1777-1778	Emily P. Hellings	1884-1903
Martha Down	1778-1785	Miss Griffiths	1903-1909
Ann Walker	1785-1791	Catherine Terry	1909-1933
Mrs Elizabeth Morris	1791-1806	Miss M. Bastable	1933-1949
Elizabeth Alder	1806- ?	Miss Elizabeth Abbott	1949-1960
Ann Lee	? -1826	Mrs Lucy M. MacDonald	1963-1974

Appendix 1e. List of presidents.

THE PRESIDENTS OF THE BATH HOSPITAL FROM ITS FOUNDATION

Year	President
1739 } 1740 }	Thomas Carew Esq, First President
1741	Hon. Marshall Wade, MP
1742	Ralph Allen Esq
1743	The Bishop of Bath & Wells (Dr. Ed. Willes)
1744	The Earl of Chesterfield
1745	Francis Colston Esq HRH Prince of Wales
1746	HRH Prince of Wales
1747	HRH Prince of Wales
1748	The Duke of Beaufort
1749	The Duke of Bedford
1750	The Lord Vis Palmerston
1751	The Lord Vis Dupplin
1752	The Duke of Devonshire
1753	Nathaniel Curzon Esq
1754	The Marquis of Rockingham
1755	Sir John Ligonier, MP
1756	The Lord Ilchester
1757	The Duke of Kingston
1758	The Right Hon Wm Pitt, MP
1759	The Marquis of Carnarvon
1760	The Archbishop of Canterbury (Dr. Secker)
1761	The Lord Henley, Lord Keeper, afterwards Earl of Northington and Lord Chancellor
1762	The Duke of Marlborough
1763	Sir John Sebright, Bart, MP
1764	Walter Long Esq
1765	The Earl of Lincoln
1766	The Duke of Beaufort
1767	HRH Duke of York (Lord Clive)
1768	The Duke of Montagu
1769	Sir Lawrence Dundas, Bart
1770	The Earl of Kerry
1771	John Smith Esq, MP
1772	Rev. Mr Hethrington
1773	Rev. Dr Domville
1774	The Duke of Devonshire
1775	The Duke of Leeds
1776	Henry Hoare Esq
1777	The Lord Clifford
1778	The Bishop of Bath & Wells (Dr. Chas Moss)
1779	The Earl of Guildford
1780	The Earl Spencer
1781	The Earl of Ailesbury
1782	The Earl Camden, afterwards Marquis Camden
1783	The Lord Rodney
1784	Abel Moysey Esq
1785	The Hon. J Jefferys Pratt, MP
1786	The Lord Vernon
1787	The Earl of Mansfield
1788	The Earl Nugent
1789	The Lord Primate of Ireland (Dr. Richard Robinson, Lord Rokeby)
1790	The Marquis of Bath
1791	The Earl of Harewood
1792	The Earl of Chesterfield
1793	The Bishop of Durham (Dr Shute Barrington)
1794	The Lord Viscount Weymouth
1795	Sir R. P. Arden, Knt
1796	The Duke of Northumberland
1797	HRH Prince of Wales
1798	HRH Duke of York
1799	The Lord Gwydir
1800	The Marquis of Stafford
1801	William Gore Langton Esq, MP
1802	William Dickinson Esq, MP
1803	The Lord Bishop of Bath and Wells (Dr. R. Beadon)
1804	The Lord John Thynne, MP
1805	John Palmer Esq, MP
1806	The Earl Manvers
1807	The Earl of Pembroke
1808	Thos Buckler Lethbridge Esq, MP
1809	William Dickinson Esq, MP
1810	The Earl of Bridgwater
1811	The Duke of Leeds

Appendix 1e. List of presidents (continued).

1812	The Earl of Guildford	1860	Jerom Murch Esq
1813	Sir Benjamin Hobhouse, Bart	1861	The same
1814	Sir James Mansfield, Bart	1862	The same
1815	Lieut-Col. Palmer, MP	1863	The Lord Bishop of Bath and Wells
1816	The Lord Bishop of Gloucester		(the Right Hon and Right Rev
	(Hon. H. Ryder)		Lord Aukland)
1817	John Parish Esq	1864	Major Thomas R. Baker
1818	Sir T. Shelley, Bart, MP	1865	David Johnston Esq
1819	Lieut-Gen. Popham	1866	The same
1820	Charles Knatchbull Esq	1867	The Earl of Cork
1821	Sir Walter James, Bart	1868	The Rev. H. M. Scarth, Prebendary of
1822	Charles Phillott Esq		Wells
1823	The Earl of Brecknock, MP afterwards	1869	Henry Duncan Skrine Esq
	Marquis Camden	1870	The Lord Bishop of Bath and Wells
1824	The Earl of Liverpool		(the Hon. and Right Rev. Lord Arthur
1825	The Lord Bishop of Bath and Wells		C. Hervey)
	(Dr. G. H. Law)	1871	The Duke of Beaufort
1826	Edward Berkeley Portman Esq	1872	The Rev. C. Kemble (Rector of Bath and
1827	Sir William Draper Best, MP		Prebendary of Wells)
1828	John H. Smyth Pigott Esq	1873	Major Ralph S. Allen, MP
1829	The Marquis of Lansdowne	1874	The Marquis of Bath
1830	The Lord Bexley	1875	G. D. Wingfield Digby Esq
1831	E. A. Sanford Esq, MP	1876	James Watson Esq, MD
1832	John Wiltshire Esq	1877	The same
1833	George E. Allen Esq	1878	The same
1834	W. Miles Esq, MP	1879	Major Ralph S. Allen
1835	The Earl Manvers	1880	The same
1836	The Lord Carrington	1881	The same
1837	The Lord James O'Bryen⋆	1882	Major Ralph S. Allen
1838	The same	1883	The same
1839	The Lord James O'Bryen	1884	The Lord Brooke, MP
1840	Joseph Neeld Esq, MP	1885	Major Ralph S. Allen
1841	Sir Orford Gordon, Bart	1886	Major-General J. Gordon Jervois
1842	Sir William S.R. Cockburn, Bart	1887	The same
1843	The Venerable W. T. P. Brymer,	1888 }	Major-General R. Q. Mainwaring
	Archdeacon of Bath	1897 }	
1844	The Duke of Beaufort	1898	HRH The Duke of Cambridge
1845	The Lord William Powlett, MP, afterwards	1899 }	Col. Theopilus Vaughton – Dymock
	Duke of Cleveland	1900 }	
1846	The Lord Bishop of Bath and Wells	1901/6	W. Kemble Esq
	(the Hon. Richard Bagot, DD)	1907/10	Col. Montague Poyntz-Ricketts
1847	The Marquis of Thomond	1910/11	William Handyside Esq
1848	G. Wm. Blathwayt Esq	1912/14	Rev. Charles E. B. Barnwell
1849	Philip Bury Duncan Esq	1915/19	Col. Handley P. Kirkwood
1850	The Lord Viscount Midleton	1920/21	Major I. M. T. Reilly
1851	Major-General Daubeny	1922	Col. C. V. Mainwaring
1852	William Sutcliffe Esq	1923	Brig-Gen. E. H. Molesworth
	J. H. Markland Esq, DCL, FRS	1924	HRH The Prince of Wales
1853	The same		(Leonard Miller V. P. substitute)
1854	The same	1925/28	Leonard Miller
1855	Thomas H. King Esq	1929/	Godfrey Lipscomb
1856	The same	1929/35	Mr. Lipscomb
1857	William Long Esq	1936	Mr. G. C. Mackay
1858	The same	1937/48	HRH The Duchess of Kent
1859	The same		

⋆ *Marquis of Thomond, 1846*

APPENDIX 2

EARLY STAFF

OCCUPATION	DATE CREATED	INITIAL PAY	1st APPOINTEE	RESIDENT/NON-RES.
APOTHECARY	1742	£60/annum	John Morris	resident
		Redesignated RESIDENT MEDICAL OFFICER in 1870		
REGISTER (HOSPITAL SEC.) renamed REGISTRAR in 19th C.				
	1742	£30/annum	Edward Brett	resident
MATRON	1742	£20/annum	Mrs Whitlock	resident
		Salary in 1853 – £40/year		
HOUSE STEWARD	1742	£15/annum	William E. Hyatt	resident
		Duties divided between matron and apothecary after 1774		
CHAIRMEN	1742	£12/annum	Thomas Pearce	resident
			William Rowe	resident
			John Brown	resident
			John Rudman	resident
BEADLE	1742	£10/annum	William Webb	resident
		Duties taken over by chairmen in late 18th cent.		
BREWER & BAKER	1742	£10/annum	Henry Smith	resident
		Baker dismissed in 1836 and bread bought.		
COOK	1742	£8/annum	Ann Jordan	resident
NURSES	1742	£8/annum		resident
LAUNDRY MAID	1742	£7/annum	Eliza Smith	resident
		Molly Doman employed in this capacity for 51 years (1795-1846)		

Hospital of the Nation

OCCUPATION	DATE CREATED	INITIAL PAY	1st APPOINTEE	RESIDENT/NON-RES.
HOUSEMAID	1742	£6/annum	Sarah Stockwell	resident
ASSISTANT COOK	1742	£5/annum	Sarah Miller	resident
ASSISTANT LAUNDRY MAID				
	1742	£5/annum	Ann Little	resident
CLOTHWOMAN	1742	2s 6d/wk	Mary Bond	resident
LABORATORY MAN	1743	4 Guin/annum	Robert Borrey	resident

Redesignated APOTHECARY'S ASSISTANT after 1826

Redesignated DISPENSER after 1836

The dispensers salary in 1846 – £80/year

LABORATORY ASSISTANT				
	1826	£4/annum	Henry Lamb	
			(a Bluecoat School boy)	
PORTER	1742	£?/annum	James Bolton	resident
BATH GUIDES	1742	5s/week	Mary Cole	resident
			Abraham Bryant	resident
			William Ryall	resident
BARBER	1742	£10/annum	Ernest West	non-resident
CHAPLAIN	1775	£30/annum	Rev. Parry	non-resident

Chaplain's salary in 1821 – £40/year (Rev. Francis Kilvert)

Chaplain's salary in 1844 – £120/year

ENGINEER	?1830		George Wheeler	non-resident
RUBBER (ie Masseuse)	1852		Mrs Isles	non-resident
LIFT OPERATOR	1861	15s/week	John Hall	?resident
WARDER	1862	£15/year	William Skinner	resident
(To observe order in men's day room)				(Retired Serg'nt, Royal Artillary)

REFERENCES

ABBREVIATIONS USED IN REFERENCE SECTION

BMJ	British Medical Journal
CB	Case Book (in possession of RNHRD)
DNB	Dictionary of National Biography
HVB	House Visitors Book (in possession of RNHRD)
IB	Incidentals Book (in possession of RNHRD)
MB	Minute Books (in possession of RNHRD)
Phil. Trans.	Transactions of the Royal Society. (London)
RNHRD	Royal National Hospital for Rheumatic Diseases (Bath)
SCRO	Somerset County Records Office (Taunton)

References to Chapter 1.

(1) Smollett, T. *The Expedition of Humphrey Clinker.* 1771.

(2) Guardian. Wed. Sept 30.1713.

(3) Peirce, Robert. *Memoirs of the Bath.* Bath. 1713 p. 135.

(4) 14th ELIZ. cap.v. sec.xxxvi. 1572.

(5) James, P.R. *The Baths in the 16th and early 17th centuries.* Arrowsmith 1938. pp. 102-103.

(6) ibid. p. 69.

(7) From a broadside published by Paul Cresswell, based on Feckenham's rules for bathers.

(8) James, P.R. ibid. p. 104.

(9) Peirce, R. op. cit

(10) James. P.R. op. cit. p. 106.

(11) Turner, W. *A book of the natures and properties of the baths of England.* Arnold Birkmann. Colen. 1562.

(12) Ward, Edward. *A Step To Bath.* London. 1700.

(13) James, P.R. op. cit. p. 66-67.

(14) Wood, J. *Description of Bath (1765).* Kingsmead Press, Bath. Reprinted edit. 1969.

(15) So called because of the high temperature in the centre of the bath.

(16) Harrison, Wm. *Description of England,* Ed. F.J. Furnival. London. 1887. also ed. by George Edelen. Ithaca. N.Y. 1968.

(17) Fiennes, Celia. *Journeys.* ed. C. Morris. p. 19. Crescent Press. London. 1947.

(18) Oliver, W. *A Practical Dissertation on the Bath Waters.* London. 1707.

(19) George Logan. Letter to Philadelphia from Bristol. Sept. 22 1776 quoted in Wriston, B. *Rare Doings at Bath.* Art Inst. of Chicago. 1978.

(20) Davis, Graham "Entertainments in Georgian Bath" in *Bath History.* Alan Sutton. 1986.

(21) Smollett, T. *The Expedition of Humphrey Clinker.* op. cit.

(22) Wood. op. cit. p. 279.

(23) Neale, R.S. *Bath – A Social History.* p. 25. Routledge & Kegan Paul. 1981.

(24) *Hoare's Bank – A Record. 1673-1932.* C. Hoare & Co. London. 1932.

(25) Mee, A. *King's England; Northamptonshire.* p. 104. Hodder & Stoughton. London 1975.

(26) Wood. op. cit. p. 282.

(27) Wood. op. cit. p. 222.

(28) Quinton, John *A treatise on Warm Bath Water and cures lately made at Bath..* Oxford. 1733/34.

(29) Phil. Trans. xli. p. 56.

(30) see notes on William Oliver in possession of Bath Ref. Library and deeds relating to Dr Oliver in S.C.R.O, Taunton.

References to Chapter 2.

(1) Wood, J. *A Description of Bath.* op. cit.

(2) Dakers, W. Sydie. *John Wood and his times.* Bath. 1954. p. 8.

(3) Wood, J. op. cit. p. 234.

(4) ibid. p. 285. I have been unable to trace any of the designs printed.

(5) ibid. p. 445.

(6) ibid. p. 290.

(7) MB. 21.487

(8) MB. 1.71

(9) The main staircase now ascends in the West Wing and dates from 1860.

(10) named Duke, Duchess, Prince and King's Wards.

(11) named Nash ward.

(12) probably on the south side of the yard, running between east and west wings.

(13) MB. 5.217.

(14) MB. 11.216.

(15) MB. 20.284.(1854).
(16) MB. 1.294.
(17) Mainwaring, Capt. R. *Annals of Bath.* Meyler. Bath. 1838.
(18) MB. 3.121.
(19) MB. 3.293.
(20) MB. 16.511.
Nathaniel Gundry was possibly related to Sir Nat. Gundry (1701?-1754), buried at Musbury, Dorset. (DNB). Nathaniel Gundry appears in the Bath street directories for 1826 and 1829.
(21) IB.
(22) MB. 10.45.
(23) Peach, R.E.M. *Street Lore of Bath.* London. 1883. p. 67.
(24) MB. 17.177.
(25) MB. 21.191.
(26) MB. 26.271.
(27) *Bath City Improvement Act (1791).*
(28) MB. 19.283.
(29) MB. 20.254.
(30) MB. 23.170.
(31) MB. 20.284.
(32) MB. 3.291.
(33) MB. 4.36.
(34) MB. 5.260/2.
(35) MB. 6.188.
(36) MB. 11.164.
(37) *Bath Chronicle.* 2.6.1791.
(38) *Bath Herald.* 3.3.1792.
(39) *Bath Chronicle.* 3.5.1792 and 24.5.1792.
(40) *Bath Chronicle.* 24.5.1792.
(41) *Council Minute Book* 10.7.1792 and *Bath Act Order Book* 14.12.1792.
(42) MB. 11.308.
(43) MB. 18.416 (1840).
(44) MB. 19.543.
(45) viz. Sydney Gardens and Hotel, Manvers Street, James Street West, Marlborough Rd, Villa Fields in Bathwick and the land in Pulteney Road on which the Convent was later built.
(46) MB. 20.144 (Copy of letter dated 25. Feb. 1852).
(47) *Museum Collections Guide.* Bath Univ. Press.
(48) MB. 20.196.
(49) MB. 20.301.
(50) ibid.
(51) Certain Governors had expressed an interest in the rectory as early as 1840, and it was almost purchased in 1850. (see Brabazon, A.B. *History of the Royal Mineral Water Hospital.* Bath. 1888. pp. 61-64).
(52) MB. 22.146/7.
(53) Brabazon. op. cit. pp. 84-86.

References to Chapter 3.
(1) Goldsmith, O. *The life of Richard Nash.* 2nd ed. Lond. 1765. p. 121.
(2) MB. 12.335.
(3) MB. 10.247.
(4) Smollett, T. *Expedition of Humphrey Clinker.* op. cit.
(5) *Gentlemen's Magazine.* May, 1745. p. 345.
(6) Penrose, Rev. *Letters from Bath.* ed. B. Mitchell. Alan Sutton. Gloc. p. 59.
(7) Letter from S. Richardson in possession of RNHRD.
(8) *Book of Transcribed Letters,* RNHRD.
(9) *A Sermon preached at the Abby (sic) Church, etc* April 25. 1749. Bath.
(10) MB. 10.72.
(11) MB. 6.191.
(12) MB. 2.246.
(13) Charles Gordon. Personal Communication.
(14) *Book of Transcribed Letters,* RNHRD.
(15) Carew was MP for Minehead.
(16) Robb-Smith, A. Unpublished paper on the life of Richard Frewin read to the Society of Apothecaries.
(17) ibid.
(18) *Bath Journal.* 13.3.1758 & 27.3.1758.
(19) *Bath Advertiser.* 29.4.1758.
(20) MB. 4.181.
(21) *A Sermon preached at the Abby (sic) Church, etc.* 1759. p. 34.
(22) *Bath Journal.* 30.4.1759.
(23) MB. 3.08.
(24) MB. 3.267.
(25) *Report of the Committee on Mr Parish's Statement.* Bath. 1822.
(26) ibid.
(27) MB. 26.73.
(28) MB. 27.525.
(29) MB. 17.144.
(30) MB. 2.7. (23 May 1744).
(31) MB. 2.145.
(32) MB. (1921) p. 555-8.
(33) MB. 31.384.
(34) MB. 23.361.
(35) MB. 36.440 (July 1948).
(36) MB. 3.63.
(37) MB. 21.320.
(38) MB. 29.912.
(39) *Bath Herald.* 9 Nov. 1904.
(40) MB. 27.437.

References to Chapter 4.
(1) Entry in Marston Parish Reg. 1754. SCRO.
(2) CB. p. 93.
(3) MB. 20.341.
(4) MB. 1.52.
(5) MB. 22.435.
(6) CB. p. 77.
(7) MB. 18.394. (Oct 1839).
(8) MB. 21.57.
(9) MB. 20.514. (8 Jan 1857).
(10) HVB. 29 Jan 1758.
(11) *Rule Book.*
(12) CB. p. 84.
(13) MB. 9.175 & 180.
(14) IB.
(15) CB. p. 92.
(16) *Narrative.* pp. 50-5 (see note 39, Chapter 7).
(17) MB. 34 76.
(18) IB. Nov 1753.
(19) IB. Dec 1757.

(20) CB. 83.
(21) IB.
(22) CB: passim.
(23) MB. 1.295.
(24) MB. 6.87.
(25) MB. 9.198.
(26) MB. 20.43.
(27) MB. 25.336.
(28) MB. (1954) 187.
(29) MB. 1.231.
(30) HVB. Mar. 1743.
(31) MB. 3.249.
(32) *Rule Book.*
(33) MB. 19.300.
(34) MB. 20.299.
(35) MB. (18.2.1795).
(36) MB. 1.238.
(37) MB. 23.368.
(38) MB. 23.224.
(39) HVB. 1742.
(40) MB. 3.200.304.
(41) MB. 10.175.
(42) MB. 19.202.
(43) MB. 12.61.63.
(44) MB. 13.57.
(45) MB. 18.198.
(46) MB. 19.171.
(47) MB. 19.396.
(48) MB. 20.386.
(49) MB. 21.55.
(50) Cleland, A. *An Appeal to the public.* Bath. 1743. passim.
(51) Cleland, A. *A full vindication of Mr Cleland's Appeal, etc* Bath & London. 1744.
(52) Cleland, A. (1743) op. cit.
(53) ibid.
(54) *A Short Vindication of the Proceedings of the Governors of the General Hospital, etc.* Bath & London. 1744. pp. 15-16.
(55) ibid. pp. 10-11.
(56) MB. 1.311.
(57) MB. 2.88.
(58) Howard, J. *An account of the principal lazarettos in Europe.* Warrington. 1789. p. 190.
(59) The hospital chairmen and porters acted as beadles.
(60) *Letters from Bath. (1766-67)* by Rev. J. Penrose. Alan Sutton. Gloucester. 1983. p. 59.
(61) HVB. 7.6.43.
(62) 9,5.53.; 23.8.86.
(63) Fighting between medical staff at the Bristol Royal Infirmary is recorded in *History of the Bristol Royal Infirmary* by Monroe Smith.
(64) MB. 19.538 (3-1-1850).
(65) MB. 19.547 (31-1-1850).
(66) MB. 21.05. (Mar 1857).
(67) MB. 21.100.
(68) Obit. Notice: Charles Empson. *Bath and Chelt. Gaz.* 1861.
(69) John Hall was appointed first lift keeper and cleaner in 1861.
(70) *Rule Book* p.4.
(71) HVB for 1743.

(72) ibid.
(73) I.B. Feb 1751.
(74) MB. 26.111.
(75) MB. 31.382.
(76) In possession of the RNHRD.
(77) HVB for 1743.
(78) ibid.
(79) MB. 7.103.
(80) MB. 7.172/3.
(81) MB. 7.48.
(82) HVB for 1754.
(83) Barlow, E. *An Essay on the Medicinal Efficacy and employment of the Bath Waters* Bath. 1822. p.130-131.
(84) MB. 17.125 (27.8.1828).
(85) MB. 17.134 (29.10.1828).
(86) MB. 23.170.
(87) MB. 17.48.
(88) MB. 17.205 and MB. 28.256.
(89) MB. 26.488.
(90) MB. 27.292.
(91) MB. 28.240.
(92) The first plaster nurse was engaged in 1932.

References to Chapter 5.

(1) Copeman, W.S.C. "The Rheumatic Diseases in the 18th century." *West Lond. Hosp. Annual Report.* 1948.

The Palsy.
(2) Huxham, J. *A Small Treatise on the Devonshire Colic which was very epidemic in the year 1724.* English ed. 1759.
(3) Charleton, R. *Three tracts on the Bath Waters.* BATH. 1774.
(4) CB. 1.
(5) Charleton. op. cit. Tract 2. p. 84.
(6) Willis, Thomas. *De Anima Brutorum.* Oxford. 1672. p. 420.
(7) Peirce, R. op. cit.
(8) Charleton. op. cit.
(9) CB.
(10) CB. 14.
(11) Charleton. op. cit. Tr.2. p. 88.
(12) ibid.
(13) Waldron, H.A. "The Devonshire Colic" in *Med. Hist.*1970.*25* pp. 387-388.
(14) Charleton. op. cit. Tr.2.
(15) Waldron, op. cit. p. 392.
(16) CB. passim.
(17) Waldron. op. cit.
(18) Charleton. Tr.1 passim.
(19) MB. 1.51.
(20) Charleton. op. cit.
(21) CB passim.
(22) O'Hare et al. *Royal Society Symposium on the Bath waters.* March. 1987.
(23) Ball, G. "Two Epidemics of Gout." *Bull. of the Hist. Med.*45. No 5. p. 407.

The Bladud Legacy.

(24) There seems to have been another leper hospital at this time, (Magdalen Hospital, Holloway), but it followed the convention of being built well away from the city. After the Reformation, it was rebuilt and used to accommodate other outcasts of society, namely the mentally handicapped.

(25) Wood, J. op. cit. p. 306.

(26) Bath Charities: see *Reports of Commissioners.* 1820. pp. 295-6. Bath City Archives.

(27) MB. 16.319.

(28) Charleton Tr.3.

(29) Falconer, W. (1795) op. cit. p. 28. Charleton. Tr.3. pp. 6 & 17.

(30) Charleton. Tr.3.

(31) MB. 19.102.

(32) Charleton Tr.3. p. 26.

(33) ibid p. 18.

(34) ibid.

(35) MB. 22.41/5.

(36) Tunstall, J. *The Bath Waters* Bath. 1850. p. 60.

(37) ibid. p. 61.

(38) ibid. p. 69.

(39) ibid.

Rheumatism – the cold-moist conundrum.

(40) CB. 99.

(41) CB. 95.

(42) Falconer, W. *An Account of the use, application and success of the Bath waters in Rheumatic Cases.* p. 20. BATH. 1795.

(43) ibid. p. 26.

(44) Peirce, R. op. cit. p. 12.

(45) Swift, H.H. et al *Rheumatic Fever as a Manifestation of Hypersensitiveness (Allergy or Hypergy) to Streptococci.* Paper read at The Bath Conference. 1928.

Hip Gout.

(46) Charleton. Tr.3. p. 56-57.

(47) ibid. p. 60.

(48) ibid. p. 56.

(49) Peirce. op. cit. p. 17.

(50) ibid. p. 33-34.

(51) Cleland, A. *An appeal to the public.* Bath. 1743.

(52) CB. p. 13.

(53) MB. 20.399.

(54) Charleton. Tr.3. p. 60.

(55) Lane, H. *Differentiation in Rheumatic Diseases* 2nd. ed. 1892. Churchill. London. p. 80.

(56) CB. 79.

(57) Kersley, George D. Personal communication.

BLOOD AND STEEL

(58) MB. 14.222.

(59) Rule XX.

(60) MB. 13.56.

(61) MB. 17.191.

(62) Plan in possession of Bath Guildhall Archives.

(63) MB. 19.152.

(64) MB. 12.7.

(65) MB. 25.539.

(66) Lowe, T.P. "Treatment of senile Rh. Arthritis by forcible movements." *BMJ.* 1894.

(67) MB. 31.433. Byelaw 13 was ammended to allow the appointment of a 4th surgeon, designated orthopaedic.

References to Chapter 6

(1) Haygarth, John. *Clinical History of Acute Rheumatism.* Bath. 1813.

(2) Spender, J.K. *Osteo-arthritis.* London. 1888.

(3) CB. 114.

(4) CB. 99.

(5) Falconer, W. (1795) op. cit.

(6) John Kent Spender (died 1916) was the son of a Bath surgeon. He qualified in 1866 and was elected honorary surgeon to the Mineral Water Hospital in the following year. In 1868, he gained his MD from London University and six years later was awarded the Fothergill Gold Medal of the Medical Society of London for an essay on pain relief. On the retirement of Wilbraham Falconer in 1881, Spender was elected physician to the hospital, an appointment he kept until his own retirement in 1894.

(7) Spender (1888) op. cit.

(8) MB. 26.204.

(9) Hugh Lane's promising career as a pioneer rheumatologist was cut short by his untimely death in 1895. His co-author, C.T. Griffiths, was resident medical officer between 1885 and 1890, and subsequently moved to Birmingham where he continued in private practice.

(10) Tunstall, J. *The Bath Waters: their uses and effects in the cure and relief of various diseases.* Churchill. London. 1850.

(11) Preston King and Arthur Wohlmann both had MD degrees.

(12) Bannatyne, G.A. *Rheumatoid Arthritis; its pathology, Morbid Anatomy and Treatment.* Bristol. 1896. p. 71.

(13) Bannatyne, G.A., Wohlmann, A. S., Blaxall, F.R. *Lancet,* 25.04.1896.

(14) *Bulletin of the Committee for study of Special Diseases.* Vol 2. p. 106. Cambridge. 1907.

(15) MB. 28.145/6.

(16) This mortuary room, in the 1860 wing, became the dispensary in 1915 (MB. 28.297).

(17) *Bulletin of the Committee for study of Special Dis.* Vol. 3. p. 4.

(18) MB. 28.221 (Sept 1909).

(19) MB. 28.194.

(20) MB. 28.461.

(21) MB. 28.461/62 (Jan 1913).

(22) see Turner. E. *A Brief History of the R.M.W.H.* Bath. 1921. p. 9.

(23) ibid. p. 21.

(24) MB. 32.63 (1932).

(25) MB. 34.227 (1938).

(26) see April 1936.

(27) Kersley, G. *The Three R's.* Bath. n.d. p. 11.

(28) A fuller account of the development of post-war research at the hospital is given by Kersley, G.D. in *The Three R's.*

References to Chapter 7.

(1) Douglas Kerr, J.G. *Popular guide to the use of the Bath Waters*. Bath. 1891. p. 47.

(2) Guidott, T. *A Discourse of Bathe and the hot waters there*. London 1676.

(3) Smollett, T. *An Essay on External Use of Water*. 1752.

(4) Kersley, G. *Rheumatic Diseases*. Heineman. 1945. p. 86.

(5) Peskett, G. and Raiment, P.C. in *Arch. Med. Hydrol*. August. 1925.

(6) *B.M.J.* 20 December 1985.

(7) See Nuttall, *Correspondence of Phillip Dodderidge*. Letter from W.O. to P.D. 1746. p. 1196. Northampton County Library.

(8) Gibbes, G.S. *A Treatise on the Bath Waters*. Bath. 1800.

(9) Hatton. J. *The Radium Waters of Bath*. Bath. nd.

(10) ibid.

(11) *B.M.J.* 12 January 1929. p. 59.

(12) Smollett. op. cit.(n.3) p. 74.

(13) MB. 3.27.

(14) MB. 9.209.(27.8.1783).

(15) MB. 1.183.

(16) HVB 1. (4.7.1743).

(17) MB. 5.212.

(18) MB. 1.229.(10.1742).

(19) Peirce, R. op. cit. p. 219.

(20) Guidott, T. *The Register of Bath*. London. 1694. pp. 83-4.

(21) Peirce. op. cit. pp. 244-45.

(22) Turner, W. op. cit.

(23) Bannatyne, G.A. *The Thermal Waters of Bath*. Wright. Bristol. 1899. p. 75.

(24) King, P. *Bath Waters*. Arrowsmith. Bath. nd. p. 124.

(25) MB. 4.232.

(26) King, P. op. cit. p. 122.

(27) HVB. 29.04.1743.

(28) Falconer, W. *An Essay on the Bath Waters*. Bath. 1772. p. 429.

(29) Oliver, W. *A Practical Essay on the use and abuse of Warm Bathing in Gouty Cases*. Bath. 1751. p. 68.

(30) Falconer, R.W. *Baths of Bath*. p. 39. quoted in Kerr. note 1. op. cit. (p. 58).

(31) Charleton, R. *Three tracts on the Bath Waters*. Bath. 1774. Tract 3. p. 20.

(32) Smollett, T. *The expedition of Humphrey Clinker*. in "Works of Tobias Smollett" Nimmo, London. n.d. p. 482.

(33) MB. 20.255.

(34) Turner. P.V. *A Brief History of the Mineral Water Hospital*. Bath. 1921. p. 20.

(35) Garrison, F.H. *An Introduction to the History of Medicine*. 4th edition. Saunders, London and Philadelphia. 1929. p. 328.

(36) Charleton. op. cit. Tr.2. p. 34.

(37) ibid.

(38) MB. 10.298. The Middlesex Hospital invested in an electrical machine in 1767; St. Bartholomew's had one in 1777; John Birch, a surgeon, was using one at St. Thomas's to treat joint disease at this time. (J. Guy).

(39) *Narrative of the efficacy of the Bath Waters in various kinds of Paralytic Disorders admitted into the Bath Hospital*. Cruttwell, Bath. 1787. p. 59.

(40) MB. 27.453.

(41) Kersley, G.D. Personal communication. 1987.

(42) John Guy. Personal communication. 1985.

(43) MB. 16.253.

(44) MB. 20.39.

(45) published 1848.

(46) Barlow, E. *An Essay in the Medical Efficacy and Employment of the Bath Waters* Bath. 1822. pp. 130-131.

(47) MB. 24.350 see Advert for Rubber in *B.M.J.* c.April 1880.

(48) Advert for Rubber placed in *BMJ* during April 1880. (MB).

(49) *Murrell on Massage* p. 14, quoted in Kerr. (op. cit., note 1). p. 72.

(50) MB. 27.230.

(51) Kerr. op. cit. (note 1) p. 86.

(52) The ward mistress was made redundant in 1904.

(53) MB. 27.380.

(54) MB. 28.416.

(55) MB. 29.502.

(56) Forbes Fraser referred to a proposed *Physiotherapeutic Department* see Harrison, F. *A Brief History of the Royal Mineral Water Hospital*. Bath. 1921. p. 23.

(57) MB. 30.226.

(58) Kersley, G.D. et al. "Insulin and ECT in the treatment of Rheumatoid Arthritis." *B.M.J.* 14.10.1950. p. 855.

(59) Advertised in Methuen's *Handbook of Massage*. 1918 and *Journal of Incorporated Society of Trained Masseuses*. 1918 editions.

(60) MB. 30.289.

(61) MB. 30.589.

(62) MB. 32.159.

(63) Rehabilitation Sub-Committee Minutes. 1.6.1943.

(64) MB. 36.271.

(65) MB. 36.276.

References to Chapter 8

(1) see *Chronicles of Pharmacy*. pp. 148-150.

(2) *Cases of Persons admitted into the Infirmary at Bath under the care of Dr Oliver*. Bath. 1760. p. 33.

(3) ibid. p. 34.

(4) MB. 10.197.

(5) IB. 1750.

(6) Nuttall. op. cit. *Correspondence of Philip Dodderidge*. p. 841.

(7) Oliver, W. *Warm Bathing in Gouty Cases*. pp. 62-3.

(8) Baylies, W. *Practical Reflections on the uses and abuses of the Bath Waters*. London. 1757. pp. 168-70.

(9) *Narrative of the efficacy of the Bath Waters in various kinds of Paralytic disorders admitted to the Bath Hospital*. N.A. Bath. 1787. p. 19.

(10) ibid. pp. 17-18.

(11) ibid. passim.

(12) IB.

(13) *Letters and Papers of the Bath Agricultural Soc.* 2nd Ed. (abridged) vol. 2. Bath. 1802.

(14) Le Strange, R. *A History of Herbal Plants.* Arco. New York. 1977. p. 87.

(15) Barlow, E. *An Essay on the Medical Efficacy and employment of the Bath Waters* Bath. 1822. pp. 81-2.

(16) ibid. p. 113.

(17) ibid. p. 113.

(18) Oliver, W. *A Practical Essay on the use and abuse of warm bathing in Gouty cases.* Bath. 1753.

(19) Lysons,D. *On the effects of a decoction of the inner bark of the common elm in cutaneous diseases* Med. Trans. 203.

(20) White, W. *Observations and experiments on the broad-leaf willow bark.* Bath. 1798.

(21) Coates, V. and Delicati, L. *Rheumatoid Arthritis and its treatment.* This textbook reflects the practice at the hospital during the 1930's.

(22) Hill, L. Review of Gout 1939-46. *Annals of Rh.* Dis. 5. pp. 171-76.

(23) Kersley, G. "Gout." *Clinical Journal.* Sept. 1936.

(24) MB. 17.87.

(25) MB. 35.417.

(26) MB. 7.93-95.

(27) MB. 7.172.

(28) MB. 17.83.

(29) Documents in possession of David Falconer.

(30) See *Dictionary of British Eighteenth Century Painters.* Ellis Waterhouse. Antique Collectors Club. 1981.

(31) Wallis, P.J. Wallis, R.V., Whittet, T.D. *18th Century Medics.* Newcastle-on-Tyne. 1985.

(32) MB. 19.538.

(33) MB. 19.461.

(34) Tunstall, J. *Rambles about Bath.* Bath. 1846.

(35) for a full account of Prince's life, see: Mander, Charles. *"The Reverend Prince and his Abode of Love."* E.P. Publishing. 1976.

(36) 1909-10 and 1943-47.

References to Chapter 9.

(1) *Tatler. 78.* Oct. 8th. 1709.

(2) Anon. *Diseases of Bath – A Satyre Unadorned with a Frontispiece* Bath. 1737.

(3) Lucas, C. *An Essay on the Waters.* London. 1756.

(4) Munk, W. in *Western Antiquary. 7.* June. 1887. p. 8.

(5) ibid.

(6) *Phil. Trans.* XXXII. p. 413.

(7) Schupbach, W. "The fame and notoriety of Dr John Huxham." *Medical History.* 25. 1981. pp. 415-21.

(8) Pallet, p. *Bath Characters* Bath. 1807. pp. 48-9.

(9) Worman, I. *Thomas Gainsborough.* Dalton. Suffolk. 1976. p. 76.

(10) Pallet, op. cit. p. 54.

(11) Letters between Charles Lucas and William Oliver. 7.11.1757. Published at Bath.

(12) Eaves, T.C.D. and Kimpel, B.D. *Samuel Richardson – A biography.* Oxford. 1971.

(13) Wallis, p. J., Wallis, R.V. and Whittet, T.D., 18th Century Medics. Newcastle. 1985.

(14) ibid.

(15) *Dictionary of National Biography.*

(16) Baylies, W. *An Historical Account of the Rise Progress and Management of the Bath Hospital.* Bath. 1758. p. 121/2.

(17) Naish, p. B. *Nelson's letters of his life and other documents.* London. 1958. p. 381.

(18) Rolleston, Sir H. "Caleb Hillier Parry." in *Ann. of Hist. of Med.* No. 3. Vol. 7. Autumn 1925.

(19) *Dictionary of National Biography.*

(20) Catholics were excluded entry to Oxford and Cambridge.

(21) Munks Roll of the Fellows of the Royal College of Physicians.

(22) Proudfitt, W.L. "The Fleece Medical Society" *Brit. Heart. J.,* 1981. 46. p. 589.

(23) McMichael, W. "Lives of British Physicians" London. 1830.

(24) Proudfitt. op. cit.

(25) MB. 2.42.

(26) MB. 1.267.

(27) Rule XII.

(28) MB. 28.82.

(29) MB. Dec. 1917.

(30) Venner. T. *Via Recta ad Vitam Longam.* p. 356. London. 1620.

(31) Tyte, W. *Tales and sketches.* p. 56. Bath. 1917.

(32) Kingsdown House, Box.

(33) Haygarth, J. *Of the imagination as a cause and as a cure of disorders of the body.* Bath. 1800.

(34) Personal communication.

(35) Kersley, G. D. *The Three R's.* p. 10. Bath. 1981.

INDEX

The names of the sickuesses/which may be healed by these bathes.

The casting of children out/ before the dewe tyme appoynted by nature.

The stoppinge of the longes and shortnes of breth when a man can not take breth/except he sit right vp.

The hardnes and binding of the bellye/ when as a man can not go to the stoole without Physick.

The palsey when as a man is quite num all the partes of his body/and hath nether mouing nor healing.

Impostemes and gatheringes of humors together with swellinge.

The rinning gout which rinneth fro one ioynte to an other.

The defenes or dulnes of hearing.

The windines or singing or tinginge of the eares

The brusing that cummeth by falling or beating.

The stone in the kidnes.

The stone in the blader.

Hard lumpes and swellinges.

The Cancre.

The headache of a cold cause.

The head ache of an hote cause.

The Reum or Pose or Catar.

The stopping of the brayne with euell humors.

Scarres and foule markes of sores or woundes.

The Colike.

The fallinge sicknes.

Crampes and drawinges together brawnes and synewes or streching furth to muche of the same.

The trimbling of the hart.

The foulnes of the skin and scruuines.

The puffinge vp of the legges with wind.

The hardnes of any place in the body.

The often and to much making of water called Diabetes.

The leannes of the hole bodye.

Agues after the mater is made rype and digested.

Tertian agues.   Quartane agues.

Fistules or hollow or false vnder crepinge sores.

Al kindes of isshues or flires.

The stickinge of yron in a bone or in the fleshe.

Breaking or bursting of bones.

Membres that are made num with colde.

The knobbes and hard lūpes that are made by the french pockes.

The lousnes and watering of the gummes.

The emrodes and pyles.

The mygram or headache in the one halfe of the head.

The diseases of the liuer.

Bursting or breakinge.

The bottel dropsey in the stomach.

The general dropsey throw all the body/rinninge betwene the fell and the fleshe.

The iaundes or guelsought.

The coldnes and stopping of the liuer.

The sciatica or hancheuel.

The lepre vpon the skin.

The hardnes of the milt / or the cake in the left syde.

Wormes in the bellye.

Membres that are num and fele not.

The madnes called melancholia.

The hurting of the memorye or forgetfulnes.